Practical Church Management

A guide for every parish

To Deborah and Emma-Jane

Practical Church Management

A guide for every parish

James Behrens

MA, LLM (Canon Law)
of Lincoln's Inn and the Middle Temple
Barrister

First published in 1998

Gracewing
Fowler Wright Books
2 Southern Avenue, Leominster
Herefordshire
HR6 0QF

ISBN 0 85244 471 0

Typesetting by James Behrens

Printed by The Cromwell Press,
Trowbridge, Wiltshire

Foreword

I am very happy to commend Mr Behrens' book. It is extremely thorough and will be a valuable supplement to the standard handbooks of church law. This particular book is concerned not just with the rules of church government but also with all the practical details of the management of a parish and the many problems that arise in the course of it. It is an illuminating picture of the church today that it includes not only computers but also the whole question of child protection and the House of Bishops' recent statement of policy. It will be invaluable to all those involved in the management of a parish, PCC members as well as the incumbent, churchwardens, organists and vergers but could also be of great interest to the ordinary parishioner and give him a very much deeper insight into the whole running of the church as an institution and the practical problems presented in connection with pastoral care. I hope the book will be widely read and used.

+Eric Chichester:

The Rt Revd the Bishop of Chichester

Introduction

Ecclesiastical Insurance was founded by churchmen to provide insurance services for the church and today, despite expansion into many other fields, we remain the UK's leading insurer of churches and provide personal insurances to many thousands of church people.

As such we, at Ecclesiastical, are pleased to be associated with James Behrens' book as it will provide support, advice and assistance to parishes and their officials.

In the ever changing market place we believe this guide will be of immense help, but we would like to remind all parishes that advice and assistance on any insurance matter is freely available from Ecclesiastical Insurance either from our head office or locally within the diocese from our team of surveyors.

We would like to thank James Behrens for allowing us to be involved in his book. We congratulate and thank him and his publishers for all their work and efforts.

JOHN COATES
Direct Operations Manager
Ecclesiastical Direct Church, Diocesan & Charities

Beaufort House
Brunswick Road
Gloucester
GL1 1JZ

Ecclesiastical is owned by Allchurches Trust Ltd which receives dividends and grants for charitable distribution from the profits of Ecclesiastical. In the five years from 1991 to 1996 that support amounted to £11.2m donated to the church and other good causes, and in 1996 ranks Ecclesiastical tenth largest corporate donor to charity in the UK.

Preface

Anyone involved in leadership has to get to grips with administration or management. This applies in the parish church as elsewhere. Many people are involved with leadership and management in the parish church – clergy (and senior clergy), churchwardens, church treasurers, members of the PCC, covenant secretaries, church administrators, musicians, and employed staff. All these should understand how the church works, and how their roles relate to each other.

I have divided the book into four parts: *church people*, *church life*, *church property*, and *church finance*. There is obviously an overlap in many cases – the work of the treasurer for example is covered in both *church people* and *church finance* – but I think it is helpful to look at the subject in this way. As much practical advice has been given as possible on a whole range of day-to-day matters within the church – areas such as finance, repairs, the annual parochial church meeting, dealing with the press, and the interregnum. There is also legal advice on subjects which churches need to be aware of, such as food hygiene, data protection, employment law, copyright, charity law, VAT, and the many aspects of safety law. The law is stated as at 1 January 1998, though more recent developments have been included where possible.

I have tried to make this book representative of all types of church life within the Church of England. My Christian experience has been mainly fairly low church, but I hope that this fact does not intrude into the text. Also it has been largely based in London, and I appreciate that many things may be dealt with somewhat differently in country parishes. I hope what I have written will be useful for all types of church, wherever they are.

It has been very difficult to decide what to include and what to leave out. I may have erred by including too much, with the result that the book is more a reference book than one to be read from cover to cover. All PCCs need to be aware of the topics I have included, but no-one needs to be an expert on everything.

PREFACE

Our Lord spoke strong words to lawyers, accusing us of loading people down with burdens they can hardly carry, and not lifting one finger to help them.[1] With this in mind, I have used the word *should* rather than the word *must* whenever possible. You should do what I say, none the less.

Many positions in the church, both lay and clerical, are held by women. For convenience I have usually used the masculine in the text, but it also includes the feminine whenever appropriate.

I have consulted with as many people and organisations as I have been able to identify for assistance on the various topics in this book. I received a great many publications and other information from the diocesan offices for Bath and Wells, Blackburn, Birmingham, Bradford, Bristol, Carlisle, Chichester, Derby, Durham, Ely, the diocese in Europe, Guildford, Leicester, Lichfield, Lincoln, Liverpool, London, Oxford, Portsmouth, Rochester, St Albans, Salisbury, Sheffield, St Edmundsbury and Ipswich, Sodor and Man, Truro, Wakefield, Winchester, Worcester and York.

The following organisations gave me assistance: the Data Protection Office, the Charity Commission, the Charities Aid Foundation, the Ecclesiastical Insurance Group, the Council for the Care of Churches, the Royal College of Organists, the Inland Revenue, the Churches' Child Protection Advisory Services, the Centre for Dispute Resolution (CEDR), the Department of Health, the Health and Safety Executive, Binder Hamlyn, the Churches' Main Committee, and the Central Board of Finance of the Church of England. Many other organisations referred to in this book sent me details of their work. As a result of my contact with CEDR I have recently completed one of its mediator training courses.

Individuals who have helped me include four archdeacons, the Ven. Hugh Buckingham, the Ven. Michael Hill, the Ven. George Cassidy, and the Ven. Timothy Raphael; the Rev. Dr Geoffrey Simpson, a team rector in Yorkshire; Fr Jonathan Redvers Harris; Dr Norman Doe, the director of the postgraduate course in canon law at Cardiff Law School; Sister Muriel, the librarian at Heythrop College in Kensington, London; Christopher Smith and Roy Martin at London Diocesan House; Stephen Finch, Richard Hargreaves and Mrs Helen Main, respectively churchwarden, covenant secretary and catering manager for St Helen's, Bishopsgate; Paul Joslin, the director of music at St Jude's church, Courtfield Gardens, London SW5; Robin Stevens, the Central Stewardship Officer of the Central Board of Finance of the Church of England; Brian Hanson, registrar and legal adviser to the General Synod; the Rev. John Rees of Winckworth and Pemberton; Mrs Barbara Hird, registered indexer; Mrs Jill Pinnock of Oxford; Tom Longford and Miss Jo Ashworth of Gracewing; and in particular my wife Sally, who has encouraged me in the whole project. She read many of the chapters in draft, and made me change anything which I had not explained clearly enough.

Without the help of these people and organisations, this book could never have been written. I am grateful to them all.

James Behrens
Lincoln's Inn
April, 1998

---

[1] Luke 11:46.

Acknowledgements

Scripture quotations taken from the Holy Bible, New International Version, Copyright © 1973, 1978, 1984 by International Bible Society. Published by Hodder and Stoughton.

The table of food hazards in Chapter 11, 'Food and drink', is taken from the Department of Health's booklet *A guide to food hazards and your business*. It is Crown copyright, and is reproduced with permission.

The table of parochial fees set out in Chapter 17, 'When the parish priest leaves', is based on the table prepared by the Church Commissioners, and is reproduced with permission.

The risk analysis questionnaire in Chapter 19, 'Security', is the copyright of Staffordshire Police, and is reproduced with permission.

The House of Bishops' policy document on child protection is referred to in Chapter 8, 'Children'. This is the copyright of the Central Board of Finance of the Church of England, and is reproduced with permission.

The Home Office report on child protection *Safe from Harm* is referred to in Chapter 8, 'Children'. The report is Crown copyright, and is reproduced with the permission of the Controller of Her Majesty's Stationery Office.

The guidelines agreed by the House of Bishops in 1997 on communion before confirmation are referred to in Chapter 9, 'Church Services'. The guidelines are the copyright of the Central Board of Finance of the Church of England, and are reproduced with permission.

The cold weather code for churches is the copyright of the Ecclesiastical Insurance Group, and is reproduced with permission.

Contents

Contents

PART II   CHURCH LIFE

CONTENTS

PART III   CHURCH PROPERTY

CONTENTS

PART IV   CHURCH FINANCE

APPENDICES

Chapter 1

WHO'S WHO?

1.　INTRODUCTION

When someone asks you what church you belong to, you probably reply by saying the name of the parish church where you normally worship. But your parish church does not exist in isolation. Year by year every parish deals with a whole host of people and organisations involved with the administration of the Church of England. It is easy to become muddled by names such as rural deans, archdeacons, bishops, archbishops, chancellors, diocesan registrars, diocesan secretaries, and various bodies with odd-sounding names such as *diocesan advisory committee* and *deanery synod*. But over a period of time you are likely to come across most of them, so this chapter is a 'who's who' guide, to explain very simply what they all do. It is intended as an over-view: filling in the details will be done in later chapters.

At the end of this chapter is an explanation of some of the terms I use when I refer to particular church rules. If I refer to a *measure* or a *canon*, for example, it may be helpful to know what these words mean, and where you can look them up if you need to.

2.   THE DIOCESE

England is divided into 43 areas known as *dioceses*, each under the charge of a *bishop*. There is also one diocese outside England called the diocese in Europe, covering the whole of Continental Europe from Norway to Russia, Greece to the Azores, and including Turkey and Morocco! 30 dioceses belong to what is known as the *province* of Canterbury, under the leadership of the archbishop of Canterbury. The remainder belong to the province of York, under the leadership of the archbishop of York. Leaving aside the diocese in Europe, the largest diocese geographically is Lincoln, and the smallest is Sodor and Man. The diocese with the largest number of parishes is Oxford.

In most dioceses there are one or more assistant bishops, some of whom are known as suffragan bishops. In some dioceses these assistant bishops are given responsibility for particular geographical areas, in which case they are known as area bishops. Thus the diocese of Chelmsford has area bishops for Barking, Bradwell and Colchester; the diocese of Chichester has area bishops for Horsham and Lewes; and there are many others.

The diocese has various boards and committees. Three that you may come across are:

- the *diocesan parsonages board*. This deals with various property matters. In particular the board maintains the houses where parish priests live, known as *parsonages*. A *parsonage* is an old-fashioned word for the place where the *parson* lives. These houses are now usually referred to as the *vicarage* (where the *vicar* lives) or the *rectory* (where the *rector* lives). Parish priests are also known as *incumbents*. There is no practical difference between these various titles.[1]
- an advisory committee for the care of churches, known as the *diocesan advisory committee*, and often abbreviated as the *DAC*.[2] The DAC has a very important role to play whenever any parish wants to carry out any building works or alterations to its church, its furnishings, or in a churchyard. Any proposal to carry out such work normally requires the approval of the DAC before the diocese authorises the work to be done.

- *the diocesan board of finance.* The diocesan board of finance acts as trustee for any land owned by the Parochial Church Council[3] of a church.[4] The diocesan board of finance has many other functions as well. For example, it pays the fee for an inspection of each church in the diocese every five years (the quinquennial inspection).[5]

The *bishop* is the chief pastor[6] of all members of the Church of England within his diocese, both the *laity* (people who have not been ordained) and the *clergy* (people who have). As the Alternative Service Book puts it:

> A Bishop is called to lead in serving and caring for the people of God and to work with them in the oversight of the Church.

He is both a leader and an administrator. His duties include ordinations, confirmations, the pastoral care and discipline of the clergy, appointing rural deans, licensing curates, pastoral reorganisation of parishes, and being the spiritual leader to the people in his diocese. He is assisted by *area* or *suffragan bishops*, and also by his *archdeacons*.

There are also what are known as *flying bishops* or, to give them their proper title, *Provincial Episcopal Visitors*. There are three flying bishops, namely the bishop of Richborough, the bishop of Ebbsfleet, and the bishop of Beverley. Under the Episcopal Ministry Act of Synod 1993 provision was made for the continuing difference of opinion in the Church of England as to the ordination and ministry of women as priests. Parishes which are opposed to women priests can request their diocesan bishop to make special arrangements for their pastoral care.[7] Such special arrangements have now been made for nearly 300 such parishes. In some cases another bishop within the diocese or in a neighbouring diocese is appointed for the parish.[8] In other cases one of the three flying bishops is appointed.[9]

The *archdeacon* works with the bishop in the pastoral care of clergy and their families within the diocese. He makes sure that the parishes are administered properly, and makes sure that the clergy, the churchwardens and the Parochial Church Councils all do their various duties. He is responsible for church buildings and vicarages. The main occasions when parishes are involved with the archdeacon are:

- once a year, when churchwardens get sworn in.

- once a year, when the diocese sends on behalf of the archdeacon a list of questions to parishes, asking about what has been going on in the church over the previous year. These questions are known as the archdeacon's *articles of enquiry*.
- when a church wants to carry out building works or alterations.
- when there is some pastoral problem within the parish, in particular some conflict between the parish priest and members of his congregation.

Each diocese has a number of paid staff working at the diocesan office. The *diocesan secretary* is the point of contact for any inquiries about administrative arrangements in the diocese. Some diocesan secretaries are clergy; others are not. In many chapters in this book I refer to guidelines issued by each diocese. Some dioceses publish all their guidelines in one handbook; others publish separate leaflets, A4 sheets or booklets covering individual topics. Most guidance is free, but in some cases dioceses make a small charge.[10] Appendix 1 contains a list of names, addresses and telephone numbers of all the diocesan secretaries in the country.

In addition, each diocese has a number of officers who are not full-time employees.

- The *diocesan registrar* is usually a solicitor. He acts as the legal advisor to the bishop, and prepares all the legal documents for any church appointments within the diocese. The diocesan registrar is paid by the diocesan board of finance an annual fee to cover a whole range of legal advice. This includes giving legal advice to clergy, churchwardens and secretaries of PCCs on any matter that arises in connection with their duties.
- The *chancellor* is a barrister or judge appointed by the bishop, whose main function is to deal with *faculties*. Before carrying out works to the church or churchyard, permission, known as a *faculty*, should first be obtained from the chancellor, or in some cases from the archdeacon. You also require a faculty in order to dispose of any of the contents of a church, and to introduce any new items into a church.
- The *diocesan surveyor* deals with the repair and maintenance of vicarages.

The *General Synod* is the main governing body of the Church of England. It conducts debates upon matters of religious or public interest, and makes laws (subject to the approval of the Houses of Parliament) governing the church. Each diocese has a form of government known as a *diocesan synod*, which acts in a similar way, making provision for matters within the diocese. The bishop consults with the diocesan synod on matters of general concern and importance to the diocese.

Your diocesan secretary can give you the names and addresses for any of the church organisations or people you may need to contact within your diocese. A complete list of names and addresses covering all the dioceses is published each year in the *Church of England Year Book* (Church House Publishing, 1998).

3.   THE DEANERY

Each diocese is divided into a number of *deaneries*, also known as *rural deaneries*. In urban areas the word *rural* is usually omitted. A deanery is a group of neighbouring parishes. Each deanery has a *rural dean*, also known as *area dean*, usually appointed by the bishop from one of the clergy of the deanery.[11]

The rural dean acts as a support to the other clergy within his deanery, giving advice and assistance to them on any matter of concern. He has a similar role to the archdeacon whenever there are pastoral problems within a parish. The rural dean has a very important role whenever there is what is known as a *vacancy* or *interregnum*, which is the time between one parish priest leaving a parish and a new person being appointed. During a vacancy the churchwardens and the rural dean are in charge of the parish.[12]

Each deanery has a *deanery synod*, which acts as a forum for the parishes to exchange views on problems affecting the deanery. One important function it has relates to finance. Each deanery is asked to contribute an amount of money (known as a *quota* or *parish share*) to the finances of the diocese. The deanery synod determines how that quota is to be shared between the various parishes belonging to the deanery.

4.   THE PARISH

There are about 16,000 parish churches in active use in England. The parish is an area under the care of a *parish priest* or *incumbent*. Some parishes are organised into *team* or *group ministries*, which is a means of sharing one or more clergy among a group of parishes close together. In this book I use the phrase *parish priest* as a generic title for an incumbent, a rector, a vicar or a priest-in-charge. Some parish priests have one or more *assistant curates* (usually known as *curates*, without the word *assistant*) to help them in their duties.

Each parish has (usually two) *churchwardens*, and a *Parochial Church Council*, generally referred to as the *PCC*. The churchwardens are chosen each year by a meeting of parishioners which is held no later than 30 April. The members of the Parochial Church Council are chosen each year at a separate meeting known as the annual parochial church meeting, which also should be held no later than 30 April.

Each year the church should prepare a list of the people who are entitled to vote at the annual parochial church meeting. The list is known as the *church electoral roll*. Anyone over the age of 16 who lives in the parish or who has attended the church for six months can be on the electoral roll. The person whose responsibility it is to prepare the electoral roll each year is known as the *church electoral roll officer*.

The *churchwardens* have many duties. They will be described more fully in other chapters, but some of the main ones are these:

- They form a direct link between the bishop and the parish. Each year they have to answer a number of written questions (known as *Articles of Enquiry*) sent to them by the archdeacon on behalf of the bishop. These articles of enquiry deal with a whole range of matters concerning the parish. The churchwardens can report to the bishop any matter that affects the parish.
- They also form a link between the congregation and the parish priest. They are to do their best to encourage the parishioners in their Christian faith, and to promote peace and unity among them.
- They should make sure that the church obtains a faculty whenever necessary.
- They are members of the PCC and of its standing committee.[13]

- They should see that the PCC carries out its responsibilities for the care, maintenance and insurance of the church, its contents, the churchyard, and any other land and buildings it owns.
- They are responsible for the allocation of seats to the congregation, and for keeping order in the church during services.
- They have a major role to play when there is a vacancy.[14]
- They should arrange to inspect the fabric of the church every year. The word *fabric* means the building itself – stones, bricks and mortar. They make a report about the state of the building to the PCC and to the *annual parochial church meeting*. (For brevity, this meeting is sometimes known as the *annual meeting* or the APCM.)

Some churches have a *deputy churchwarden*. In a team ministry, where a parish has two or more churches where services are held, deputy churchwardens may be appointed to look after each of the subsidiary churches.[15] Some churches have a deputy churchwarden as an assistant to the churchwardens, for example if one of the churchwardens is ill or temporarily absent. Some deputies are appointed so that they can be trained up by the existing churchwardens, with a view to the deputy being elected as churchwarden the following year.

The PCC and the parish priest consult together on matters of general concern and importance to the parish. The PCC's functions include:

- controlling expenditure within the parish.
- looking after the maintenance of the building.
- 'co-operation with the minister in promoting in the parish the whole mission of the Church, pastoral, evangelistic, social and ecumenical'.[16] (*Ecumenical* means our relationship with other Christian denominations. The ecumenical movement is the impetus to restore unity amongst all Christian churches and denominations.)
- discussing matters concerning the Church of England.
- having representatives on the deanery synod.

The PCC should meet at least four times each year.[17]

Each PCC should appoint a *standing committee* of five or more members, consisting of the parish priest, the churchwardens, and at least two other members from the PCC. The treasurer should normally be a member of the standing committee. The standing committee carries out the routine work of the PCC between each PCC meeting. It acts as a committee of the PCC, not as an independent body. It is therefore accountable to the PCC for everything it does. The practical advantage of a standing committee is that it is smaller than the PCC. It is easier to discuss and decide routine matters in a meeting of five to ten people than in a full PCC meeting of fifteen to twenty. In some churches the standing committee meets a couple of weeks before each PCC meeting to consider what should be on the agenda for the PCC meeting.

Each PCC has a *treasurer* to deal with church finance and the church accounts. The annual parochial church meeting appoints an *auditor* or an *independent examiner* who has to audit or examine the church accounts each year.[18]

Many people give money to their church using a deed of covenant, as this enables the church to recover from the Inland Revenue a payment that adds to the value of the gift. At the rates of tax payable from April 1998, the payment made by the Inland Revenue amounts to almost 30 per cent of the gift.[19] The person who deals with the administration of these covenants is usually known as the *covenants secretary*.

The PCC has a *PCC secretary*, who deals with the paperwork for all meetings of the PCC. He or she sends out notices, makes sure everyone has the necessary papers, takes notes of the meetings, chases up action afterwards, and generally makes sure that records are properly kept and filed.

Some churches, especially ones with large congregations, have an *administrator*. He or she is an employee of the Parochial Church Council, and acts as its executive officer to implement its decisions. His responsibilities may include the employment of staff, some aspects of church finance, the organisation of home groups and other groups within the church, organising conferences, organising the maintenance of the building, parish outings, publications and bulletins, and many other matters. He does not take over the functions or the ultimate responsibility of the churchwardens, the PCC and the treasurer: rather, he assists them and the parish priest in their respective tasks by taking day-to-day matters off their hands. The duties of the administrator vary according to the needs of the particular church where he is appointed. Some administrators spend most of their time dealing with financial matters, others with the church building, and others in assisting the secretary to the PCC.[20]

Some churches have a *parish priest's secretary*. He or she may also be the secretary to the PCC, but the two roles are different. The main function of the secretary to the parish priest is to deal with his personal correspondence and to organise his appointments.

Sidesmen are appointed at the annual parochial church meeting.[21] Officially, they assist the churchwardens in keeping order during services. In practice they greet people as they come into church, show them to their seats, and if they are new to the church try to make sure they feel welcome. During communion they guide people up to the altar at the appropriate time.

Readers are members of the Church of England who have not been ordained as priest or deacon, but who have undergone quite extensive training, and who have been licensed by the bishop to perform various duties within the church. (They are sometimes referred to by the public as *lay readers*.) Readers can visit and pray for the sick, teach in Sunday school, preach, and distribute the communion bread and wine. Some readers are authorised also to conduct funeral services. Most of what readers do is now done by ordinary members of the congregation in many churches.

The organist or *director of music* is employed by the PCC. The parish priest should consider the organist's advice on the choice of music for the services, but the final responsibility and decision rest with the parish priest.

The *verger* has three main areas of work:
- He welcomes and cares for visitors to the church, members of the regular congregation, and people in need.
- He needs to know about the church buildings, architecture, ceremony and forms of worship.
- He needs to be practical, able to deal with communication and lighting systems, forms and registers, security, and sometimes elementary maintenance.[22]

He is appointed and dismissed by the parish priest jointly with the PCC.

The *sacristan* has no legal responsibilities, but the term is used for the person who looks after the sacred vessels used for holy communion.

Once every five years, every church has to be inspected by an architect or surveyor. The architect or surveyor makes a report on the state of repair of the church, saying what needs to be put right. This is known as the *quinquennial inspection*, and the person who carries out the task is known as the *quinquennial inspector*. The quinquennial inspector is chosen by the church, and must be approved by the DAC before being appointed. The fee for the five-yearly or *quinquennial inspection* and the architect's report is paid by the diocese rather than by the parish, though of course parishes pay for it indirectly through the quota system.

5.   RULES IN A CHRISTIAN COMMUNITY

Every church is also a human institution. Any human institution involving a large number of people requires rules. The Church of England is no exception.

What are the rules that govern the Church of England?

As I have mentioned, the *General Synod* makes laws governing the Church, subject to the approval of Parliament. Sometimes these laws are called *measures*, at other times they are called *canons*.

(a)   Measures

Measures are like Acts of Parliament. Most of the ones you are ever likely to need are printed in *A Handbook for Churchwardens and Parochial Church Councillors*, by Kenneth MacMorran and Timothy Briden (Mowbray, 1996). For example, during an interregnum,[23] it is helpful to have a copy of the Patronage (Benefices) Measure 1986, which sets out how a new parish priest is chosen,[24] and the relevant parts of this measure are set out in MacMorran and Briden. The Measures are published by HMSO, and can be purchased from HMSO bookshops. They are also printed in *Halsbury's Statutes* volume 14 (and a continuation volume also numbered 14), and are available in any law library, and in some public libraries.

(b)   The Canons

The Canons of the Church of England are published by Church House Publishing.[25] They are issued in a A5 ring binder with loose-leaf pages, and are available from

CHURCH HOUSE BOOKSHOP
31 Great Smith Street,
London SW1P 3BN

Tel: 0171 340 0276

The whole collection runs to just under 200 pages. Most of the Canons are a page or less in length, and in fairly simple language. The Canons are divided into eight sections, sections A to H, each covering a different part of church life, and then into numbers within each section. For example, Section B deals with services and the administration of the sacraments. Within this section, taking two examples, Canon B 11 deals with Morning and Evening Prayer, and Canon B 22 deals with infant baptism.

Quite a few clergy have a copy of the Canons. They are useful to have around for reference.

(c)   *Acts of Synod and Statements by the House of Bishops*

Two other forms of law which come from the General Synod are *Acts of Synod* and *statements by the House of Bishops*.[26] The only Act of Synod of importance to parishes is the Episcopal Ministry Act of Synod 1993, which makes arrangements for those parishes which continue to oppose the ordination of women to the priesthood. The House of Bishops' statements on child protection and on communion before confirmation are set out in the Appendices.

(d)   Case law

The Church of England is the *established* church in this country. Amongst other things, this means that Church of England law is part of the general law in England. The courts have sometimes had to determine questions dealing with the Church of England, and if the decision is important, people may want to refer to it as a precedent. The judgment is therefore printed and published as part of a set of law reports.

(e)   *General English law*

Many of the ordinary laws in this country apply to the church. To take one example, the church is subject to the licensing laws concerning alcohol. So the PCC should get permission from the licensing justices before selling alcohol at a church function. A second example concerns computers. If a church uses computers, it should make sure it obeys the rules about data protection. A third example is the law of copyright. If a church makes use of material that is copyright, it should make sure that it has permission to do so. These are all topics covered in this book.[27] Indeed, one of the main purposes in my writing this book is to gather together all the general laws which people involved in church administration need to know.

(f)   *Local laws for each diocese*

Each bishop can issue rules relating to his diocese. Sometimes they are called *guidance* rather than *rules*, but they are still there to be used. The diocesan secretary supplies a copy of the diocesan rules to all parish priests in the diocese, and also sends to PCCs and churchwardens a copy of any rules that they need to know.

---

[1] See Timothy Briden and Brian Hanson, *Moore's Introduction to English Canon Law*, 3rd edn. (Mowbray, 1992), page 30.

[2] See the Care of Churches and Ecclesiastical Jurisdiction Measure 1991 section 2.

[3] For the Parochial Church Council, see page 8.

[4] Parochial Church Councils (Powers) Measure 1956 section 6.

[5] See page 12.

[6] The term *pastor* derives from the Latin *pastor* meaning *shepherd*. It is used for example in the Book of Common Prayer, in the Collect for St Peter's Day (June 29):

> O ALMIGHTY God, who by thy Son Jesus Christ didst give to thy Apostle Saint Peter many excellent gifts, and commandedst him earnestly to feed thy flock; Make, we beseech thee, all Bishops and Pastors diligently to preach thy holy Word, and the people obediently to follow the same, that they may receive the crown of everlasting glory; through Jesus Christ our Lord. Amen.

[7] For full details on these arrangements, see Chapter 3, 'The PCC'.

[8] For example, the bishop of Fulham is appointed for any parish within the London diocese which asks for such arrangements.

[9] For example, All Saints', Houghton Regis is a traditional Anglican church in the diocese of St Albans but within the care of the bishop of Richborough, one of the three flying bishops. For the relationship between the flying bishops and the diocesan bishop, see Norman Doe, *The Legal Framework of the Church of England* (Clarendon Press, 1996), page 176.

[10] Some dioceses make a small charge (£2 to £3) for their guidelines relating to child abuse. Almost everything else is available free.

[11] In Exeter and Truro dioceses, rural deans are elected by the deanery clergy.

[12] See Raymond Ravenscroft, 'The Role of the Rural Dean' (1988) 5 Ecc LJ 46.

[13] Provided they receive Holy Communion and their names are on the electoral roll: Church Representation Rules, rule 14 (1) (d).

[14] See Chapter 17, 'When the parish priest leaves'.

[15] See Chapter 16, 'Team ministries'.

[16] Parochial Church Council (Powers) Measure 1956, section 2. The meaning of this phrase is explained on page 32.

[17] In rural parishes PCCs often meet less frequently than this.

[18] See generally, Chapter 4, 'The Treasurer', and Chapter 26, 'Church Accounts'.

[19] The arithmetic is explained in Chapter 25, 'Covenants and Gift Aid'.

[20] For examples of the job descriptions for a church administrator in three different parishes, see Chapter 7, 'The verger, the organist and the administrator'.

[21] Canon E 2.

[22] See Chapter 7, 'The verger, the organist and the administrator'.

[23] The time between one parish priest leaving a parish and a new parish priest being appointed.

[24] See Chapter 17, 'When the parish priest leaves'.

[25] *The Canons of the Church of England*, 5th edn. (Church House Publishing, 1993 plus second supplement 1996). The canons were promulgated by the Convocations of Canterbury and York in 1964 and 1969. They replaced almost the whole of the existing set of canons, which dated from 1603. The canons are formally known as the *Revised Canons Ecclesiastical* to distinguish them from the *Canons Ecclesiastical* (1603).

[26] The legal status of an Act of Synod is controversial. One view is that they have no statutory force, and are only morally binding: see Lynne Leeder, *Ecclesiastical Law Handbook* (Sweet and Maxwell, 1997), page 8, and Norman Doe, *Legal Framework of the Church of England* (Clarendon Press, 1996), page 77, where he describes them as *ecclesiastical quasi-legislation*. Acts of Synod

derive from the Synodical Government Measure 1969 Schedule 2 article 6 (a) (iv), and therefore, I consider, do have the force of law. Further, the Episcopal Ministry Act of Synod 1993 is worded just like a statute. Statements by the House of Bishops may not be laws in the technical sense, but they are very important guidance to the church.

[27] For alcohol licensing, see Chapter 11, 'Food and drink'; for data protection, see Chapter 12, 'Computers'; for copyright, see Chapter 13, 'Copyright'.

Chapter 2

THE CHURCHWARDENS

1.   INTRODUCTION

One archdeacon[1] recently described the role of a churchwarden as *management, maintenance, and ministry.* That is not the analysis I propose to follow in this chapter, but it is a useful starting point. *Management* refers to the churchwarden's relationship with the clergy, the PCC and the members of the congregation; *maintenance* refers to his responsibilities to look after the church building; and *ministry* refers to his pastoral role with regard to his parish priest and to the congregation.

I see his role more as a leader than a manager. It is a shared leadership, but it is leadership rather than management. The churchwarden should be someone who the congregation respects as a leader, and who can take charge when needed. He may have to take a service at ten minutes' notice. He may have to deal with the press when some scandal occurs. He needs to guide the PCC to make the right decisions. He should be wise, and, if needed, firm. He should not be frightened when dealing with senior clergy. He should maintain his own Christian faith, and not let it become stale.

Many of the churchwarden's responsibilities are connected with maintenance. But he also has responsibilities in connection with the Sunday services, for keeping order in the church, and for collecting the church offerings. He has to make various reports each year to the annual parochial meeting and to the archdeacon. He may be a trustee of some charitable trust connected with the church. He has to go to all the meetings of the PCC and the standing committee, and should meet and pray regularly with the parish priest. His work is not just the maintenance of the church building, but helping the smooth running of the church.

His third and most important role is on a personal level. He cares for his parish priest and his parish priest's family. He should also care for the congregation, to encourage its members in their Christian faith, and to help heal any quarrels or disagreements that arise between them or between the congregation and the parish priest.

If you want a brief three-point summary of the churchwarden's role, all beginning with the same letter, I would describe it as *leadership, labour, and love.*

2.   WHO MAY BE A CHURCHWARDEN?

The qualifications for being a churchwarden are that he or she
- should be resident in the parish or on the electoral roll.
- should be over 21.
- should consent to being appointed.
- should have been confirmed, and should have received communion at least three times in the previous year. A person who is ready to be confirmed and wants to be confirmed also qualifies.[2]

The churchwarden's duties involve the handling of money and the ownership and care of valuable property. This calls for as much financial integrity as a charity trustee. Indeed in many parishes the churchwardens become trustees of some charity linked to the church. People who have been convicted of certain offences of dishonesty, and people who have been disqualified as company directors, are not allowed to be charity trustees. Such people should not be appointed as churchwardens either.

3.   APPOINTMENT OF CHURCHWARDENS

(a)   *Choosing the churchwardens*

Churchwardens are chosen annually at the *annual parish meeting,* known also as the *meeting of the parishioners* and the *Easter vestry meeting*.[3] This is a separate meeting from the annual parochial meeting of the church, though the two meetings are almost always held together. At the meeting for the choosing of churchwardens, the people entitled to vote are:

- anybody on the electoral roll of the parish.
- anybody who lives in the parish and whose name is on the register of local government electors.

After the churchwardens have been chosen, only those on the electoral roll of the parish are entitled to vote on the business of the annual parochial meeting.

The two churchwardens should be chosen by the parish priest and the people present at the meeting of parishioners agreeing on who should be appointed. Many people still believe that the parish priest chooses one warden and the people choose the other. This should only happen if the parish priest and the people present cannot agree on the choice of both wardens.

If there are no other candidates, the parish priest should propose a motion to appoint as churchwarden the two people who have been proposed as candidates. A vote is taken on a show of hands. If there are more than two candidates, then an election is taken either on a show of hands or by ballot.

Under new rules proposed for 1999, all candidates for the position of churchwarden should be proposed and seconded at least two days before the meeting. This gives the parish priest time to consider the suitability of the candidates. If the parish priest has no objection to any of the candidates then the meeting chooses two of them, with the two candidates who get the most votes being chosen. If the parish priest is concerned about any of the candidates he may state at the meeting that he will choose one warden and the meeting will then choose the other, and this is what then takes place.

Some churches encourage people to stand for more than one year, to provide continuity and enable a churchwarden to grow into the job. Under the new rules proposed for 1999 a churchwarden may remain in office for a maximum of six years. There should then be a break of at least two years before he or she is appointed again.[4]

(b)   Admission to office

Churchwardens become members of the PCC from the date they are elected. They become the officers of the bishop only after they take up this role (known as being *admitted* to their office) at a special service known as the *archdeacon's visitation*. The outgoing wardens retain office and continue to serve as members of the PCC until their successors are admitted as officers of the bishop. So their legal responsibility continues after the election of their replacements, until they have been admitted to office. For one PCC meeting a year there may be four churchwardens present.

The archdeacon's visitation usually takes place during the course of a mid-week service in early summer. There are usually at least two of these occasions, so that churchwardens can choose the one that is most convenient to attend. All the churchwardens in the area have to attend one or other of these occasions to be admitted to their office. If a new churchwarden is needed sometime in the middle of the church's year, then the archdeacon will arrange a special occasion when he can be admitted to office.

The archdeacon's visitation has something of the feel of a court of law. The churchwardens are summoned to attend by a formal document written in very legal-sounding language. The visitation usually takes place during a church service. During the formal part of the procedure the churchwardens have to make a public declaration, usually in the following form:

I do solemnly and sincerely declare that I will faithfully and diligently perform the duties of the office of Churchwarden.

This declaration is usually made in front of the registrar of the diocese, who wears his wig and gown as though in court. The archdeacon then delivers a *charge* to the churchwardens, that is, a talk or sermon in which he sets out some of the things he wants to make sure they know. Then there is usually food and drink, which is a good opportunity for the archdeacon and all the churchwardens to meet and get to know each other.

4.   A SHARED LEADERSHIP

(a)   *Relationship with the bishop*

The churchwardens are officers of the bishop. In practice, their main duty as the bishop's officers is to ensure that a report is made to the archdeacon each year on a printed form called the archdeacon's *articles of enquiry*. If there have been any serious complaints about the state of the parish or the parish priest's discharge of his duties, the churchwardens should make a serious attempt to deal with such complaints locally in a constructive and co-operative spirit. If this fails to resolve the situation, the churchwardens ought to report the matter to the bishop or archdeacon. The churchwardens owe a duty to the bishop before any duty to the parish priest. For more on resolving complaints, see Chapter 15, 'Resolving Conflicts'.

The bishop, through his archdeacons, may carry out a *visitation* of the parish. The archdeacon will examine the state of the building with the churchwardens, and will check with them that all the church records and registers are being properly kept. It is the churchwardens who are responsible for making and keeping everything in order.

The churchwardens together with the parish priest are the direct link between the bishop and the parish. He has admitted them all to their offices and together they all share in caring for the parish.

(b)   *Relationship with the archdeacon*

The archdeacon is the person who leads the service where churchwardens are admitted to their office. He meets the churchwardens there, and encourages them to make contact with him whenever they need to.

It is most important that churchwardens consult the archdeacon at the beginning stage of any proposal for work of maintenance or alteration of the parish church. He will advise the best way to proceed, and whether or not a faculty is required. In cases where the inside of a church is being reorganised, he can give permission for changes to be made on a temporary basis (for up to twelve months) without the need to apply for a full faculty. The archdeacon will discuss proposed building works to a church with other members of the diocesan advisory committee (the DAC). He is also responsible for advising on state aid grants for church repairs (by English Heritage and the National Lottery). He is likely to know about any local charities who may be able to assist with funds.[5]

The archdeacon is also involved when there are proposals for altering parish boundaries, or altering the way parishes are served by clergy, a process known as *pastoral reorganisation*. If there are proposals for joining parishes together or creating team or group ministries,[6] and these affect your parish, you should consult the archdeacon.

(c)   Relationship with the rural dean

The rural dean has special responsibilities to care for parishes between the time one parish priest leaves and the new one arrives, the time known as a *vacancy* or *interregnum*. But even in ordinary times, he is a person to talk to whenever help is needed in any of his parishes. He is likely to have more local knowledge than the archdeacon. Deaneries have regular meetings where the clergy discuss local issues together. Both the parish priest and the churchwardens should feel free to seek advice and assistance from the rural dean on any matter they feel worried about, or in case of sickness or other emergency.

(d)   Relationship with the parish priest

Churchwardens are supposed to co-operate with the parish priest! This does not mean agreeing with everything he says, but it does mean having a close working relationship with him. The best way to develop this relationship is to have regular meetings for prayer and for sharing a vision of the parish's life and mission.

Churchwardens have a duty to care and pray for the clergy. This includes a concern for his family, his expenses, and his time off. It involves feeding back to the clergy both positive and negative comments of parishioners. It also involves, with the parish priest, sorting out any problems either between the parish priest and members of the congregation, or between members of the congregation themselves.

The churchwarden's job and expertise are not the same as those of the parish priest, and therefore a proper respect for the position of each other should exist.

The churchwardens should try to make sure that the parish priest does not have to do administrative work such as insurance, heating, lighting, cleaning and maintenance of the church and its furnishings, and the repair and replacement of such things as hassocks, hymn and prayer books, notice boards and the like. This is largely achieved through proper use of members of the PCC, the treasurer, and members of the congregation who can help with any of these things. The parish priest should be free from these duties so that he can prepare sermons, lead services, and look after people.

The churchwardens have to make sure there is bread and wine available for Holy Communion. In practice, it is usually left to the parish priest to order fresh supplies when required.

If the parish priest is away and the service is taken by a visiting priest, the churchwardens should check that he is authorised by the bishop to officiate. They should also check that he is paid the proper fee and his expenses. If the parish priest is away, the churchwardens should make sure that there is someone to lead the service, or they should lead it themselves.[7] Of course, if the churchwardens know in advance that the parish priest will be away, they can contact the rural dean for help. But if the parish priest is ill at the last minute, the churchwardens will have to lead the service themselves. How to do this is described in Chapter 9, 'Church Services'.

During a vacancy, the churchwardens have special duties. These are set out in Chapter 17, 'When the parish priest leaves'. In particular, they have to arrange every week for someone to take Holy Communion.

They are also likely to be very much involved in the process of choosing the new parish priest.

(e)   Relationship with the PCC

The churchwardens are members of the PCC, and do not need to be elected to it. They should lead and help the PCC to carry out all its duties. The PCC is called to co-operate with the parish priest in *promoting the whole mission of the church in the parish – pastoral, evangelistic, social and ecumenical.*[8] The church is called to be *pastoral* – to look after individual people; *evangelistic* – to tell people the Good News and invite them to accept it; *social* – to help the poorer members of society, and those suffering from racial, economic and other forms of injustice; and *ecumenical* – to encourage good relations with other Christian denominations. The churchwardens may need to remind the PCC of this.

The churchwardens should try to ensure that the PCC pays the parish contribution to the diocese (the quota or parish share), pays in full all the working expenses of the clergy in the parish, pays for the church to be insured, and pays all its bills. In practice, the treasurer is likely to know the financial state of the parish rather better than the churchwardens, and it is for the treasurer to sound the warning if he thinks there is not enough money to pay these sums.

If no other member of the PCC is willing to be the treasurer, the churchwardens should do the job together.

(f)   Relationship with the congregation

Canon E 1 says that churchwardens are

> to use their best endeavours by example and precept to encourage the parishioners in the practice of true religion and to promote unity and peace among them.

They should be known to parishioners, and available to them. Of course they have their own private lifes, but they should be approachable by anyone in the congregation, and they may become directly involved in looking after such people.

5.   THE PROPERTY OF THE CHURCH

The churchwardens should see that the PCC carries out its responsibilities for the care, maintenance and insurance of the church building and its contents, and for the fencing of the churchyard. The church should be inspected every five years by an architect or suitable chartered surveyor. (This is called the *quinquennial inspection.*) The churchwardens should be familiar with the recommendations made by the architect in the quinquennial inspection report.

The churchwardens, together with the parish priest, should make sure various record books concerning the church property are kept up to date. These are:

- a *terrier*, not a breed of dog, but a list of land belonging to the church.
- an *inventory* of all the items belonging to the church. The churchwardens should ensure that the items on the inventory are inspected at least once a year to check they have not gone missing.
- a *log book* of all alterations, additions and repairs to the church, its lands and articles.

These record books can be purchased from the Council for the Care of Churches. The terrier and inventory are now published together as a *Church Property Register*.

Each year the churchwardens should submit these records to the PCC, and sign a statement saying that they are accurate.[9]

Every year the churchwardens should prepare a written report on the fabric, fixtures, fittings and furniture of the church, and present this to the PCC meeting before the annual parochial church meeting. (The word *fabric* refers to the building itself – stones, bricks and mortar.) The PCC can change the report, and the final version is then presented to the annual parochial church meeting. The report should summarise all the maintenance done or proposed during the past year, and also set out plans to carry out the work recommended in the *quinquennial report.*[10]

The legal title to the plate, ornaments, furniture and furnishings of the church is in the name of the churchwardens. They should ensure that a faculty is obtained before any item is added or disposed of, and before any major repairs are carried out. The parish priest usually obtains all the necessary forms for a faculty, but the churchwardens usually join in signing them.

They should ensure that valuable furnishings, alms boxes and any valuable items are secure against theft. They should make sure items of particular value are kept in the bank, especially when they are not in regular use. Further guidance on this subject is given in Chapter 19, 'Security'.

The PCC has various duties in relation to the church's registers and records.[11] The churchwardens should make sure that these are properly maintained and kept safe.

Each diocese has a set of regulations governing the care of churchyards. The churchwardens should be familiar with the regulations, and make sure that any necessary faculty applications are made. They should see that the PCC maintains the fencing of the churchyard. They should also see that the PCC makes a numbered plan of the graves together with a list of names, and that both are kept up to date.

6.   WORSHIP

The churchwardens are responsible for the seating of the congregation in the church, and for maintaining good behaviour in the church building and churchyard. In practice the sidesmen are the people who welcome people into the church and show them into their places, but they do so on behalf of the churchwardens. The churchwardens should arrange the sidesmen's rota, and ensure that sidesmen are trained to welcome all worshippers, especially visitors.

If there is any trouble during a service, it is the churchwardens who are responsible for restoring order. They can use reasonable force if necessary.

On one occasion I restrained an unruly six-year-old who was running wild in the church. I was promptly set upon by the child's irate mother who considered I had no right to touch her child. There is obviously a conflict between the rights of parents and children and the duties of churchwardens in such situations. The PCC should try to ensure that proper control of children is exercised so that this kind of situation does not arise.

The churchwardens are responsible for the taking of offerings and collections (helped by the sidesmen), for recording the sums received in the service register, and for the proper disposal of the money as directed by the parish priest and the PCC. The churchwardens together with the treasurer should ensure that there is a proper system in place for the collection to be counted by (at least) two people together, and for the money to be properly recorded and banked.

7.   TRAINING FOR CHURCHWARDENS

Many dioceses have training days for churchwardens. When I was a newly-elected churchwarden I found the one I attended invaluable. The courses often cover the topics of repairs, security and insurance. There is often a question and answer session, with two favourite questions being, what happens in an interregnum, and how to deal with disagreements within the parish. All these are the topics of specific chapters in this book.

8.   RESIGNATION

Once in office, a churchwarden cannot resign without the permission of the bishop. He also needs the written consent of the parish priest and any other churchwarden in the parish.

Perhaps it should be said that a parish priest cannot require a churchwarden to resign merely because they have had some serious disagreement. In such situations, a churchwarden may wish to telephone his archdeacon or rural dean on an informal and private basis for advice. The circumstances should be kept quiet so as not to give rise to scandal. The archdeacon or rural dean will arrange to see both parties if necessary to assist a reconciliation. Remember that innocent actions can be misunderstood by the other party; and that saying 'I am sorry' can do more than almost anything else to heal a rift. Remember, too, that one or other party may be going through a bad time, and may just need support.

If a churchwarden leaves the parish, and wants to resign as churchwarden, he should inform the parish priest of the fact, and write to the bishop offering his resignation. Once it is accepted, another person can then be appointed as churchwarden for the remainder of the year until the next annual parochial church meeting. That person is chosen in the same way as at the annual parish meeting. A notice is put up on the church door advertising the meeting to appoint the new churchwarden, and at the meeting an election is held. After the election, the new churchwarden becomes a member of the PCC, and the parish priest should arrange with the archdeacon a service when the new churchwarden can be admitted to his office.

When a churchwarden goes out of office, he should hand over to his successor anything he has which belongs to the church, and the inventory, which his successor should then check.

9.   FURTHER INFORMATION

To help with the running of church services, and with work in the parish context, each churchwarden should have available a copy of the following:

- The Alternative Service Book.
- The Book of Common Prayer.
- The lectionary for the year.
- The diocesan directory or handbook (Dioceses have various names for this publication – the *Blackburn File* and the *Bradford Diocesan Manual* are two examples).
- Your diocese's churchyard regulations, if your church has a churchyard.
- The *Church Representation Rules* (Church House Publishing, 1996), giving all the rules concerning qualification of membership and elections for PCCs and deanery synods.

In addition, the following items are likely to be useful:

- Kenneth MacMorran and Timothy Briden, *A Handbook for Churchwardens and Parochial Church Councillors* (Mowbray, 1996).

- The publications of the Council for the Care of Churches. A list of the most important ones is included in Chapter 20, 'Repairs and maintenance'. They can be obtained from:

THE COUNCIL FOR THE CARE OF CHURCHES
Fielden House
Little College Street
London SW1P 3SH

Tel: 0171 222 3793.

Fax: 0171 222 3794

---

[1] The Ven. Timothy Raphael, now retired archdeacon of Middlesex, at a churchwardens' training day in 1994.

[2] The bishop can permit someone to be appointed who does not satisfy this requirement. A person who is about to be confirmed may well not have taken communion at all.

[3] In the case of Guild churches in the City of London special rules apply.

[4] Under the proposed new rules, a parish may pass a resolution saying that these provisions should not apply in their parish.

[5] See also the section 'Grants and Loans' in Chapter 20, 'Repairs and maintenance'.

[6] In a team ministry, there is one priest (known as the team rector) who is the principal member of the team. In a group ministry, all the incumbents assist with each other's parishes, and there is no one person with overall leadership. See Chapter 16, 'Team ministries'.

[7] In practice the parish priest will usually have arranged for some other priest to take the service.

[8] Parochial Church Councils (Powers) Measure 1956 section 2.

[9] There are many more records which a church has to maintain than just these. See Chapter 24, 'Church records'.

[10] The report made by the inspecting architect following the quinquennial inspection.

[11] Under the Parochial Registers and Records Measure 1978. See Chapter 24, 'Church records'.

Chapter 3

THE PCC

PART I. CHURCH PEOPLE

1. WHAT IT IS

T he PCC is what is called in law *a body corporate*. This means that the PCC is a separate body from the people who serve on it. So no one on the PCC can be made liable for its debts.

I was a churchwarden for just under four years, from 1993 to 1997. At one stage, the PCC wanted to employ someone as a lay assistant to the parish priest. We were going to pay him a salary of £1,000 a month, and were not sure we would have the money to do so. Members of the PCC were worried that if we could not afford to pay him his salary, we might be liable to him as individuals. I told them we would not be, because the members of the PCC are not liable for the PCC's debts. We went ahead and employed him, and God gave us the money to pay his salary.

Being a body corporate also means that a change in the membership of the PCC does not affect the PCC's liability for its debts. So each new PCC should honour the contracts and pledges undertaken by the members of the previous PCC.

2. WHAT IT DOES

The PCC's general functions are set out in the Parochial Church Council (Powers) Measure 1956, section 2. The section starts:

> It shall be the duty of the minister and the PCC to consult together on matters of general concern and importance to the parish.

The section then sets out some of the functions of the PCC. The first is:

> co-operation with the minister in promoting in the parish the whole mission of the Church, pastoral, evangelistic, social and ecumenical.

The church is called to be *pastoral* – to look after individual people; to be *evangelistic* – to tell people the Good News and invite them to accept it; to be *social* – to help the poorer members of society, and those suffering from racial, economic and other forms of injustice; and to be *ecumenical* – to encourage good relations with other Christian denominations.

This point is so important that it has to be set out every year in the annual report presented to the annual parochial church meeting.[1]

The next function is:

> the consideration and discussion of matters concerning the Church of England or any other matters of religious or public interest, but not the declaration of the doctrine of the Church on any question.

Note that it is not the function of the PCC to declare doctrine. Doctrine means the official teaching or beliefs of the Church. As Canon A 5 states:

> The doctrine of the Church of England is grounded in the Holy Scriptures, and in such teachings of the ancient Fathers and Councils of the Church as are agreeable to the said Scriptures.

> In particular such doctrine is to be found in the Thirty-nine Articles of Religion, the Book of Common Prayer, and the Ordinal.

This statement makes it appear as though what is sound doctrine is straightforward. Unfortunately that is not so. There is a large range of views within the Church of England on many matters of doctrine. Ultimately it is for Parliament to decide what is or is not true doctrine for the Church of England, but unless Parliament takes this course, doctrine is left to the Church to work out for itself.[2]

No member of the church or of the PCC should feel pressurised into agreeing some statement which is contrary to his or her beliefs.

Take one example, the question of tithing.[3] There is a clear duty on Christians to support the church financially,[4] but Christians differ on whether we should tithe our income. The parish priest may preach his thoughts and beliefs on the subject, and he and the PCC may encourage members of the church to give in accordance with it. But it remains a matter for individual conscience, and it is not for the PCC to declare an 'official' line for all members of the church or the PCC to follow.

The next functions mentioned are:

> making known and putting into effect any provisions made by the Diocesan Synod or the Deanery Synod, but without prejudice to the powers of the Council on any particular matter.
>
> giving advice to the Diocesan Synod and the Deanery Synod on any matter referred to the Council.
>
> raising such matters as the Council consider appropriate with the Diocesan Synod or Deanery Synod.

This shows the link between the PCC, the deanery synod, and the diocesan synod. Each PCC has on it one or more members of the deanery synod,[5] who act as a link between the deanery synod and the council.

3.   THE PCC AND THE PARISH PRIEST

The key-note here is that the parish priest and the PCC should work together, support each other, and that they should 'get on'. Ideas and plans should be freely discussed between them, and decisions should be taken jointly. The PCC is involved with a lot more than just controlling the spending of money, and looking after the church building. Almost everything to do with the church's work in the parish, and its relationship with the deanery and the diocese, are matters which the PCC and the parish priest should be able to discuss together. The only matters which can not be on the agenda are matters said in confidence to the parish priest on a one-to-one basis as part of his ministry.

4.   THE PCC AND THE CONGREGATION

At the annual parochial church meeting, when the PCC is elected, the parishioners have an opportunity to discuss matters of general concern to the parish. It is important that the PCC takes account of the views expressed at this meeting (or at any other meeting of the parishioners). The section says:

> In the exercise of its functions the Parochial Church Council shall take into consideration any expression of opinion by any parochial church meeting.

At the church where I was churchwarden, the PCC decided that it would be good to remove the wooden pews and replace them with chairs. We talked this through at the annual parochial church meeting, and it was clear from what was said that many members of the congregation had concerns about this course. So we did not go ahead immediately with our proposals. Only after much further discussion, and when we considered that almost all the congregation were now in favour of the change, did we apply for a faculty.

Of course, any good PCC should always try to be aware of the views of the other members of the congregation, to take into account in reaching its decisions. The more the PCC know about the views of the members of the congregation, and the more the members of the congregation know that their views are considered and respected by the PCC, the better it is for everybody in the church.

5.   RIGHTS AND DUTIES

These are considered in detail in other chapters, but it is useful to have a summary of them here.

(a)   The church building

The PCC is responsible for the maintenance and repair of the church and the churchyard, and for the movables in the church. Movables are furniture, equipment, paintings, valuables – anything that can be moved. The topics mentioned below are all considered in detail in Chapter 20, 'Repairs and maintenance', and Chapter 21, 'Insurance'.

(i)   The quinquennial report.

Every five years the inspecting architect makes a report on the state of the church building. The report will usually list urgent works, works of a less urgent nature, and longer-term items for future planning and budgeting. If possible, the PCC should arrange to carry out all works recommended by the inspecting architect. The PCC needs to obtain a faculty before carrying out any major repairs.

(ii)   Insurance

Each year, about one in four churches suffers from a theft, a burglary or a fire. The PCC should insure the church and its contents against fire, theft and other usual risks.

(iii)   Annual inspection and report

Each year the churchwardens carry out or arrange an inspection of the church and its contents, and prepare a report known as the *Fabric Report*. The Fabric Report is presented to the meeting of the PCC before the annual parochial church meeting. The PCC can change this report, and it is then presented to the annual parochial church meeting.

(iv)   Terrier, inventory and log book

The terrier is a record of all land belonging to the church. The inventory is a record of everything else that belongs to the church. The log book is a record of all repairs and alterations carried out to the church building. The churchwardens have a responsibility to keep all these documents up to date, and to give them to the PCC each year to check.

(b)   Other property

The PCC should not acquire any interest in land longer than a yearly lease without the consent of the Diocesan Board of Finance.[6] Similarly, if any property is given to the church on what is known as a *permanent trust*[7] the Diocesan Board of Finance needs to be involved.[8] The title deeds will show the Diocesan Board of Finance as *custodian trustee*, with the PCC as the *managing trustee*. What this means in practice is that any legal arrangements concerning the land have to have the Diocesan Board of Finance's consent. So, for example, the Diocesan Board of Finance needs to be involved if the PCC wants to sell the land, lease it, offer it as security, or take any legal proceedings in relation to it.

Church conveyancing is more complicated than ordinary conveyancing. If you need the name of a firm of solicitors who know about it, your diocesan secretary or the diocesan registrar should be able to recommend one. While I was a churchwarden, the PCC acquired a 21-year lease of a flat from a trust connected with the church. The lease involved (i) the Official Custodian for Charities, (ii) the parish priest and churchwardens (who were the trustees of the trust), (iii) the PCC, and (iv) the London Diocesan Fund. We used a firm of solicitors who understood what was needed.

(c)   Conduct of the financial affairs of the parish

The PCC has overall charge of all expenditure. The treasurer is of course automatically a member of the PCC. The PCC should make an annual budget, and should take steps to raise the money required. At the end of each church year, the PCC should present to the annual parochial church meeting the audited or independently examined accounts of the PCC, and be ready to answer questions relating to the accounts.[9]

The PCC is the employer of staff who work for the church, and pays the salary (or retainer) of people such as the organist, lay workers, administrators, secretaries and the verger.[10] If any formal contract is to be signed on behalf of the PCC, the parish priest needs to sign together with two other members of the PCC.[11] In practice, ordinary contracts such as ordering more stationery and other everyday matters do not need this formality.

The PCC and the parish priest together decide how money collected in church should be divided between the various needs of the church. Some churches make a point of giving a proportion of their collection to some Christian mission abroad.

(d)   Rights regarding women priests

There are widely differing beliefs and positions concerning the ordination of women to the priesthood. Many people welcome the ministry of women priests in all their roles. Some people do not believe that that a woman should lead the Holy Communion service, or pronounce the absolution in church. Some people do not believe that a woman should be appointed as the parish priest. We should respect those who hold different views from our own on the subject.[12]

Under the Priests (Ordination of Women) Measure 1993 a PCC can, if it wishes to, take steps to prevent a woman acting as a priest in the parish. To do this, the PCC needs to vote on and pass one or both of the following resolutions:

PART I. CHURCH PEOPLE

A   That this parochial church council would not accept a woman as the minister who presides at or celebrates the Holy Commnion or pronounces absolution in the parish.

B   That this parochial church council would not accept a woman as the incumbent or priest-in-charge of the benefice or as a team vicar for the benefice.

The resolution should follow these exact words. If you want to pass the resolutions, make sure you keep the following rules so that no-one can challenge them afterwards.

- The PCC secretary should give to the members of the PCC at least four weeks' notice of the meeting. The notice calling the meeting should say the time and place of the meeting, and that the purpose of the meeting is to discuss the resolution. As with any other PCC meeting, you should put a copy of the notice on or near the main door of the church.
- The agenda should set out clearly the text of the resolution you want the PCC to agree.
- At least half of the PCC should be present.
- A simple majority (51 per cent) is all that is required to pass the resolution.
- Once the resolution is passed, you should send a copy to the bishop of the diocese, to the rural/area dean, to the lay-chairman of the deanery synod, to an officer appointed by the bishop,[13] and to the patron.

If your parish is part of a team ministry, and there is already a woman priest as part of the team, you are not allowed to consider either of the resolutions.[14]

A PCC may consider the subject of women priests at any time, whatever the views of the present parish priest are on the subject. The only time when PCCs *have* to consider whether to pass these resolutions is when a new parish priest is to be appointed.[15]

Approximately 850 parishes have passed one or both of the resolutions under the Priests (Ordination of Women) Measure 1993.

Some bishops are in favour of the ordination of women to the priesthood; others are opposed to it. Parishes which are opposed to the ordination of women priests may be in a diocese whose bishop supports this practice. Under the Episcopal Ministry Act of Synod 1993 such parishes can ask their diocesan bishop to make arrangements for some other bishop, who is opposed to women priests, to provide pastoral care for the parish. This other bishop may be another bishop within the same diocese, or a bishop in a neighbouring diocese, or one of the three 'flying bishops' from the dioceses of Canterbury and York.[16]

A parish can only ask for arrangements under the Episcopal Ministry Act of Synod 1993 if it has already passed resolution A or resolution B (or both A and B) under the Priests (Ordination of Women) Measure 1993. PCCs therefore need to pass resolutions A or B first, and then call a second meeting to pass a resolution under the Act of Synod.[17]

Unlike the the Priests (Ordination of Women) Measure 1993, the Episcopal Ministry Act of Synod 1993 does not lay down a form of words for the necessary resolution. A suitable form would be:

> That the Parochial Church Council of .... hereby resolves to petition the Bishop of [*diocese*] to the effect that appropriate episcopal duties in the Parish of .... should be carried out in accordance with the Episcopal Act of Synod 1993.

Again, you should be careful about procedure. The PCC secretary should give at least four weeks' notice of the time and place of the meeting. The agenda should set out the words of the proposed resolution.

If the resolution is passed by a simple majority, send a copy to the diocesan bishop.[18] The bishop *may* act, but he is not *bound* to act unless

- the meeting was attended by at least one-half of the members of the PCC.
- at least two-thirds of the members of the PCC who attended and voted were in favour of the petition.
- the parish priest is in favour of the resolution, whether or not he was present and voted.

The arrangements made by the diocesan bishop for the care of the parish should be reviewed by the PCC every five years.[19] That does not mean that the PCC needs to reconsider every five years its resolution under the Act of Synod. The subject of the arrangements simply needs to be on the agenda, and reviewed by the meeting. No resolution whatever is needed. If the PCC does have any concerns over the arrangements this is the occasion for them to be discussed, and the PCC can then raise the matter with either the diocesan bishop or the new bishop as appropriate.

Nearly 300 parishes have arrangements under the Episcopal Ministry Act of Synod 1993. Many of these parishes are registered with the organisation Forward in Faith. Forward in Faith is a charity giving advice and support to parishes that are opposed to the ordination of women. For further details contact

FORWARD IN FAITH,
Faith House,
7 Tufton Street,
London SW1P 3QN

Tel: 0171 976 0727

Fax: 0171 976 0737

(e) Rights in relation to church appointments

When the parish priest leaves, there is what is known as a vacancy or interregnum. The PCC has an important part to play in choosing the successor. It prepares a written summary or profile, describing the conditions, needs and traditions of the parish, and the kind of parish priest the PCC feel the parish needs. It also appoints two people known as the *parish representatives* (who should be lay persons) to discuss with the patron and the bishop who should be appointed.

An interregnum is one time when the PCC should consider the issue of women priests. At its first meeting after the interregnum starts, the PCC may pass a resolution that it would not accept a woman as a minister who presides at the Holy Communion and pronounces the Absolution. It may also pass a resolution that it would not accept a woman as the new parish priest.[20]

Full details on this subject are in Chapter 17, 'When the parish priest leaves'.

(f)   Functions in relation to church services

The PCC and the parish priest decide what form of service to have on Sunday, whether the formal prayer book service, the service from the Alternative Service Book, or the new *Service of the Word*. The PCC and the parish priest should also agree what version of Scripture to use at the services, and what robes the parish priest is to wear.

These topics are considered in full in Chapter 9, 'Church Services'.

(g)   Miscellaneous

The parish priest cannot dismiss the organist without the agreement of the PCC. (In exceptional circumstances this rule does not apply, but the archdeacon has to consent instead. The effect is that the parish priest can never act single-handedly.)[21]

The PCC can make representations to the bishop on any matter affecting the welfare of the church. In practice, the PCC would normally first raise the matter with the rural dean or the archdeacon, who act as the bishop's officers for this purpose.

The PCC has a right to be consulted if the parish is to be the subject of a *pastoral scheme*. A pastoral scheme is an arrangement under which the area of land in the parish, or the arrangements for clergy to serve in the parish, is altered. So, for example, the PCC should be consulted where a *team ministry* or a *group ministry*[22] is proposed.

The PCC should agree to any church-sharing agreement. A church-sharing arrangement is one where the church building is shared by members of different denominations. In some cases joint services are held,[23] in other cases the building is used at different times by each denomination.

6.   MEMBERSHIP OF THE PCC

(a)   Appointment of the PCC

Certain people are by law members of the PCC. They are:

- all priests and deacons licensed to the parish. This does not include retired clergy who just take services in the parish.

- any deaconesses or lay workers licensed to the parish.
- the churchwardens.[24]
- any person on the electoral roll who is a member of the Deanery Synod, the Diocesan Synod or the General Synod.

Readers are not automatically members of the PCC unless the annual parochial church meeting decides that they (or some of them) should be. If a reader is not automatically on the PCC, he or she may be elected as one of the lay representatives, or he or she may be co-opted onto the PCC. It is obviously sensible that readers should be on the PCC unless there are strong reasons why they should not be (for example, where a parish has a large number of such persons).

In addition there are *elected* members, and *co-opted* members. Elected means chosen by the annual parochial church meeting. Co-opted members are chosen by the PCC during the course of the year, usually to make up numbers if someone has left.

The number of elected members of the PCC is decided by the annual parochial church meeting, but if the meeting alters the existing number, the alteration only takes effect from the next meeting. So, if the 1998 meeting alters the number from 18 to 16, it remains 18 for the 1998 year and becomes 16 for the election in 1999.

The number who can be co-opted during the year is two, or one-fifth of the number of elected members if that produces a greater number.

A person who is to be elected should

- be on the electoral roll.
- be over 16.
- consent to being appointed.
- have been confirmed (or he should be ready to be confirmed and want to be confirmed), and should have received communion at least three times in the previous year.[25]

The bishop can dispense with this last requirement in a suitable case.

A person who is to be co-opted does not need to be on the electoral roll, but he or she should be over 16, and receive communion. Clergy can be co-opted onto the PCC.

(b)   Length of service

Members of the deanery synod elected by the annual parochial church meeting hold office for three years. These members of the deanery synod are members of the PCC for the same period.

The normal rule for everyone else is that they are elected for one year, from the conclusion of one annual parochial church meeting until the conclusion of the next.

Some parishes prefer that members of the PCC should serve for three years. The annual parochial church meeting can decide to adopt this course, in which case a third of the elected members of the PCC retire each year, being those who have served the longest.

The annual parochial church meeting can decide to put a limit on the number of years a person can serve on the PCC without a break. The annual parochial church meeting can also decide how many years such a person should remain off the PCC after serving this number of years, before he or she stands for election once again.

(c)   Removal

A person ceases to be a member of the PCC during the course of the year:

- if his name is removed from the electoral roll, for example because he moves away from the parish and ceases to worship there for six months.
- if he does not apply for his name to be put on the new electoral roll when this is being compiled.
- if he becomes disqualified from being a charity trustee, for example if he becomes bankrupt, or is disqualified from acting as a company director.
- if the bishop disqualifies him from being on the PCC.

Sometimes a person on the PCC is involved in some scandal, and the parish priest or other members of the PCC are concerned that that person should not continue to serve on the PCC. Of course, the person may be willing to retire on account of what has taken place; but if he is not willing, the only way he can be removed from the PCC prior to the next annual parochial church meeting is for the bishop to make an order disqualifying him from being on the PCC.

7.   PCC MEETINGS

A PCC meeting can fall into two errors. It can be too formal, or too informal. At one extreme it can become like the annual general meeting of a large company, where major decisions seem to be rubber-stamped, and the meeting sometimes gets bogged down with arguments about matters of procedure. At the other extreme, meetings can drag on interminably with discussion on one or two matters. Important business then gets left to the last five minutes when everyone is wanting to get home, so not enough time is left to deal with it properly.

It is a mistake to think that just because we are all Christians, there should not be some rules on how meetings should be run. Equally, there is a world of difference between a PCC meeting and a company meeting. That difference is our Lord's presence in the hearts of the members of the PCC, and at the meeting itself. That is one reason why PCC meetings usually begin with prayer. We ask for His blessing, His guidance and His wisdom, for ultimately it is His church, not ours, that we are responsible for.

(a)   Arranging the meetings

The PCC should meet at least four times a year. It can of course meet more often than this.[26] If there are only four meetings, they should be at three-monthly intervals. The parish priest can arrange extra meetings if necessary, and the members themselves can arrange a meeting if one-third of them have asked the parish priest to do so and he has declined to call a meeting.[27]

Except in an emergency, a notice of the meeting should be posted on the door of the church at least 10 days before the meeting. Again, except in an emergency, at least 7 days before the meeting a copy of the agenda should be sent to every member of the PCC. If a meeting has to be postponed, the new meeting should be within 14 days of the date originally fixed for the meeting.

(b)   What happens at a PCC meeting?

The parish priest is the chairman of the PCC, and at least one-third of the members of the PCC should be present. (If fewer than this number turn up nothing done at the meeting is binding on the others.)

It often happens that new items for discussion crop up in the seven days before the meeting. If an item is not on the agenda, it can only be dealt with under the heading of *any other business*.[28] An item can only be taken under *any other business* if three-quarters of the people present at the meeting agree to discuss it. If the item is important, members of the PCC may be reluctant to discuss it if they have not had sufficient time to consider it before the meeting.

Matters which cannot be agreed at the meeting can be put to the vote, and the side with the greater number of votes wins. If there is an equal division of votes the chairman has a second, or casting, vote.

That is the strict legal position. But in a Christian spirit of charity it may not be right to have a vote on important issues of principle. A parish priest may be able to feel the sense of a meeting on a particular point without needing to put it to a vote. Voting on major issues can lead to divisions within the PCC, and to a lack of charity amongst its members. Needing to vote on a major issue often indicates that there are serious difficulties with what is proposed, and that it would not be right to proceed, whichever side wins. Voting on unimportant issues is neither here nor there. A vote whether or not to hire a bouncy castle for the church fete is not going to make or break relationships on the PCC. Voting on whether or not to dismiss the choir may be another matter.

Sometimes a formal vote is needed or is useful, either for legal reasons or on a personal level. In an application for a faculty, the chancellor needs to know whether or not the PCC approves of the proposal, and this is indicated by a vote in support or against the proposal. A unanimous vote in support of a particular candidate for a position in the church can be a good boost to the morale of that person. Important property transactions involving the church often need to be formally approved by the PCC.

PCC meetings normally follow a fairly standard pattern.

PART I.   CHURCH PEOPLE

After prayers, and noting any apologies from people who are absent, the first item is to *approve the minutes* of the previous meeting. The minutes are the official record of each meeting. They are prepared by the PCC Secretary, and it is important that they are a fair record of what took place. Those who were present should confirm that they are, or point out any mistakes so that the minutes can be corrected. The parish priest will then sign his copy of the minutes (corrected if necessary), and this becomes the official record of the previous meeting. All this should only take a couple of minutes.

Next is the item known as *matters arising*. The purpose of this is to report any action taken as a result of decisions made at the last meeting. It is not to re-open the discussion on what has already been decided. So, if the PCC decided at the last meeting to re-paint the parish room, and this had taken place, this could be noted under this heading.

If there has been a meeting of the Standing Committee, *the minutes of the Standing Committee meeting* should also be available for the PCC meeting to see. A member of the Standing Committee who was present at the Standing Committee meeting should confirm that the minutes of the Standing Committee meeting are accurate (and they should be corrected, if they are not).

The point of seeing the minutes of the meeting of the Standing Committee is that the Standing Committee is not an independent body from the PCC. It is a part of the PCC, and is *accountable* to the PCC. That word means it should give an account to the PCC of what it has done. Thus, the PCC should see the minutes of the Standing Committee. The PCC can also ask questions and comment on what the Standing Committee has done.

Then there are the *main items* for discussion. These of course vary each time.

The last item on the formal agenda is an item called *any other business*. This is an opportunity to deal with matters which are not on the agenda but which need to be said. Strictly, three-quarters of the meeting have to agree to discuss any item mentioned under this heading. In practice, if they are short matters of a few minutes, nobody bothers with this rule. If they are large matters needing 20 minutes' discussion, then people might feel they should have been given proper warning, and need time to think before deciding the issue. The moral, for the parish priest or anyone else seeking to raise an important matter under *any other business*, is to give people as much notice of the item as possible before the meeting. It helps too if the person who wants to raise an important item can summarise it on paper in time for a copy to be sent to all members of the PCC well before the meeting.

That is the end of the formal agenda. But it should not be the end of the meeting. As at the start, there should be prayer, to commit to God the decisions that have been made. And I suggest it should end with the Grace.

(c)   Practical tips for the PCC meeting

These are offered not as rules, but as tips which many parishes have found helpful.

(i)   The layout of the chairs

If the PCC sits in a circle or horseshoe where everybody can see everybody, each person can be useful to the whole group. It is also clear that everybody counts and has a part to play.

(ii)   Major items of business

For major items such as planning a budget for the next year, a mission to the parish, or a major building plan, it is useful for one person to explain the subject first. Many PCCs find it helpful to have a screen and overhead projector or a flip chart so that people can take in what is being said.

Next, ask for any questions, purely to clarify what has been said.

It is very useful if the members then talk to each other in twos and threes, not going into groups, just turning round to their neighbour for a couple of minutes. This enables all present to take part in the meeting, and possibly test out their ideas on their neighbours.

Then open up the discussion to everybody. The result is that everyone has given some thought to the proposals, and a much more useful discussion will follow.

(iii)   *Action*

It can save much embarrassment if the Secretary checks with the whole PCC at the end of each item who is going to be responsible for doing what has been agreed. The Secretary should then put at the end of that paragraph of the minutes:

> Action: Mary Jones/the building committee/the parish priest (whatever has been agreed).

(iv)   *Timing*

If meetings end at 9.30 p.m. often useful and friendly chat follows. If the meeting ends at 10 p.m., everybody rushes off home. Anything after 10 p.m. is a waste of time because people are too tired.

(v)   *The vice-chairman*

In some parishes and in some situations it may be useful if the vice-chairman actually chairs the meeting even while the parish priest is present. In others, the chairman and vice-chairman alternate in chairing meetings. (It has been known for them to vie for the shortest meeting.)

8.   FURTHER INFORMATION

For the conduct of the elections for the PCC, see Chapter 10, 'The annual parochial church meeting'.

For the responsibilities for repairs, insurance and other matters connected with the church building, see Chapter 20, 'Repairs and maintenance', Chapter 21, 'Insurance', and Chapter 19, 'Security'.

For the financial responsibilities, see Chapter 4, 'The Treasurer', Chapter 25, 'Covenants and Gift Aid', and Chapter 26, 'Church Accounts'.

All members of the PCC should understand the benefits of giving money using a covenant or Gift Aid, so that they can encourage members of the congregation to give to the church in this way. For this, see Chapter 25, 'Covenants and Gift Aid'.

A Handbook for Churchwardens and Parochial Church Councillors, by Kenneth MacMorran and Timothy Briden (Mowbray, 1996).

An ABC for the PCC, by John Pitchford (Mowbray).

Administry publishes two guides on how to run PCC meetings:

- *We can't go on meeting like this!*
- *In the hot seat* (chairing meetings).

ADMINISTRY
PO Box 57,
St Albans,
Herts AL1 3DT

Tel: 01727 856370

Administry also runs a one-day training course for parish priests and church staff on running meetings. The course covers planning and chairing church business meetings, and taking decisions in a group.

---

[1] Church Accounting Regulations 1997, paragraph 27.

[2] See *Williamson, ex p.* (1994) Times, 9 March 1994. The full judgment is printed in Mark Hill, *Ecclesiastical Law* (Butterworths, 1995), page 77.

[3] Tithing means giving one tenth of your income to the Church. It is specifically ordered in the Old Testament: Lev. 27: 30–2, Deut. 14:22–4. It is however only implied in the New Testament: Matt. 5:17–19, 23:23. The New Testament places much greater emphasis on voluntary giving: 2 Cor. 9:6–7. See the article on tithing in the *Oxford Dictionary of the Christian Church*, 3rd edn. (Oxford University Press, 1997). And see the section 'How much should we give?' in Chapter 4, 'The Treasurer'.

[4] Thus, for example, in *A Short Guide to the Duties of Church Membership*, issued by the Archbishops of Canterbury and York at the request of the Church Assembly in May 1954, the archbishops call upon all baptised and confirmed members of the Church:

> to give money for the work of parish and diocese and for the work of
> the Church at home and overseas.

The text of the short guide can be found reprinted in John Stott, *Your Confirmation* (Hodder and Stoughton, 1958), page 117.

[5] The actual number is decided by each diocesan synod. The secretary of the diocesan synod writes to the secretary of the PCC to say how many people the parish should supply for the deanery synod the following year.

[6] Parochial Church Councils (Powers) Measure 1956 section 6.

[7] When property is held on *permanent trust*, you can only use the *income* from the property, not the *capital*. So you cannot sell the property and spend all the money.

[8] See the Incumbents and Churchwardens (Trusts) Measure 1964.

[9] See Chapter 4, 'The treasurer'.

[10] See Chapter 6, 'Employees and office holders', and Chapter 7, 'The verger, the organist and the administrator'.

[11] Parochial Church Councils (Powers) Measure 1956 section 3.

[12] See the Episcopal Ministry Act of Synod 1993 recital (3) (a).

[13] Under the Patronage (Benefices) Measure 1986 section 7 (5). If no officer has been appointed under this provision, send a copy to the secretary of the diocesan pastoral committee.

[14] See the Priests (Ordination of Women) Measure 1993, section 3 (3). For team ministries generally, see Chapter 16, 'Team ministries'.

[15] Patronage (Benefices) Measure 1986, section 11 (1) (f). See Chapter 17, 'When the parish priest leaves'.

[16] The proper title for these *flying bishops* is *Provincial Episcopal Visitors*: see Chapter 1, 'Who's who?'.

[17] Resolutions A and B arise under the Priests (Ordination of Women) Measure 1993. For obvious reasons the resolution under the Episcopal Ministry Act of Synod 1993 has come to be known as Resolution C.

[18] The *Encyclopaedia of Forms and Precedents* 5th edn. vol. 13 (2) 1996 reissue (Butterworths, 1996) page 110 gives a suitable form to use for the petition to the bishop. However, a letter is all that is required. The letter should enclose a copy of the resolution, and simply ask the bishop to make arrangements for the parish in accordance with the Episcopal Ministry Act of Synod 1993. The letter should confirm that 4 weeks' notice was given to the members of the PCC. The letter should say how many people attended the meeting, how many were entitled to attend, how many voted in favour of the resolution, how many against it, and how many abstained. The letter should say whether the parish priest is in favour of the resolution, or against it.

[19] Episcopal Ministry Act of Synod 1993 section 9 (2).

[20] Four weeks' notice is not required before passing resolution A or resolution B in the case of the statutory meeting under section 11 of the Patronage (Benefices) Measure 1986.

[21] This is likely to apply where there is a dispute concerning the choir and many members of the choir are also members of the PCC, or where some improper relationship has developed, and there is a risk of scandal.

[22] In a team ministry, there is one parish priest (known as the rector) who is the principal member of the team. In a group ministry, all the parish priests assist

with each other's parishes, and there is no one person with overall leadership. See Chapter 16, 'Team ministries'.

[23] Under what is known as a *local ecumenical project.*

[24] Provided they receive Holy Communion and their names are on the electoral roll: Church Representation Rules, rule 14 (1) (d).

[25] Church Representation Rules, rule 10 (1) and rule 54 (1).

[26] In rural parishes PCCs often meet less than four times a year.

[27] The request should be in writing, and they should give him one week to convene the meeting before deciding to hold it themselves.

[28] See page 46.

Chapter 4

THE TREASURER

PART I.   CHURCH PEOPLE

1.   INTRODUCTION

I have split the work of the treasurer into four chapters: this one, which gives a summary of the work of the treasurer, Chapter 25, 'Covenants and Gift Aid', Chapter 26, 'Church Accounts', and Chapter 27, 'VAT'. The treasurer will need to read all four chapters in detail. The covenant secretary will no doubt concentrate on Chapter 25. Other people need to read this chapter fairly fully, but the other chapters only in outline. Everyone should have some understanding of how covenants and Gift Aid work, and members of the

PCC need to be able to understand the accounts otherwise they may be failing in their duty of care.

2.   THE WORK OF THE TREASURER

The Church of England has no official guidelines covering the sort of person who should be a treasurer. He is much more than just a book-keeper.

- There should be no doubt about his honesty.
- For a normal-size church, the treasurer does not need to be a qualified accountant, but he does need to know more than just how to keep a cash book. For a very large church, or if the church's financial affairs are complex, he should be a qualified accountant.
- He needs to understand the work of the church in the parish. Through this he will understand what the needs of the church are, and also what its resources are, both in human and in money terms.
- He needs to be able to explain things both simply and gently. He should be sympathetic to the views of other PCC members.
- He is a full member of the PCC, and should be at all the PCC meetings. Even if there is nothing about money on the agenda, he ought to know about all that is being done in the parish, and the plans for the future.
- He will come to know how much or how little money some of the members of the church have, and how much they give to the church. He should be able to keep this strictly confidential.

Some of these standards are no different from those than any member of the PCC should have: honesty, understanding the work of the church, and being sensitive to other views.

In April 1998 there is being formed an association of church accountants and treasurers. This is a very welcome development, and should be of great assistance to parish treasurers throughout the country. For further information contact:

PART I.   CHURCH PEOPLE

THE ASSOCIATION OF CHURCH ACCOUNTANTS AND TREASURERS
Jeremy Hopkinson Esq.
Binder Hamlyn,
20 Old Bailey,
London EC4M 7BH

Tel: 0171 489 4000

(a)   His main tasks

The treasurer has a number of jobs, which are listed below. But the PCC should remember that it is the PCC which is in charge of the church's money, and that the treasurer is only acting on the PCC's behalf. This is important as some treasurers think they can dictate how money should be spent.

(i)   Carry out the financial policy of the PCC

The PCC decides how much money it is going to spend each year, and where that money is going to come from. The treasurer carries out this policy, by keeping control of the money the church spends, and by keeping watch over the church income.

(ii)   Prepare a budget

The treasurer needs to prepare for the autumn PCC meeting a rough budget for the following year, for the PCC to approve.

(iii)   Record all cash transactions

He should make sure that all cash received or paid by the church is written down in the cash book.

(iv)   Keep a watch on the finances of the church

All through the year he should keep an eye on how much money the church has, to make sure that there is always going to be money when it is needed. If he thinks the church is not going to have enough, he should make sure the PCC knows what is happening, and why, as soon as possible.

(v)   Keep the PCC aware of its duties

This means reminding the PCC to pay the quota or parish share, to pay for insurance, to pay back the clergy their expenses, and to pay any other church expenses which the PCC may not know about. He needs to be able to advise the PCC and members of the congregation on matters such as covenanting and other ways of giving.

(vi)   Encourage the wider mission of the church

He should remind the PCC of its duty to support other Christian charities and missions, both in England and abroad.

(vii)   Set up a system of book-keeping

He will need to:

- Make sure all money coming in is recorded, comes to him, and goes into the bank.
- Pay and keep a record of all expenses which are paid.
- Keep clear and accurate account books, and the necessary documents to explain his entries in the accounts.

How to do this is described below.

(viii)   Prepare the annual accounts for the annual parochial church meeting

How to do this is described in Chapter 26, 'Church Accounts'. The accounts are presented first to the PCC, and then on behalf of the PCC to the annual parochial church meeting. They also have to be inspected by an independent examiner or auditor.

In most churches, the treasurer will personally prepare the accounts for the PCC. In some cases the treasurer may prefer that they should be professionally prepared, and this is quite in order provided the PCC agrees. The treasurer should of course have kept proper records for the accountant to carry out this task.

(ix)   Free the parish priest from worry over the church finances

The vicar's role is to be pastor to his congregation and his parish. He is not trained to be a financial expert, and he needs to be free to exercise his spiritual ministry without becoming too involved in parish finance.

(b)   Appointment

The treasurer is an officer of the PCC. He is appointed by the PCC from the members of the PCC. He is not appointed by the annual parochial church meeting. It is better not to combine the jobs of churchwarden and treasurer, but if no-one is willing to be the treasurer, the churchwardens should take on the position of treasurer as well as being churchwardens.

The appointment is made at the first meeting after the annual parochial church meeting. A person not on the PCC may be co-opted so that he can then be appointed treasurer.

(c)   Relationship with the PCC

It is the PCC which is responsible for the financial affairs of the church. The treasurer only does his job on behalf of the PCC. When he presents the accounts to the annual parochial church meeting, he presents them on behalf of the PCC.

In practice, the PCC delegates a good deal of its authority to do with money to the treasurer. It is important however that he should always remember that the final authority and responsibility over money is the PCC's, not his.

The treasurer needs to be on good terms with the parish priest, with the members of the standing committee, and if possible with all members of the PCC. Through this everyone will learn to understand his concerns as treasurer, and he in turn will be able to understand their wishes as members of the church.

The treasurer should be a member of the standing committee.

(d)   The treasurer's main records

His main records will consist of:

- the cash-book(s).

- a file of invoices and documents relating to payments for the current year.
- bank statements, cheque book stubs, and investment records.
- a file of the budgets and annual statement of accounts for previous years.
- a file for correspondence.

Cash-book(s), invoices, cheque book stubs, bank statements and all other records should be kept for six years plus the current year. It is best to label them clearly for storage.

3.   SOME TERMS

To avoid confusion, there are some terms which need to be understood.

(a)   A fund

A fund is a sum of money which can be used to make payments. The church may have more than one fund, and some funds may be earmarked for specific purposes.

Each fund has its own account in the PCC's records, though not necessarily its own bank account.

There are three different types of fund, and the treasurer should keep them separate. Funds which can be used for any purpose are known as *unrestricted funds*. The *general fund* is the church's main unrestricted fund, and all unrestricted income is paid into it. Most expenses are paid out of it.

Funds which can only be used for a special purpose are known as *restricted funds*. If money is given to the church on condition that it is only used for one purpose, then it should be used for that purpose and for nothing else. For example, one lady in her will left a large sum of money to her parish church for the music in the church. That fund was used to pay for the restoration of the organ. It would have been both morally and legally wrong to have used it for the general expenses of the church.

The last type of fund is known as an *endowment*. An endowment is where money or some property has been given to the church with the specific instruction that only the interest gained from the money or property can be spent.

Some PCCs like to set aside or 'earmark' part of the general fund for a particular purpose – e.g. for mission giving. A fund set aside for a particular purpose is known as a *designated* fund. Although the PCC may decide to use the designated fund for one particular purpose, it could if necessary be used for *any* purpose. Designated funds are therefore a type of *unrestricted* funds.

So, here is a summary of the different types of fund:

- *unrestricted*: can be used for any purpose. If the PCC chooses to sets aside a sum for a special purpose, that sum is a *designated* fund. The church's general fund is the main unrestricted fund.
- *restricted funds*: can only be used for the purpose for which the money was given.
- *endowments*: a special form of trust. Only the income can be spent.

(b)   An account

An account is simply the record of the receipts and payments relating to one fund, e.g. the fabric fund account, or the choir account.

(c)   The parish accounts

The parish accounts are the accounts of all the funds which the parish has. It also means the complete record of the parish's financial transactions. Keeping these records properly is 'keeping the accounts'.

The PCC is in charge of all the funds in the parish accounts. That does not prevent the PCC giving the day-to-day control of some fund to a person who is involved with it; but the PCC remains in overall control.

4.   THE MAIN EXPENSES OF A CHURCH

The Charities Act 1993 introduced new accounting rules for almost all charities, including money given to the church.[1] In 1997 the Church of England itself introduced new accounting rules for churches.[2] The Central Board of Finance (the CBF) has prepared a set of guidance notes to the new requirements, *The Charities Act 1993 and the PCC* (Church House Publishing, 1997).

Expenses should now be divided into four main areas:

- Grants.
- Activities directly relating to the work of the church.
- Fund-raising and publicity.
- Church management and administration.

(a)   Grants

This covers all missionary and charitable giving.

In some cases money will be collected in the parish for a particular mission or charity, and will be paid through the parish accounts. In other cases, the PCC may decide to give some money to missionary work from its general funds. Amounts collected specifically for missionary giving should be shown in the annual accounts as a restricted fund.

(b)   Activities directly relating to the work of the church

This covers the following areas:

- Ministry expenses.
    - Diocesan quota/parish share.
    - Working expenses of the parish priest.
    - Expenses of the vicarage.
    - Expenses of assistant staff.

    Further details on these items is set out below.
- Church running expenses.
    - Heating, lighting, cleaning, insurance.
- Church maintenance.
    - Minor repairs and routine maintenance.

    Some parishes pay for regular maintenance out of the general fund; others have a fabric fund for this purpose. A large-scale project for restoration and extension is best dealt with in a separate fabric fund.
- Upkeep of services.
    - Service books, music leaflets, choir robes, candles, communion wine and bread.
- Upkeep of churchyard.
- Expenditure on parish magazine and bookstall.
- Support costs.

Parish training and mission.
Education (Sunday school, lay training).

- Hall running costs.
- Other PCC property upkeep.
- Major repairs to structure.
- Major repairs/replacements of installations.
- Interior and exterior re-decoration.
- Salaries and payments made to verger, clerk, sexton, organist, choir.
- New building or major works.
- Depreciation (for accounts which are prepared on the accruals basis only).[3]

The first item, *Ministry Expenses*, covers a large range of expenses:

(i)   The quota or parish share

Each parish contributes to the total costs of the diocese through the quota or parish share system. The biggest elements of diocesan costs are clergy stipends and housing. The best way to pay the quota is by monthly standing order. Some dioceses offer discounts for regular payments.

(ii)   Working expenses of the parish priest

The expenses of the parish priest carrying out his duties should be budgeted for and met in full by the PCC. The PCC should pay for the following:

- Telephone.

The account should normally be paid direct, by the PCC. If the parish priest refunds the cost of private calls to the PCC, that is income for which the PCC has to account.

- Postage and stationery.
- Secretarial assistance.
- Office equipment.

The PCC should pay the cost of all secretarial assistance given to the parish priest, and also the cost of necessary office equipment. This includes the cost of a computer and software if the parish priest uses this for his work.

- Books.

The parish priest should be reimbursed for the cost of books and periodicals which he needs for his work.

- Robes.

The PCC should pay for repairs and replacements of all robes which the parish priest needs to use.

- Hospitality.

A small monthly hospitality allowance from the PCC is probably the best way of meeting expenses the parish priest incurs in entertaining visitors to the parish and members of the congregation.

- Visiting clergy.

The PCC should pay in full the expenses of all visiting clergy.

- Travel.

Where the parish priest uses public transport, the PCC should reimburse his fares in full. Where he uses his private car, he should be reimbursed at a suitable rate per mile. The diocese will have information on what rate should be allowed.

Some PCCs and trusts may want to be more generous and pay for other expenses as well – for example the cost of ministry retreats.

A free handbook entitled *The Parochial Expenses of Clergy – A Guide to Their Reimbursement* is available from The Stipends Department, The Church Commissioners, 1 Millbank, London SW1P 3JZ.

(iii)   *Expenses of the vicarage*

This covers repairs, water rates and interior redecoration.

(iv)   *Assistant staff*

This covers assistant clergy, pastoral staff, youth workers, visiting clergy and speakers.

(c)   **Fund-raising and publicity**

This covers

- fees paid to a professional fund-raiser.

- costs of a particular fund-raising campaign.
- cost of fetes, bazaars and other fund-raising events.

(d)   Church management and administration

This covers administration costs and the salary of a parish administrator. The salaries of the organist and other lay assistants come under the heading of activities directly relating to the work of the church.

5.   HANDLING RECEIPTS

The weekly collection sheet on the following page may be useful. Details should agree with the amounts banked.

It is important to keep to the following rules.

- All collections and envelopes should be checked by two people together as soon as possible after receipt. Make sure the checkers sign the record so that they can be identified.
- Make sure that all receipts are promptly and regularly banked.
- Make all payments only by cheque or through a petty cash float, not straight out of income. How to run a petty cash float is described in 'Handling payments', below.
- For every amount that you bank, record where the money came from. Check your record agrees with the bank statement when it arrives.
- Some payments are made directly into the church bank account, e.g. interest received on a deposit account, and covenanted payments paid by standing order. When you receive the bank statement showing these items, you should enter up the items into the cash book. By doing this, you make sure that for every item shown as income in the bank statement, there is a corresponding item in the cash book.
- Make sure that records of covenant income and Gift Aid donations are kept properly. See Chapter 25, 'Covenants and Gift Aid'.

WEEKLY COLLECTION SHEET

.... Parochial Church Council

Collections	_____
Specific collections	_____
Donations	_____
Covenants (envelopes)	_____

(Envelopes should have donor's
number and be dated, and contents
written in ink on envelope)[4]

Fees	_____
Hire of Church Hall	_____
Other income	_____
Banked cash	_____
Banked cheques	_____
Total banked	_____

Date _____ Signed _____

Name _____

6. HANDLING PAYMENTS

Most payments made by the treasurer are of a routine nature, and the amounts can be predicted fairly accurately. If the lighting, heating and water last year cost £3,000, it is reasonable to predict that this year it will cost somewhere between £2,500 and £3,500. The treasurer prepares a budget, and once the PCC has approved it, the treasurer has the authority to spend the amount allotted for each item in the budget.

The treasurer needs to come back to the PCC or the standing committee if he considers that any item will cost more than the figure mentioned in the budget. The PCC or standing committee can then decide whether or not to authorise the extra amount to be spent.

All payments should be made by cheque, wherever possible. All invoices should be filed. If there is no invoice for an item, then a piece of paper should be written out giving details of the payment – the date, the amount, what it was for, who it was paid to, and perhaps why there was no invoice. Invoices and details of payments where there is no invoice should be kept in the order in which they are paid, with a note of the cheque number used to pay them, so that easy cross-reference is possible.

If it is necessary to pay for certain small items in cash – e.g. postage stamps, matches, or a bus ticket, a *petty cash float* should be used. It works as follows:

- The treasurer decides on the float amount – say £40.
- He writes a cheque for £40 payable to 'cash'.
- He opens a petty cash book in which all petty cash receipts and payments are entered.
- Receipts or their substitutes are kept to support every payment entry. That means, if he does not get a receipt for a payment, he should write out on a sheet of paper what he spent the money on.
- At any one time, the receipts and details of other payments, plus the amount left of the original £40 should total £40.
- When the £40 is nearly exhausted, the treasurer draws another cheque to cash for the amount needed to bring the float back to £40. The payment is entered in the main cash book, described as *transfer to*

petty cash. The receipts for the original float are filed, and he starts again with the new float.

7. BANK AND BUILDING SOCIETY ACCOUNTS

It is easiest to keep all the money from all the funds of a parish in one branch of one bank or building society, except for any money which is invested separately to get a better rate of interest (e.g. in the CBF Church of England deposit fund, described below).

It is best to have only a current account for receipts and payments, and a higher rate interest account for short-term surplus cash. Where money is placed on deposit, make sure that interest is paid gross. You may need a tax reference from the Inland Revenue to be able to have interest paid gross.

If there is only one account, there will only need to be one cheque book and one paying in book in use at one time. If the parish has more than one fund, then the cheque stubs, paying in book and bank statements will have to be marked to show which fund each item relates to.

Whenever you receive a statement from your bank or building society, you should reconcile the statement with your accounts. That means that you should check that each item shown in the bank statement is for the correct amount, and corresponds with an item in your cash book.

Obviously, banking charges should be kept to a minimum. Most banks and building societies now operate treasurers' accounts which give free banking to charities with modest income and outgoings. Free banking depends on the number of transactions rather than their value.

The PCC needs to pass a resolution whenever a new bank or building society account is to be opened, and whenever the bank account signatories change. It is good practice, and it protects the individual, if the signatures of two people are required on each cheque. It is useful to have (say) four people who are authorised to sign cheques, and to specify that any two of them may sign a cheque (provided they are not two people from the same household). You need to make special arrangements to cover times when one or more of the people authorised to sign cheques is ill or away on holiday.

A list should be kept of those who are authorised to sign cheques, and this should be kept up to date. This is easily dealt with annually when the PCC appoints its treasurer.

No-one should ever sign a blank cheque. This may well be inconvenient, but if it is done, the whole point of needing two signatures is lost. If it is *essential* to pre-sign a cheque, the cheque should be limited in amount.

8.   INVESTMENTS

The Central Board of Finance of the Church of England (sometimes referred to as the CBF), through its investment office provides a choice of suitable investments for funds which are surplus to immediate parish requirements.

The *Central Board of Finance Church of England deposit fund* is intended for cash balances at short notice. It almost always offers a higher rate of interest than that paid by the banks, and close to money market rates even on small sums. Interest is always paid gross. Deposits may be made at any time, and withdrawals can be made very quickly.

The *Central Board of Finance investment fund* is the main fund for long-term capital. Its portfolio is mainly invested in UK and overseas equities. Its aim is steady income and capital growth.

The *Central Board of Finance Fixed Interest Securities Fund* invests only in fixed interest stocks, and is useful to supplement the initial lower income yield on the *Central Board of Finance investment fund.* It offers no protection against inflation.

Dividends and interest on all the Central Board of Finance funds are paid quarterly without deduction of tax. The money can be transferred directly to a PCC bank account, or it can be retained in a Central Board of Finance Deposit Fund or reinvested in additional shares.

For further details of any of the Central Board of Finance funds, contact

THE CENTRAL BOARD OF FINANCE INVESTMENT OFFICE
St Alphage House,
2 Fore Street,
London EC2Y 5AQ

Tel: 0171 588 1815

In any case of doubt on investment matters, advice should always be sought from someone qualified and authorised to give it. The secretary of each diocesan board of finance is a person authorised to give investment advice in relation to church funds to parish priests, churchwardens and PCCs.

9. THE CHURCH BUDGET

(a) What is a budget?

A budget is an estimate of the income and expenses for the calendar year. An example is shown on page 70.

The categories of expenses in this example are those described earlier in section 4 of this chapter, 'The main expenses of a church'.[5] The categories of income are also based on the guidance in *The Charities Act 1993 and the PCC*.

(b) Why does a parish need a budget?

The parish needs to estimate the total expenses for the calendar year, in advance, so as to

- give authority to the treasurer to pay bills up to the budget figure for each item.
- stimulate and support parish giving. The example budget shows a deficit, so either income needs to go up, or expenditure should be cut down.
- let the PCC know where the money is going.
- calculate the total income needed.
- calculate the amount to be raised from giving.
- provide an early warning system.

Budget for the Year ending 31/12/1998	Budget 1997	Actual 1997	Budget 1998
INCOME	£	£	£
Covenants (incl. Tax recoverable)	18,000	18,600	19,800
Uncovenanted	8,000	7,700	7,900
Collections in church	5,500	5,800	5,900
Fund raising events	6,500	6,800	6,500
Legacies, special donations and grants		1,400	
Investment income			
Dividends and interest	500	300	300
Church Hall	1,500	700	800
Trust Income	500	500	500
Charitable trading			
Magazine and bookstall	800	700	600
TOTAL INCOME	41,300	42,500	42,300
EXPENDITURE			
Grants			
To other Christian missions and charities	2,000	2,700	2,900
Activities directly relating to the work of the church			
Ministry expenses (quota, working expenses of parish priest, vicarage, staff)	16,000	15,700	16,500
Church running expenses (heating, lighting, cleaning, insurance)	8,500	9,000	9,500
Church maintenance	4,600	5,200	5,400
Upkeep of services, altar, books, music, robes	1,300	1,600	1,800
Churchyard	500	600	600
Parish magazine and bookstall	1,000	1000	1,200
Support costs (Sunday School)	400	400	500
Church Hall	1,000	1,000	1,200
Organist's salary	1,800	1,800	1,800
Fund raising and publicity			
Summer fete	500	600	600
Management and administration			
Printing, stationery, postage, legal expenses, salary of administrator	1,300	1,400	1,500
TOTAL EXPENDITURE	38,900	41,000	43,500
SURPLUS OF INCOME OVER EXPENDITURE	2,400	1,500	(1,200) deficit

(c)   Monitoring a budget

A budget will never be 100 per cent accurate. During the year expenses will vary because of unknown factors: an unusually mild or severe winter can radically change the cost of fuel bills, or emergency repairs to buildings can add a large sum to the budgeted repair bill. You need to keep a careful watch on the expenses throughout the year, in case the total looks as if it is going to exceed the figure in the budget. If you think this is going to happen, you should take action. You should tell the PCC either to cut down some other expenditure, or to encourage the congregation to increase its giving, so that at the end of the year you do not make a loss. You should also consider keeping reserves for some future expenditure.

(d)   When should the budget be made?

The treasurer is appointed after the annual parochial church meeting, which should be held before 30 April. The church accounts run from January to December. Between May and December the treasurer bases his expenses on the budget made the previous year. During that time he should prepare a budget for the next calendar year, for the PCC to approve.

The treasurer should start preparing the budget soon after the annual parochial church meeting has approved the previous year's accounts. So, for example, the accounts for the calendar year January–December 1997 are approved by the annual parochial church meeting held in April 1998. The treasurer can then start to prepare the budget for the calendar year January–December 1999.

(e)   How do you prepare a budget?

You start with the previous year's income and expenditure. Much church expenditure is of a regular nature. From these figures, and the most up-to-date information and indicators for the current year in progress, calculate the increases in quota, fuel, wages and any other expenses for the current year.

(f)   Consulting the PCC

In preparing the budget, the treasurer should consult the PCC about

- capital expenditure e.g. replacement of books, and refurbishment of the church.
- specific appeals to cover capital expenditure.
- accumulating reserves for future expenses – for example repairs following the quinquennial inspection.
- the church's giving to missions and charities.
- any special expenses which need to be provided for.
- recommendations for change in investment policy.

The PCC's role is not just a question of comparing figures, noting trends and trimming certain areas of expenditure. The PCC should relate the budget to the church's mission in the parish. Many parishes are being encouraged to have a parish plan setting out their priorities and agenda for action. The budget should take into account the parish plan.

The following questions should provoke lively discussion and debate:

- Is our work organised as effectively and efficiently as possible?
- Which of the main areas of expenditure could we cut down, and still be just as effective?
- Are there any areas we should stimulate by spending more?
- Are there some areas of expenditure missing in our budget?
- What are our priorities?
- Are the proportions between the various areas of expenditure sensible?
- Does it stretch us?

The budget is really a picture in financial terms of the church at work, and the PCC should take great care in giving approval.

(g)   Making a final budget

By November the treasurer should be close to having a final budget for the following year. The PCC should approve the budget, and also recommend how sufficient income is to be raised – e.g. giving, special events, investment income.

Having approved the following year's budget, people should be told about it. How much each person gives should be determined by their response to the love of God, but it is helpful for them to know what their money is to be used for.

(h)   What if the budget shows a deficit?

The example budget[6] shows an estimated deficit. This is not unusual. The PCC will need to re-examine its expenditure or its giving, or both, to make sure that income and expenditure balance.

10.   KEEPING THE ACCOUNTS

The parish accounts should run from 1 January to 31 December each year.

This section covers the normal week by week work of the treasurer throughout the year. Preparing the final accounts is covered in Chapter 26, 'Church Accounts'.

(a)   The cash book

The cash book contains a record of every item received or paid, analysed into as much detail as is required. Each fund has its own account, but all accounts are kept in basically the same way.

One cash book can be used for all funds, provided the details of each are kept on separate pages.

The key thing to remember when operating your cash book is that *All money is cash until you bank it.* This may sound obvious, but to some treasurers coins and notes count as cash and cheques count as bank. Not so – all is cash until banked.

The example below show the process for receiving cash or cheques and paying into the bank. All receipts, from whatever source, are recorded in the *Cash column*. When money is transferred to the bank a 'cash to bank' entry is made in the *Cash column* on the *Payments side* of your cash book, and a similar 'cash to bank' entry is made in the *Bank column* on the *Receipts side* of your Cash book.

Here is the receipts side of the general fund account.

GENERAL FUND RECEIPTS		CASH, CHEQUES, etc.			
DATE	PARTICULARS	RECEIVED		BANKED	
	Totals brought forward	87	40	747	50
14 Jun	Collection	78	20		
"	Envelopes	40	00		
"	Donation	10	00		
17 Jun	Insurance claim	176	00		
18 Jun	Hall rent	50	00		
"	Cash to bank			441	60

The £441.60 banked is the total of the items in the 'received' column. Here is the payments side of the same account.

GENERAL FUND PAYMENTS		CASH, CHEQUES, etc.			
DATE	PARTICULARS	By Cash or into Bank		By Cheque	
	Totals brought forward	33	90	43	20
17 Jun	Communion wine			17	20
18 Jun	Weedkiller	4	95		
"	Toilet rolls	3	00		
"	Quota			500	00
"	Cash to bank	441	60		

Follow this process, and your cash column will always equal the cash (including cheques) you have in your cash box or safe, and the bank column will always equal what you have in your bank account.

These examples show only the first few columns of the cash book. The remaining columns enable you to allocate each item to a particular category of income or expenditure. This is described below.

Three points need to be considered before the precise form of the cash-book is decided:

- What separate funds are there (or should there be) which need to be shown separately in the final accounts?
- Funds need to be grouped together according to whether they are restricted funds, unrestricted funds, or endowments.
- What headings are going to be used to analyse receipts and payments in the final accounts, especially in the general fund account?

Headings should:

- have names which are clearly understood.
- if possible, be the same from one year to the next, to allow comparisons to be made.
- relate to the Central Board of Finance recommended headings for income and expenditure, as set out in *The Charities Act 1993 and the PCC*.

All these are important when the final accounts are prepared for the year. The treasurer needs to decide in some detail how the final accounts are going to be laid out before he starts his cash book. For more detail on these, see Chapter 26, 'Church Accounts'.

(b) *Choosing a cash book*

A parish needs a proper cash book, and should be prepared to spend a reasonable amount of money on one. A suitable one can be purchased from Church House Bookshop, entitled *Parish Accounts*.

CHURCH HOUSE BOOKSHOP
31 Great Smith Street,
London SW1P 3BN

Tel: 0171 340 0276

Or you can use one of the cash books published by Guildhall, Cambridge or Collins, which are obtainable at good stationers.

(c) *Computerised accounts*

Several systems are available at reasonable prices. Some systems are designed to handle covenant administration. These are described in Chapter 25, 'Covenants and Gift Aid'. Other systems are designed to handle the accounting requirements under the Charities Act 1993, described in Chapter 26, 'Church Accounts'. Contact the following:

DATA DEVELOPMENTS LTD
Wolverhampton Science Park,
Stafford Road,
Wolverhampton,
West Midlands WV10 9RU

Tel: 01902 824044

Fax: 01902 824046

SUNRISE SOFTWARE
Scorrier Park,
Scorrier,
Cornwall TR16 5AU.

Tel: 01209 821821

Fax: 01209 822125

THE KUBERNESIS PARTNERSHIP
36 Acomb Wood Drive,
York YO2 2XN,

Tel: 01904 788885

In choosing church accounting software, check that the system can support fund accounting, and can produce accounts in the form required by the Church Accounting Regulations 1997. The *Kubernesis Accounting System* produced by the Kubernesis partnership of York has been chosen by many PCCs as suitable. The *Kubernesis Accounting System* costs £175. Another popular program, used by many churches, is *Cashcall 3*. This is a Windows based program produced by Data Developments Ltd. *Cashcall 3* costs £69.

Many standard programs may be used for church accounts. For example, a well-known computer program *Quicken*® is particularly good at dealing with bank accounts.

Any church using computers for its accounts should make sure that the computer files are backed up regularly, and that printouts are made regularly on paper, in case of data loss. This is covered in Chapter 12, 'Computers'.

11.   PRINCIPLES OF GIVING

A treasurer will often find himself in the difficult role of telling other church members that more money needs to be found if quota payments, building repairs and other vital expenses are to be met. What this means is that the treasurer often has to ask people to increase their giving to the church.

Some churches have regular teaching spots on the principles of giving. It is helpful for the treasurer to be able to refer to these principles when he speaks to individuals about their personal giving. There are many ways of expressing these principles. I offer the following as a suggestion.

(a)   *Why should we give?*

See 2 Cor. 8:1–15; 2 Cor. 9:12–13.

- To show our gratitude for what God has given us.
- To help God's work.
- To help those in need.

Giving is both a duty and a privilege. But we should give as a response to God's love for us, rather than as a duty. By giving we also recognise that:

> All things come from you, and of your own do we give you.[7]

(b)   *How much should we give?*

There is no fixed rule. We should give in proportion to our income. Many Christians give 10 per cent of their income, in accordance with the Old Testament.[8] The General Synod in 1982 and again in 1992 recommended that we give 5 per cent of our take-home pay or pension to the Church, and 5 per cent for other charitable purposes.

(i)   *Give with cheerfulness, not grudgingly*

2 Cor. 8:3–4

> For I testify that they gave as much as they were able, and even beyond their ability.   Entirely on their own, they urgently pleaded with us for the privilege of sharing in this service to the saints.

2 Cor. 9:7

> Each man should give what he has decided in his heart to give, not reluctantly or under compulsion, for God loves a cheerful giver.

(ii)   *Seek God's guidance*

Your giving is part of the surrender of your whole life to the Lord, so seek His guidance.

In the words of the well-known hymn by Frances Ridley Havergal (1836–79)

> Take my life, and let it be
> consecrated, Lord, to Thee;
> take my moments and my days,
> let them flow in ceaseless praise.
>
> Take my hands, and let them move
> at the impulse of Thy love;
> take my feet, and let them be
> swift and beautiful for Thee.
>
> Take my voice, and let me sing
> always, only, for my King;
> take my lips, and let them be
> filled with messages from Thee.
>
> Take my silver and my gold,
> not a mite would I withhold;
> Take my intellect, and use
> every power as Thou shalt choose.
>
> Take my will, and make it Thine;
> it shall be no longer mine:
> take my heart, it is Thine own;
> it shall be Thy royal throne.

> Take my love; my Lord, I pour
> at Thy feet its treasure store:
> take myself, and I will be
> ever, only, all, for Thee.

The church in Corinth appreciated this point.

2 Cor. 8:5

> ... they gave themselves first to the Lord and then to us in keeping with God's will.

Everyone should decide their own response to God's love, and express this in their giving.

(c)   *How should we give?*

(i)   *Give regularly*

That means weekly, monthly, quarterly or annually. Many give by setting up a monthly standing order with their bank. Others give every week.

1 Cor. 16:2

> On the first day of every week, each one of you should set aside a sum of money in keeping with his income, saving it up, so that when I come no collections will have to be made.

(ii)   *Give discreetly*

You are bringing glory to God, not to yourself: Matt. 6:1–4.

(iii)   *Give wisely*

The government encourages people who want to give to charity to make use of two recognised tax schemes which add to the value of the gift. The two schemes are a covenant and the Gift Aid scheme. If you pay income tax and use one of these schemes, the church can then claim from the Inland Revenue a refund of basic rate tax amounting to almost 30 per cent of the amount you have given. Making a gift using a covenant or the Gift Aid scheme makes it worth almost 30 per cent more to the church.

PART I.   CHURCH PEOPLE

–   A COVENANT

A covenant is a formal written promise to pay the church a sum of money each year (or each week, month, or quarter) for a minimum of 4 years, or until you die. You fill in a simple printed form saying how much you wish to give, and when the payments will begin, and then sign it in front of a witness. The form is then given to the church. At the end of the first year you also have to sign a certificate of deduction of tax, confirming that you have made the agreed payments, and that you pay UK income tax.

–   THE GIFT AID SCHEME

The Gift Aid scheme is available for individual gifts of £250 or more. It is not available where you make a series of smaller gifts which, over a period, total £250; nor where two people – say, a husband and wife – join forces to make a single gift of £250. You can make more than one Gift Aid gift to the same charity in a year, but each gift should be over £250 to qualify for the tax benefit.

No forms have to be filled in before the gift is made. All that is required is that at some stage you fill in a Gift Aid Certificate, so that the church can recover the tax.

–   THE CHARITIES AID FOUNDATION

If you want to support several charities, but do not want to make more than one covenant, you may prefer to make that covenant with the Charities Aid Foundation. The CAF acts like a bank: you write CAF cheques in favour of as many charities as you want, up to the amount of your gift to the CAF plus the tax to be recovered, less a 5 per cent administration charge. For further details, contact

THE CHARITIES AID FOUNDATION
Kings Hill,
West Malling,
Kent ME19 4TA

Tel: 01732 520 000

(d)   Help from the diocese

All dioceses can give advice on stewardship campaigns. Contact your diocesan secretary if you do not know who is responsible for this.

12.   SECURITY AGAINST FRAUD

Every year, sums of money are lost by churches through fraud.[9] In most cases where money has been lost in this way, too much trust has been placed in one individual. Even treasurers are not immune from temptation, and Judas Iscariot is not the only church treasurer to have given in to it.[10]

It may be embarrassing to start taking precautions against fraud if there has been a long-serving treasurer, because it may suggest that you do not trust him. The answer is that you do trust the treasurer, but these controls are for his protection as well as for the benefit of the PCC. He should not take it as a criticism or sign of distrust that you want to tighten up on your security.

These are some of the steps you should take:

(a)   Take up references

Take up references for potential employees.

Some people suggest that you should always take up a reference for the treasurer before appointing him . If the person to be appointed treasurer has only recently joined the church, it may be right to ask for a reference. But it is surely unnecessary to insist on a reference in the case of someone who has been coming to the church for years and who is well known to the parish priest and the congregation. In quite a few churches it is difficult to find anyone willing to take on the task of being treasurer, and to insist on a reference would only add to the difficulty.

(b)   Collections

Collections should always be counted by two people together, and the amount signed by the people who do the counting.

(c)   Banking

Make sure the amounts banked agree with the amounts given at the collection.

(d)   Cheques

Cheques should be made out to the church or to the PCC of the church, not to an individual.

Only one cheque book should be in use at any one time. Cheques should always require two signatures. They should never be signed in advance. This can cause major difficulties over holiday periods. There are two ways round this problem. The best way is to make arrangements with the bank for extra people to have authority to sign cheques over these periods. The second way is to have a single emergency cheque limited in amount but signed in advance. The second way involves a risk.

(e)   Bank statements

Someone other than the treasurer should be asked to check the bank statements from time to time. Check them regularly for large or unexpected payments or receipts.

Check the balance in the cash book with the balance on the bank statement regularly. Long-term deposit balances should be checked regularly.

The computer program *Quicken*® can be used to check the church bank statements.[11]

(f)   The auditor or independent examiner

The church accounts have to be checked by an auditor or an independent examiner. In some frauds, although the accounts appeared to have been signed by the independent examiner, he had never in fact even seen them. Someone other than the treasurer should check by speaking to the independent examiner that everything is in order.

[1] The detailed regulations are contained in the Charities (Accounts and Reports) Regulations 1995 and a Statement of Recommended Practice *Accounting by Charities* issued by the Charity Commission in 1995.

[2] The Church Accounting Regulations 1997.

[3] All churches with an income over £100,000 have now to prepare their accounts on what is known as the accruals basis. See Chapter 26, 'Church Accounts'.

[4] For details on envelope schemes see Chapter 26, 'Covenants and Gift Aid'.

[5] See page 60.

[6] See page 70.

[7] From the Order for Holy Communion in the Alternative Service Book. See also 1 Chr. 29:14.

[8] See also note 3 in Chapter 3, 'The PCC'.

[9] See the article 'Trust in God – audit everybody else' by James Blewett-Mundy in the *Church Times*, 30 August 1996.

[10] See John 12:6 and 13:29.

[11] See 'Computerised accounts', page 75.

Chapter 5

THE PCC SECRETARY

1.   INTRODUCTION

A PCC secretary has a vital role in helping both the parish priest and the PCC. Leading a PCC meeting is the parish priest's job. Some parish priests are better at it than others. But a good PCC secretary is one of the best helps any parish priest can have. The PCC secretary helps the parish priest before the meeting, during the meeting, and after the meeting. That way the parish priest can concentrate on giving an overall lead, knowing that he has the backing to ensure that the decisions reached by the PCC will be carried out.

2.   WHAT DOES A SECRETARY DO?

The secretary
- cares about proper procedure.
- sends out notices of meetings in good time.
- makes sure reports are prepared on time.
- prepares the agenda for the meeting.
- deals with letters.
- prepares minutes of the meeting.

- keeps a check on the parish diary.
- knows what is going on.
- acts quietly and efficiently.

He or she should be

- a good organiser.
- tidy and methodical.
- calm and clear-headed.
- tactful and friendly.

3.   PCC MEETINGS

(a)   *Before the meeting*

At least ten full days before the meeting (unless it is an emergency meeting) the secretary should post a notice of the date, the time and the place of the meeting at or near the main door of the church. The notice should be signed by the priest or on his behalf.

At least seven full days before the meeting, a notice of the date, time and place of the meeting signed by the secretary has to be sent to every member of the PCC. The notice should include the agenda for the meeting.

Once the notice about the PCC meeting is put on the church notice board, members of the congregation will know that the meeting is to take place, and they can make sure that their views are known before the meeting by talking to members of the PCC.

(b)   *Postponement of the meeting*

Each PCC has a chairman and a vice-chairman. The chairman is the parish priest. The vice-chairman is elected by the PCC, and is often one of the churchwardens.

Sometimes it is necessary to postpone a meeting which has already been arranged. If for a proper reason the chairman, the vice-chairman and the secretary (or any two of them) consider that a meeting which has been arranged should be postponed, notices should be sent out to every member of the PCC. The new date for the meeting should be within 14 days of the original date.

(c)   *During the meeting*

During the meeting, the PCC secretary

- makes sure that he has spare agenda papers, the Minute Book, reports, copies of letters, and any other necessary papers with him.
- takes a note of the meeting.
- makes sure he understands and notes exactly what has been decided on each issue. Where a clear decision is needed, he may suggest a form of words to be put to the vote.
- makes sure that nothing on the agenda is left out by mistake.
- makes sure that decisions are practical and constitutional.
- keeps a watch on the pastoral affairs of the Committee. So, for example, the secretary makes sure that thank-you letters are sent to visiting speakers, or to people who have helped the parish in some way. The secretary helps the parish have a good relationship with other church denominations and organisations.

(d)   *After the meeting*

After the meeting, the PCC secretary

- prepares the minutes from his notes, and sends them to the members of the PCC before the next meeting.
- puts into action any decision made by the PCC, or makes sure that the person who should do something, does it.

4.   MINUTES

It is an old joke that committees take minutes and waste hours. Minutes are a written record of what occurred at the meeting, and they are important. Some months or even years later, it may be necessary to find out what was decided on a particular point, or whether a particular matter was discussed. Properly prepared minutes will give the answer.

Minutes should be condensed and to the point. They should therefore record all important facts, and the outcome of discussions, but details of the actual words used and mere chat should be left out. For instance, it is not usually necessary to record the details of what any person said, or who said it, only what was finally agreed on each matter.

Minutes usually include the following items:

- *Names of those present.*
- *Apologies for absence.*
- *Minutes of the last meeting.*

Everyone should have received a copy of the minutes of the last meeting. The reason for having them on the agenda is not to re-open the matters which were discussed last time, but to make sure that the minutes are a correct record of what took place at the last meeting. If someone wants to correct a passage in the minutes, the meeting should be asked whether it agrees with the change, and if it does (after a vote, if necessary), the correction should be made in the copy which is signed by the parish priest. The minutes of the new meeting should say:

> The minutes of the last meeting were approved [subject to the following corrections ....]

- *Matters arising out of the last meeting.*

This is to report action taken as a result of decisions made at the last meeting. For example, where the subject of the children's church had been in the last minutes:

> Sarah has now obtained a copy of the recommendations of the diocese concerning child protection. She, James and the vicar will study them, and will report to the next meeting on what needs to be done.

If, as in this example, you use Christian names only, beware of confusion as to which James or which Sarah.

Normally the items *apologies*, *minutes* and *matters arising* occupy the committee for only a couple of minutes. Sometimes however the topic of *matters arising* can need much more time.

- *A report on the main topics which were discussed.*

This of course forms the main part of the meeting.

- *Any other business.*

This gives a time for the parish priest or anyone else to raise matters not listed on the agenda. If they are important, it is not a good idea to raise them at 9.25 p.m. when everyone is thinking about getting home. (If a member of the PCC has a burning item which needs to be talked through, and which is not on the agenda, he should raise it with the parish priest well before the meeting. The parish priest can then re-plan the agenda to give it plenty of time for discussion, possibly at the expense of some other less important item.)

- *Date of next meeting.*

    A good time to fix the date is when everyone is present with their diaries. The minutes should mention the date which was agreed.

5.   FURTHER INFORMATION

Administry publishes two guides:

- *A meeting will be held* (how to prepare agendas).
- *How to write minutes* .

    Administry also runs a one day training course for PCC secretaries, called *Just a minute!* For details, contact

ADMINISTRY
PO Box 57,
St Albans,
Herts AL1 3DT

Tel: 01727 856370

Chapter 6

EMPLOYEES AND OFFICE HOLDERS

1.   INTRODUCTION

Many parishes employ lay people to assist in the work of the Church.[1] Some of these are employed part-time, and some full-time. Some do secretarial or administrative duties; some people have a skill or training which they wish to use for the service of the Church – for example musicians, cooks, builders and craftsmen. Many parishes have a paid verger or caretaker, paid cleaners, or a paid organist. This chapter applies to all these types of employment.

In most cases the employer will be the PCC. There are many rules which employers need to know, and also many good practices which employers should follow. PCCs therefore need to know about them when they employ people.

Employment law is one of the areas where parishes may need the legal advice of the diocesan registrar. This advice is available free to parishes, and if they take advice from the diocesan registrar they may prevent a serious problem arising later.

2.   BEFORE THE EMPLOYMENT

(a)   A job specification

Before employing someone, the PCC needs to decide fairly clearly what it wants the employee to do, and it needs to put this it in writing. This is known as writing a *job specification* or *job description*.

A job specification should set out clearly what you expect the person to do, and who he or she has to answer to. It should cover the following points:

- The name of the job.
- The place of work.
- Why the job is needed. Give some past history to explain the reasons for setting up the job.
- Who is the person's immediate boss or supervisor? How often should he report to that person?
- What are the most important tasks of the job?
- Who or what is he in charge of?
- What type of person are you looking for to fill this position?
- Put down any important terms and conditions. For example, you may need someone with a current driving licence. Or you may be offering with the job somewhere to live. You can state what the wage or salary is, or leave that to be discussed in the interview.
- Is this description of the job likely to change from time to time? If so, how will you do this?

For examples of job specifications for a church administrator, see Chapter 7, 'The verger, the organist, and the administrator'.

(b) Unlawful discrimination

Under the Sex Discrimination Act 1975 you should not allow the sex or marital status of a person to influence you when you look for an employee, or in the terms you offer the employee. This means, for example, that in advertisements and job descriptions you should say that either sex can apply for the job. You are not allowed to refuse to offer someone a job because of their sex or marital status.

The Employment Appeals Tribunal has held that discrimination against a person on the basis of his or her homosexuality is not sexual discrimination under the Sex Discrimination Act 1975.[2] Such discrimination may however be contrary to the EEC Equal Treatment Directive,[3] and two such cases (not involving the church) have been referred to the European Court of Justice.[4] The Human Rights Bill 1998 contains provisions which, it has been suggested, may prevent a church from lawfully refusing to employ a person on the grounds of his or her homosexuality.[5] In short, the law on discrimination against homosexuals may change in the near future, and if you are faced with this issue you should take the legal advice of the diocesan registrar.

Under the Race Relations Act 1976 you should not allow the race of a person to influence you when you look for an employee, or in the terms you offer. Refusing to consider someone who looks or sounds foreign, for example, is likely to be unlawful.

There is also discrimination against people with a disability. The rules on this are set out in the Disability Discrimination Act 1995. The Disability Discrimination Act 1995 only applies where an employer has 20 or more employees,[6] so it is unlikely to apply to most church employments. However the church should be willing to offer employment to disabled people whenever possible.

Parishes often want to insist that someone should be a practising Christian before employing him or her. Others want to proclaim that the church is an 'equal opportunities employer', and that people of other faiths can apply for a job. It should not matter for certain posts whether or not a person is a Christian. For other posts, it may be essential for a proper working relationship that the employee is a Christian. If you consider that the person you want to employ should be a practising Christian, you should say so in the job specification. If you do not, you may wish to include the following statement (or something similar) so that you make it clear that you need someone who is at least sympathetic to the Christian faith.

> Staff are expected to have regard to the essentially Christian basis of their work, and to their role in serving the Church of England.

The best way to avoid all kinds of discrimination is to have a policy that you treat all applicants in the same way.

(c)   *Immigration rules*

Anyone with a right to live in the UK or in the EEC is allowed to work in the UK. It is a criminal offence to employ a person who is not entitled to live or work in the United Kingdom.[7]

You can make certain basic checks before taking on new employees which will give you protection against being taken to court. To provide yourself with a full defence you should make sure that before a new employee starts working for you:

- you see one of the documents listed below.
- you check that the document appears to be genuine, and that it relates to the person you are considering employing.
- you obtain a copy of the document.

The documents you could see to establish a defence include:

- a document from a previous employer, the Inland Revenue, the Benefits Agency, the Contributions Agency, or the Employment Service showing the person's name and National Insurance Number. This could be a P45, a pay slip, a P60, a National Insurance card or a letter. This should cover most new employees.
- a passport confirming that the person is either a British citizen or a EEC national, or which shows that he or she is otherwise entitled to live and work in the UK.
- a birth certificate confirming birth in the UK or the Republic of Ireland.
- a letter from the Home Office confirming that the person named is allowed to work.

If they have any of the above documents, it does not matter if they do not have a national insurance number. You may employ them.

For further information, see the Home Office booklet *Prevention of illegal working – Guidance for employers*. This is available on the Internet at http://www.homeoffice.gov.uk/ind/emg1.htm, or from

HOME OFFICE PUBLICATIONS UNIT
Room 1024
50 Queen Anne's Gate
London SW1H 9AT

A helpline is available on 0181 649 7878.

Some churches offer sanctuary to illegal immigrants who are seeking asylum in this country. Sanctuary is discussed in Chapter 18, 'Lotteries and other matters'. As I explain there, churches offering sanctuary to illegal immigrants may be committing the crime of 'harbouring' under the Immigration Act 1971. If they offer employment to asylum seekers as well as giving them sanctuary, churches run an additional risk of prosecution.

(d)   *Interviewing*

Here are a few tips on interviewing people for jobs.

- Be polite to all candidates.
- Pay for any travelling expenses to the interview.
- Provide tea and coffee, and lunch if needed.
- Before interviewing someone for a job, plan the questions you expect to ask him or her, and prepare a list to go through.
- Have a clear idea of the job description, and the type of person you are looking for.
- Be fair to all candidates: that means asking the same range of questions to all of them. You can always add questions when needed.
- Begin the interview by introducing other people in the room.
- Ask 'open' questions, rather than ones that can simply be answered 'Yes' or 'No'. Ask *how, what, why* type questions. 'What experience have you had of ....?' 'Why do you think ......?' 'Tell us why you like ....' 'Tell us why you think this job might be right for you'.
- Keep notes. Note facts during the interview, and note your opinion about the person afterwards. It sometimes helps to have a separate person taking notes throughout the interview.
- Avoid making quick decisions based on your first impression.
- Be prepared to probe areas of doubt in the candidate's past career.
- Always appear interested.
- Keep control over the way the interview is going, and of the time.
- If more than one person is running the interview, share the questions equally between them.

THINGS TO AVOID

- Do not tell the person face-to-face that they do not dress properly, or are not from the right social background, or that you do not approve of their hairstyle. Personal remarks such as these have no place in an interview, and you cannot refuse to employ someone on these grounds.

- Do not ask female candidates whether they are pregnant or are likely to be, or about other personal domestic arrangements. They may volunteer such information, but that is a different matter. Questions which indicate prejudice against a person on the grounds of marital state, age, race, skin pigment, background or education indicate illegal discrimination under the Sex Discrimination Act 1975 or the Race Relations Act 1976.

An example of a letter to be sent to the person you decide to employ is set out on page 114.

(e) Child protection procedures

The main topic in Chapter 8, 'Children', is safety and good practice in church youth and children's work. This covers all aspects of safety, including protecting children from child abuse. All dioceses have a code of practice in order to protect children's safety, and all parishes are now required to adopt their own code of practice for dealing with children.

All employees and voluntary workers should be required to co-operate with a parish's child safety code of practice. Employees and voluntary workers should be aware of good practice in working with children and young people.

When appointing an employee or a voluntary worker, the PCC should consider:

- Could the job involve one-to-one contact with minors outside their parents' home?
- Could the job offer the chance to form close relationships which would lead to contact outside work?
- Could the job offer regular contact with minors?
- Could the job offer access to minors who are vulnerable due to their circumstances or needs?
- Will the employee regularly work alone?
- Is the work place isolated or unsupervised?

Many lay posts in the church are very flexible and involve a high degree of trust. Almost all posts in the church offer the possibility of abuse in one or more of these areas. Therefore you should make sure that *both existing and future staff* are aware of the parish's policy concerning children's welfare, and that they agree to follow it. Amongst other matters, this involves all employees, all people applying for jobs, and those applying for voluntary positions being required to disclose their criminal convictions. Job applicants should also be required to give their consent to any police or local authority checks that the PCC may consider appropriate.

Job descriptions should contain a requirement that the employee will follow the parish policy on child protection.

Problems have arisen with the written declarations which people have been asked to sign under the new child protection procedures. If you have reason to disbelieve a declaration, you should contact the diocesan registrar for advice as to whether or not you should employ the person.

3.   DURING THE EMPLOYMENT

(a)   *Employment law*

Under the Employment Rights Act 1996 employees have various rights, which PCCs need to be aware of

- a right to a statement setting out the main terms of their employment contract.[8]
- a right to a pay slip or statement showing what sums have been deducted from their pay.[9]
- rights concerning what deductions the employer can make from wages, for example tax.[10]
- a right to time off for ante-natal care.[11]
- a right to maternity leave.[12]
- a right to return to work after childbirth.[13]
- a right to a minimum period of notice.[14]
- a right to a written statement saying why they were dismissed.[15]
- a right not to be unfairly dismissed.[16]
- a right to a payment if they are made redundant.[17]

In addition, PCCs should be aware of

- the rules relating to sickness pay.

- suitable pension arrangements for employees.
- health and safety requirements for employers.

There are a large number of free employment law pamphlets available from DTI local employment services offices giving details of many of these matters. Health and safety advice is available from the Health and Safety Executive.[18] So far as churches are concerned, health and safety is enforced by the local authority, not the Health and Safety Executive.[19]

A brief description of these topics follows.

(b)   A statement of employment particulars

Within two months of starting work, you should provide your employees with a written statement showing the major terms of their contract. This includes:

- the name of the employer and employee.
- the date the employment began.
- the job title or a brief job description.
- the rate of pay, how it is calculated, and when it is to be paid.
- the normal hours of work.
- the place of work.
- holiday pay and entitlement.
- details of sick pay and pension schemes.
- the length of notice to be given by both employer and employee.

If the number of employees is less than 20, the statement should also contain the name of a person the employee should go to in order to sort out any problems or grievances. If the number of employees is 20 or more, then the statement should give details of disciplinary and grievance procedures.[20]

A model statement is set out on page 118. It does not need to be signed.[21]

(c)   Pay

Whenever you pay your employee his wages, you should give him a written statement showing the amount of the gross pay, and what has been deducted for PAYE, national insurance and pension contributions.

(d)   Sickness pay

An employee is normally entitled to *statutory sick pay* from his employer during the time he is off work through sickness. The employee is entitled to statutory sick pay for up to 28 weeks' sickness over a three-year period. The employer can then recover from the state a proportion of the amount paid to the employee.[22]

Since 6 April 1998 the standard rate of statutory sick pay has been £57.70 per week.[23]

Statutory sick pay is taxable, and is subject to national insurance contributions.[24]

Many employers pay their employees more than the minimum statutory sick pay when they are sick. In many cases the employee receives his normal wages, for a period such as three or six months. In deciding whether you want to extend the statutory provision in this way, you need to balance Christian compassion with the parish's need to employ someone else (if need be) to get the job done during the employee's absence. Parishes are often run on a shoestring budget, and may not be able to afford to be as generous as they would wish to be.

(e)   Maternity rights

Pregnant mothers have the right to take time off for ante-natal care. They have a general right to 14 weeks' maternity leave. Employees with at least two years' continuous employment are entitled to return to work at any time up to 29 weeks after childbirth. Failure to offer a mother her job back after childbirth normally amounts to unfair dismissal.[25] But there are special rules for employers with five or less employees. If a PCC has only five or less employees, and it is not practical to offer the mother her job back, then the PCC does not have to do so.[26]

All employees are entitled to *statutory maternity pay* for up to 18 weeks' maternity absence. The employer can claim back from the state money paid to the employee as statutory maternity pay.[27] Many employers pay their employees their normal wages while they are on maternity leave.

(f)   Pension arrangements

The Church Workers Pension Fund is run by the Church of England Pensions Board, and has been in existence since 1953. It is available for any Church of England organisation (such as a PCC) to use for its employees. It is an 'occupational' or employer-sponsored scheme, and not a personal pension arrangement. It should therefore be set up by an employer, and the employer should make contributions to it.

The Church Workers Pension Fund runs two types of scheme.

- The *Church of England Defined Benefits Scheme*. This is for long-term employees. The pension depends on how long the employee has been employed, and what his final salary was before he retired. This type of scheme is sometimes referred to as 'final salary'.
- The *Church of England Defined Contributions Scheme*. This type of pension depends on how much the employer and the employee have paid in to the scheme, and investment returns. This type of scheme is often referred to as 'money purchase'.

Most PCCs will want a *Defined Contributions Scheme*. It is more suitable than the *Defined Benefits Scheme* for short-term employees and for PCCs with only a few employees. Many PCCs have set up a *Defined Contributions Scheme* for a single person.

Everyone who pays national insurance contributions is entitled to the basic state pension. The State Earnings Related Pension Scheme (SERPS) is an additional pension above the basic state pension, and is based on a person's earnings. Under some pension schemes a person's retirement income from the scheme is paid *instead* of his SERPS pension. He continues to receive the basic state pension, but the additional SERPS pension is paid under the employer's scheme rather than from the state. This is known as *contracting out of SERPS*. Both the employer and the employee pay a lower rate of national insurance contributions if the scheme is contracted out of SERPS. The *Defined Benefits Scheme* may be contracted out of SERPS. The *Defined Contributions Scheme* is not contracted out of SERPS.

Most employers within the *Defined Contribution Scheme* set the contribution rate (the amount to be paid to the pension fund) somewhere in the range of 7 per cent – 10 per cent of salaries. The PCC can also choose whether or not the employee has to make a contribution and, if so, how much this should be (provided it is no more than the PCC's contribution). Employees are free to make extra payments (known as *voluntary contributions*) to the scheme, up to a maximum of 15 per cent of salary (this limit applies to the total of compulsory and voluntary contributions).

For further details, and to set up a scheme, contact

THE CHURCH OF ENGLAND PENSIONS BOARD
7 Little College Street,
Westminster,
London SW1P 3SF

Tel: 0171 222 2091.

(g) *Grievance provisions*

Employees sometimes feel that they need to complain about their employer's actions. These often arise over the following areas:

- pay issues, such as bonus or overtime calculations.
- holiday entitlement, such as a disagreement over when a person is allowed to take his holiday.
- discretionary benefits, such as the right to unpaid leave of absence.
- disciplinary action, such as a dispute over whether something was serious enough to lead to the person being warned about it.

There should be a simple written procedure to resolve such disputes. First, the issue should be raised informally with one person (possibly the parish priest or the church administrator). Then, if there is no agreement, it should be raised with the PCC, or a committee of the PCC.

At the second stage, the employee should be allowed to be represented by a colleague.

The whole thing should be resolved speedily, within a week if possible. This means being willing to call a special meeting of the PCC or a PCC committee to deal with the matter at short notice. The longer it takes, the more harm is done.

(h)   A check list for the contract of employment

The contract should deal with the following subjects.

(i)   The employer's name

This should be the PCC, not the parish priest. If the parish priest is named as the employer he would be personally liable under the contract.

(ii)   Continuous employment

Some rights only apply after the employee has been employed for a certain time: for example, the right to claim for unfair dismissal generally arises only when a person has been employed for two years. People who move from one job to another within the same organisation can use their total time with the organisation when claiming these rights, unless the contract says otherwise. The contract should therefore say whether or not the person's previous employment counts for this purpose.

(iii)   The job title and description

Refer to the job description already given to the employee. If you need the employee to be flexible about the work done, emphasise this.

(iv)   Pay

You should say

- what the rate of pay is.
- whether it is paid weekly/every two weeks/monthly.
- the method of payment: cash, cheque, or directly into a bank account.
- what overtime rates are payable.

(v)   Hours of work

Set out the normal working hours each week.

- What are the person's total hours? What are their daily hours?
- Do they work on Sunday?
- Is there a rota system?
- Can hours be varied?
- Is overtime compulsory?

- Do they have a regular day off?

The question of Sunday working is very important to consider. Do you want the employee to attend one or more of the Sunday services? Do you want him or her to be on duty for other Sunday events? Some parishes seem to get in rather a muddle over this: they strongly encourage the administrator to attend every service, but equally strongly they encourage the congregation not to raise 'business' with the administrator on Sundays.

(vi)   *Holiday pay and entitlement*

- How many paid days' holiday can the employee take each year?
- How many paid bank holidays can the employee take each year?
- When does the holiday year run from?
- Can a person carry leave forward from one year to the next?
- How does leave accrue – e.g. 2 days per completed month?
- What arrangements apply for outstanding holiday when the contract comes to an end?
- What arrangements apply for fixing the holiday dates?

(vii)   *Sick pay arrangements*

- Is the employee entitled to full pay while sick?
- If so, for how long?

(viii)   *Pensions*

Has the church taken out any pension scheme for employees?

(ix)   *Grievance provisions*

Who should the employee go to with any grievances?

(x)   *Disciplinary rules*

Has the church adopted any disciplinary rules for its employees? If so, these should be referred to.

(xi)   *Notice provisions*

- How much notice is the employee entitled to?
- Is there a trial period?

(xii)   Any other provisions

In the case of a verger, a typical example would be accommodation linked to the job.

Two model contracts of employment are set out on pages 115 and 117.

(i)   Health and safety at work

These are the main requirements.

- The PCC should display the statutory notice *Health and Safety Law – What you should know.*[28]

The poster can be purchased from HSE Books either on its own, or as part of a health and safety 'starter pack'. This 'starter pack' contains the statutory notice, an accident book, an incident at work wall-chart, and the book *Essentials of health and safety at work.*

- The PCC should assess the risks to the health and safety of employees and others using the church. If there are five or more employees, the PCC needs to write down the important findings from its risk assessment.[29]

A leaflet called *5 Steps to Risk Assessment* is available free of charge from HSE Books, which explains how to do this.

- If there are five or more employees, the PCC should have a written safety statement.[30]

A leaflet called *Writing a safety policy statement, advice to employers* is available free of charge from HSE Books.

- The PCC should discuss with all employees matters affecting their health and safety, before making any decisions on health and safety.[31]

A leaflet called *Consulting employees on health and safety: a guide to the law* is available free of charge from HSE Books.

- The PCC should make sure that employees who are exposed to risks are taught how to protect themselves and how to prevent accidents.
- The PCC should make sure employees and others using the building know emergency and evacuation procedures.
- The PCC should share with any other employers using the premises information on health and safety hazards and risks.

- The PCC needs to keep records of injuries and first aid treatment.
- Serious accidents and illnesses, and other dangerous events need to be reported to the local authority.[32]

You should report any major injury to any employee or a member of the public. You should report even a minor injury if the employee is off work for three days or more. Dangerous events which clearly could have led to an injury should also be reported. These include equipment falling over or collapsing, electrical fires or explosions, and the collapse of scaffolding over 5 metres high.

A leaflet called *Everyone's guide to RIDDOR 1995 (Reporting of Injuries, Diseases and Dangerous Occurrences Regulations)* is available free of charge from HSE Books.

- The PCC should keep a watch on health and safety arrangements, and review them when necessary.

Most new employers have to register with the local authority under the Offices, Shops and Railway Premises Act 1963 before they take on employees.[33] A parish church does not.[34]

A lot of free information can be got from the Health and Safety Executive. The following publications are recommended, in addition to the leaflets mentioned above:

Catalogue No.	Title
IND(G)259	*An introduction to Health and Safety for Small Firms*
MISC071	*Health and safety in small firms*
IND(G)173L	*Officewise*
HSC 13	*Health and Safety Regulation – a short guide*
IND(G) 36L	*Working with VDUs*
IND(G) 251L	*First Aid: Basic Advice on first aid at work*

To order or purchase any of these publications, contact

HSE BOOKS
PO Box 199
Sudbury
Suffolk CO10 6FS

Tel: 01787 881165

Fax: 01787 313995

For health and safety enquiries, contact

HSE INFOLINE

Tel: 0541 545500

(j)   Fire regulations

Under the Fire Precautions (Workplace) Regulations 1997 employers should make sure that:

- the workplace is fitted with suitable fire-fighting equipment, detectors and alarms.
- employees are properly trained to use this equipment, and know where emergency exits are.
- routes to emergency exits and the exits themselves are kept clear, and provided with suitable signs and lighting.
- all emergency equipment and devices are maintained in efficient working order and in good repair.

(k)   Insurance

The PCC should take out employers' liability insurance, and display a certificate from the insurance company in the place of work. Accidents at work do happen.[35]

For further details, see the section 'Third party liability insurance' in Chapter 21, 'Insurance', or contact the Ecclesiastical Insurance Group.[36]

ECCLESIASTICAL INSURANCE GROUP
Beaufort House,
Brunswick Road,
Gloucester GL1 1JZ.

Tel: 01452 528533.

4.   ENDING THE EMPLOYMENT

(a)   Disciplinary provisions

Minor faults can be dealt with informally, but sometimes the matter is more serious, and can lead to the employer wanting to sack the employee.

Even if the conduct of the employee is serious, the PCC should not normally sack him without first giving him a series of warnings. The first stage is normally an oral warning, the second a written warning, the third a final written warning, and the fourth is dismissal itself.

The following are examples of minor misconduct:

- poor time-keeping.
- taking time off work without permission.
- time-wasting.
- minor disobedience.
- not doing work properly.

More serious matters include:

- refusing to obey proper instructions.
- gambling on church premises.
- smoking in an area where this is not allowed.
- failing to follow safety rules.

Very serious or gross misconduct covers such matters as:

- a serious breach of confidence (telling something which is confidential).
- major disobedience, or being rebellious.
- stealing or fraud.
- fighting or assaulting another person, or threatening them.
- deliberate damage to church property.
- being drunk or under the influence of drugs.
- sexual offences or sexual harassment.

For gross misconduct, PCCs should suspend the employee from work on full pay for no more than five working days while the alleged offence is investigated. There should then be a disciplinary hearing, that is, a meeting by the PCC or a committee of the PCC to consider what took place, with the employee being allowed to state his version of events. If at that meeting it is clear that the employee did do what he is accused of, and the PCC considers it is right to dismiss him, they may do so.

A PCC which is considering dismissing a person who has been employed for two years or more should take care that its disciplinary action is conducted fairly. Otherwise the employer may bring an action against the PCC in the Industrial Tribunal, and recover damages for unfair dismissal.

To ensure fairness, PCCs should adopt the following guidelines:

- No disciplinary action should be taken against anyone until the case has been fully investigated.
- At every stage in the procedure, the employee should be told the case against him or her, and given the opportunity to respond before any decision is made.
- Employees may have a friend or colleague present during the disciplinary interview.
- No employee should be dismissed for the first breach of discipline except in the case of gross misconduct.
- All employees should have the right to appeal against any disciplinary penalty. So, if the parish priest gives an employee a warning, and the employee thinks this was not fair, he should be able to appeal to the PCC or a PCC committee. Some contracts give the employee a final right of appeal to the archdeacon. The model contracts at the end of this chapter do not, but you may want to consider this.
- The disciplinary procedure may be started at any stage if what the employee has done justifies it. This means that for serious matters, an employee can be given a written warning without having to give him a verbal warning first.

For further advice, PCCs should consult the advisory handbook *Discipline at work* (ACAS, 1997).

(b)   Giving notice

Employees who have been employed for one month or more but for less than two years are entitled to at least one week's notice. After two years' employment, they are entitled to one week's notice for each year of continuous employment, up to a maximum of 12 weeks' notice.

Many parish contracts of employment allow the employee longer notice than this minimum requirement. A minimum of one month's notice or even three months' notice is common. If the contract gives them this period of notice, then it should be honoured.

If you dismiss someone without giving them proper notice, that is wrongful dismissal, and can lead to a claim for damages against you. If you do not want someone to work out their notice, you should pay them the money they would have earned during their notice period.

(c)   A written statement of reasons for dismissal

If you dismiss someone who has been employed for more than two years, you should give them a written statement saying why you dismissed them.

If you employ a person for a fixed period, and when the contract comes to an end you do not renew it, this counts as dismissing the person. If they have been with you for two years, you should give them a written statement saying why you dismissed them.

If the employee appeals to an industrial tribunal on the grounds of unfair dismissal, the written statement of reasons can be used in evidence in those proceedings.

(d)   Unfair dismissal

Fair reasons for dismissal include the employee not being capable of doing the job, misconduct, and redundancy.

The PCC should make sure that it carries out fair disciplinary procedures before dismissing an employee. This is discussed above.[37]

It can also be unfair dismissal not to renew a fixed-term employment contract when it comes to an end. A PCC can protect itself from such a claim by including a special term in the contract of employment.[38] The term says

> You [i.e. the employee] agree to waive any right to a redundancy payment and any claim in respect of unfair dismissal under the Employment Rights Act 1996 if this agreement is not renewed when it expires.

The model contract of employment at the end of this chapter includes such a term.[39] Some people think that such provisions are immoral, others that they are essential for proper employment practice. Parishes should consider whether they wish to protect themselves from such a claim, as they are entitled to do.

(e)   *Redundancy*

Redundancy is where a person is dismissed because the employer needs to reduce the work force. The job should no longer be needed: it is not redundancy if a new worker is taken on for the same job.

In general, only employees who have been employed for two years can claim a redundancy payment.

If an employee is made redundant, he or she is entitled to a redundancy payment. The amount of redundancy payment is:[40]

(i) ½ week's pay for each year of service between the employee's 18th and 22nd birthday.

(ii) 1 week's pay for each year of service between the employee's 22nd and 41st birthday.

(iii) 1½ week's pay for each year of service between the employee's 41st and 65th birthday.

(iv) Only the 20 most recent years are to be taken into account.

Special rules apply for employees made redundant in the year before retirement age.

5.   ADVISORY CONCILIATION AND ARBITRATION SERVICE (ACAS)

The Advisory Conciliation and Arbitration Service (ACAS) publishes a wide range of employment law booklets, and is available to assist in resolving employment disputes. A list of ACAS publications may be obtained from the ACAS inquiry office.

ACAS INQUIRY OFFICE
Clifton House,
83–117 Euston Road,
London NW1 2RB

Tel: 0171 396 5100

ACAS have offices in Birmingham, Bristol, Cardiff, Fleet, Glasgow, Leeds, Liverpool, London, Manchester, Newcastle upon Tyne, and Nottingham.

The following ACAS publications are likely to be useful:

- *Employing people: a handbook for small firms.*
- *Discipline at Work.*
- *Employment handbook.*
- *Job evaluation: an introduction.*
- *Introduction to payment systems.*
- *Personnel records.*
- *Recruitment and induction.*
- *Employee communications and consultation.*
- *Employment policies.*
- *Employee appraisal.*
- *Redundancy handling.*

In 1997 ACAS published a number of free leaflets useful as guides for small firms. They are also available on the Internet at http://www.modus.co.uk/clients/acas.

- *The role of ACAS.*
- *Contracts of employment.*
- *Dealing with grievances.*
- *Discipline at work.*
- *Induction training.*
- *Recruitment and selection.*

6.   FURTHER INFORMATION

The Department of Trade and Industry and the Department for Employment and Education publish a range of free employment law pamphlets. For a list contact:

THE DEPARTMENT OF TRADE AND INDUSTRY
Cambertown Ltd,
Goldthorpe Industrial Estate,
Rotherham S63 9BL

Tel: 01709 888688

DFEE PUBLICATIONS
PO Box 5050,
Sudbury,
Suffolk,
CO10 6ZQ

Tel: 0845 6022260

The Inland Revenue publishes two guides to Pay As You Earn and National Insurance contributions:

- *Employer's Quick Guide to PAYE and NICs* (Inland Revenue guide CWG1, 1998)
- *Employer's Further Guide to PAYE and NICs* (Inland Revenue guide CWG2, 1998).

To obtain a copy contact the Inland Revenue Order-line.

Tel: 0345 143143

There is also a short leaflet about Pay As You Earn, written from the employee's perspective: *PAYE* (Inland Revenue leaflet IR34, 1996). This is available from all tax offices, and on the Internet at http://www.open.gov.uk/inrev/ir34.htm.

Employing Lay Staff – Guidelines to good practice (ACCM occasional paper No. 35. June 1990).

Administry publishes two guides:

- *Any questions?* (techniques for interviewing)
- *An inspector calls* (how churches treat their employees)

ADMINISTRY
PO Box 57,
St Albans,
Herts AL1 3DT

Tel: 01727 856370

7.   FORMS

(a)   *A model letter of appointment*

Dear

On behalf of St John's Church, I am very pleased to offer you the job of .... following your interview last ......

The starting salary is £...... per [*year* or *week* or *hour*]. You have already had a copy of the job description which outlines the work you will be doing. The other terms are set out in the contract of employment I enclose, and these will apply to you from the day you start work.

Please let me know whether you would like to accept this job, and please confirm that you will be able to start work on [*date*]. If you agree, please sign one copy of the contract and return it to me by [*date*].

Please may I have your P45 and your National Insurance Number. If you have no P45 please refer to your Tax Office.

If you need any help, do get in touch.

I look forward to seeing you on ....

Yours sincerely

(b) *Model contract of employment*

1. This contract of employment is made between [*insert name of employee*] ('you') and the Parochial Church Council of St Mary's Church, Bishopmitre ('the PCC').

2. This contract of employment is for the post of [insert job title], a description of which is attached.

3. No service with a previous employer counts towards your continuous employment with the PCC.

4. NORMAL PLACE OF WORK: The parish office.

5. SALARY: £...... per year, payable on the [*last working day* or *as required*] of every calendar month. Your salary will be reviewed [*on or around the anniversary of this employment* or *at the beginning of each calendar year*].

6. HOURS OF WORK: Normal working hours will be [*insert daily working hours*] a total of [*number*] hours per week, but subject to some flexibility as and when required.

7. OVERTIME: Any hours more than the above total per week will be paid at the rate of £.........

8. HOLIDAYS: You are entitled to Christmas week and [*four*] other weeks as paid holiday per year, to be taken from time to time as agreed with the parish priest, [*together with Bank Holidays*], [*Maundy Thursday and Ascension Day*]. You should take all your holiday entitlement by 31 March in the year following the year in which your holiday has been earned.

9. PENSION: The PCC has set up pension arrangements with the Church Workers Pension Fund. If you wish to join this scheme, please ask for details.

10. SICKNESS OR INJURY: You will be paid your normal salary for up to three months during a period of illness, unless as a result of your illness it is plain that you will be unable to start work again for a long period. In that event, the PCC may end this contract by giving you one month's notice.

11. ACCOMMODATION: The PCC will provide you with accommodation. You will not be required to pay rent or rates or any repairs. This accommodation is only available for you while you are

employed by the PCC, and should be vacated on the day this contract expires.

12. GRIEVANCE PROCEDURE: If you have a grievance relating to your employment, including any complaint about a disciplinary decision, you should first bring the matter to the attention of the parish priest. If it is not resolved at that stage, you should bring it to the attention of the PCC.

13. TERMINATION: The contract is for a fixed term of [*insert number of years*] years from [*insert starting date*] to [*insert finishing date*]. The first six months are a trial period, during which either of us can end the contract by giving one month's written notice. After six months, either of us can end the contract by giving three months' written notice.

14. You agree to waive any right to a redundancy payment and any claim in respect of unfair dismissal under the Employment Rights Act 1996 if this agreement is not renewed when it expires.[41]

Signed on behalf of the PCC   --

Signed by the employee   --

(c)   *Model contract of employment (alternative form)*

Here is another form of contract, setting out the terms in a letter. You can use either method. Several of the clauses are very different from the model contract shown above.

Date

Dear ......

This letter sets out the terms of your appointment as

PARISH ADMINISTRATOR
St Mary's, Phillimore.

1. Employer: the Parochial Church Council of St Mary's, Phillimore.

2. Job Title and Description: You will be known as Parish Administrator, and the duties and responsibilities of this post are set out in the Job Description which you already have. As the work develops, it will be necessary to review these duties and responsibilities from time to time.

3. Commencement Date: Your employment will commence on ....

4. Place of work: The parish office.

5. Salary: Your salary is £3,000 per year. You are paid at the end of each month.

6. Hours of Work: Your hours of work will amount to 10 hours per week, to be fitted in to suit your own time table. You should be in the office on Monday mornings to cover when the Parish Secretary is normally not on duty.

7. Holidays: You are allowed 30 working days paid holiday in each calendar year. Your holiday entitlement accrues at the rate of 2½ days' holiday per month worked. In addition you will be entitled to the normal public holidays.

8. Absence from work: If you are ill and cannot come to work, you should tell the parish priest straight away. While you are sick you will only be paid statutory sick pay, not your normal salary.[42]

9. Pension: No pension scheme is provided.

10. Grievance/Disciplinary: Any grievance relating to the employment should be raised with the parish priest in the first instance. If he is unable to sort the matter out, you should discuss it with the PCC. The PCC's decision on any disciplinary matter is final.

11. Termination: This contract of employment may be ended by either of us giving three months' notice in writing.

    If you agree these terms, please sign one copy of this letter at the place shown below, and return it to me.

Yours sincerely

(*signature of parish priest*)

I accept the terms of employment for my appointment as Parish Administrator as set out in this letter.

Date ....   Signature ....

(d)   *Model statement of terms of employment*

Your terms of employment

Diocese of ....

Parish of ....

Employee's name...

Employed by...
address..

Job Title..

Directly responsible to..
or else...

Date employment began ....

Previous service counting as continuous...

118

1. Salary: Your rate of pay will be .... payable weekly/ monthly in arrears. It is the employer's intention to review this rate in .... each year.

2. Hours of Work: Your hours of work will be .... per week.

3. Overtime: Any hours in excess of the above total of hours will be paid at the rate of ....

4. Holidays: You are allowed .... working days paid holiday in each calendar year, together with the normal public holidays. You should agree the dates of your holiday in advance with the person to whom you are directly responsible. The holiday year runs from .... to .... Major church festivals should be avoided.

5. Absence from work: If you are ill and cannot come to work, you should inform .... straight away. You will need a medical certificate if you are sick for seven days or more. You will be paid your normal salary while sick for up to .... months in any year. Thereafter the statutory sick pay rules will apply.

6. Accommodation: Housing is provided for you at .... at which you will be required to live. You will not be required to pay rent or rates or any repairs. This accommodation is only available for you while you are employed by this church, and you should vacate it on the day your employment ends.

7. Pension: You are eligible to become a member of the Church Workers Pension Fund at a contributory rate of .... per cent. If you wish to join the scheme we your employers will contribute at the rate of ...... per cent. If you prefer, you may make private pension arrangements with an Insurance Company of your choice.

8. Grievance/Disciplinary: If you have a grievance to your employment, including any complaint about a disciplinary decision, you should raise this first with the person to whom you are directly responsible, then to the parish priest. If you are unsatisfied with the outcome, you have a right of appeal to the PCC who will give a written decision within 30 days. The PCC's decision on any disciplinary matter is final.

9. <u>Termination</u>: You may give us ...... weeks' notice to end your employment. We may end your employment by giving you .... weeks' notice, or the statutory period of notice if that is greater.

10. <u>Retirement</u>: The retirement age for this post is ....

---

[1] This chapter concerns the employment of lay people only. For the rights of clergy you will need to consult specialised law books such as Mark Hill, *Ecclesiastical Law* (Butterworths, 1995). In 1997 the Court of Appeal held that an assistant curate in the Church of England is not an employee, and therefore can not bring proceedings for unfair dismissal: *Southwark (Diocese of) v Coker* (1997) Times, 17 July 1997; (1997) 94(29) LSG 29; (1997) SJLB 169; (1998) 5 Ecc LJ 68.

[2] *Smith v Gardner Merchant Ltd* [1996] 1 IRLR 342.

[3] Equal Treatment Directive 76/207/EEC.

[4] *R v Secretary of State for Defence ex p. Perkins* [1997] IRLR 297, *Grant v South West Trains* (1998) Times, 23 February 1998. In the *Perkins* case there was held to be unfair discrimination; in the *Grant* case there was not. See *Harvey on Industrial Relations and Employment Law* (Butterworths, 1972–1997) section L 11.

[5] David McClean and Martyn Percy in their letter to the *Church Times*, 27 February 1998, argue that the Human Rights Bill 1998 has nothing to say about employment. Paul Diamond's letter in response in the *Church Times*, 6 March 1998, argues that it does. For the church's concerns generally about the Human Rights Bill 1998 see *The Times,* 20 January 1998: 'Peers challenge human rights law'; *The Times,* 5 February 1998: 'Churchmen urge Human Rights Bill rethink', and letters by Mr Philip Gore and others in the same issue; *Church Times*, 5 December 1997: 'C of E fears mugging from rights law'.

[6] Disability Discrimination Act 1995, section 7.

[7] Asylum and Immigration Act 1996, section 8.

[8] This is known as a *statement of employment particulars*: see the Employment Rights Act 1996, section 1.

[9] Employment Rights Act 1996, section 8.

[10] Employment Rights Act 1996, section 13.

[11] Employment Rights Act 1996, section 55.

[12] Employment Rights Act 1996, section 71.

[13] Employment Rights Act 1996, section 79.

---

[14] Employment Rights Act 1996, sections 86 and 87.

[15] Employment Rights Act 1996, section 92.

[16] Employment Rights Act 1996, section 94.

[17] Employment Rights Act 1996, section 135.

[18] See 'Health and Safety at work', page 105.

[19] See the Health and Safety (Enforcing Authority) Regulations 1989 schedule 1 paragraph 13. Churches do not need to register with the local authority unless they are providing food. For this see Chapter 11, 'Food and drink'. The local authority circular *The inspection of churches and other places of worship*, LAC (Local Authority Circular) 22/3 (30 April 1996) gives guidance to local authorities on the enforcement of health and safety regulations in churches.

[20] Employment Rights Act 1996, section 3 (3).

[21] If the employee is asked to sign it, you should make it clear that this is only to acknowledge that he has received it.

[22] See the Social Security Contributions and Benefits Act 1992, section 159A (as inserted by the Statutory Sick Pay Act 1994, section 3), and the Security Sick Pay Percentage Threshold Order 1995 (1995 SI No. 512).

[23] Social Security Benefits Up-rating Order 1998.

[24] Social Security Contributions and Benefits Act 1992 section 151 (3).

[25] Employment Rights Act 1996, section 96 (1).

[26] Employment Rights Act 1996, section 96 (2).

[27] Social Security Contributions and Benefits Act 1992 sections 165 and 167. Small employers can recover 105 per cent of statutory maternity pay: Statutory Maternity Pay (Compensation of Employers) Amendment Regulations 1995 (SI 1995 No. 566). The extra 5 per cent is intended to compensate the employer for costs incurred in administering statutory maternity pay.

[28] Health and Safety Information for Employees Regulations 1989.

[29] Management of Health and Safety at Work Regulations 1992.

[30] Health and Safety at Work Act 1974 section 2(3) .

[31] Health and Safety Consultation with Employees Regulations 1996.

[32] The Reporting of Injuries, Diseases and Dangerous Occurrences Regulations 1995 requires the reporting of work-related accidents, diseases and dangerous incidents.

[33] See the Offices Shops and Railway Premises Act section 49, and the Notification of Employment of Persons Order 1964.

[34] Because the definition of *premises* in section 1 of the 1964 Act plainly does not include a church.

[35] Employers Liability (Compulsory Insurance) Act 1969.

[36] A leaflet called *Employers' Liability (Compulsory Insurance) Act 1969, A short guide* (HSE Books, 1996) is available free of charge from the publisher.

[37] See 'Disciplinary provisions', page 107.

[38] Employment Rights Act 1996, section 197 (1).

[39] See the 'Model contract of employment', page 115.

[40] Employment Rights Act 1996, section 162.

[41] If a contract for a fixed term is not renewed, the employee can claim unfair dismissal or redundancy against the employer. The PCC can protect itself from such a claim by including this term in the contract: see the Employment Rights Act 1996, section 197 (1).

[42] Compare this provision with clause 10 on page 115.

Chapter 7

THE VERGER, THE ORGANIST AND THE ADMINISTRATOR

1.   INTRODUCTION

This chapter follows on from Chapter 6, 'Employees and office holders'. Vergers, organists (sometimes called *directors of music*), and administrators are examples of people employed by PCCs. That is why they have been grouped together in this chapter. Everything said in Chapter 6 is therefore relevant when PCCs want to employ a verger, an organist or an administrator.

2.   THE VERGER

(a)   *The work of the verger*

The name *verger* means the man or woman who carries a *virge* or rod of office. He welcomes those who come to church as worshippers or as visitors. People who see the verger robed approach him or her for information and advice. He knows the history of the church, and will give practical advice about the services in the church and about local facilities. At times the verger should politely but firmly bar a visitor from some part of the church, or even refuse entry altogether. But the verger's authority should be exercised with kindness; he or she should in a real sense be a pastor.

Many vergers have responsibility for the security of the church building, for the church safe and its contents, for the handling of the church collections and for their transfer to the bank. Others may have responsibility for the cleaning and maintenance of the building, and for simple repairs. Some vergers help prepare the church for services, by preparing the altar vessels, vestments and books, or by arranging chairs. Some vergers also look after the church hall as well as the church.

Vergers may be full-time or part-time. They may be paid a proper salary or only a small sum. Many are provided with accommodation by the church.

(b)   Training for vergers

The 1990 report *The Verger's Role in Today's and Tomorrow's Church* sets out in an appendix the training scheme for vergers as used in Worcester Cathedral. Other dioceses use very similar training schemes. An example is set out below.[1]

Training will be under these headings

1. Historical

The history of church buildings
Architectural styles
How to convey the history to different ages – schools etc., and to special interest groups
To know about misericords
Stained glass
Monuments
Memorials
Organs
Vestments including copes, frontals and other embroideries

2. The Church's Year

Use of lectionary
Liturgical colours

3. The Church as a Place of Worship

How to prepare for daily services
How to prepare for Sunday services
How to prepare for special services
How to prepare for baptisms, weddings and funerals
How to take part in daily services
How to take part in Sunday services
How to take part in special services
How to take part in baptisms, weddings and funerals
How to operate the public address system
How to operate the lighting

4. The Verger's Ministry

To the visitors
To the congregations
To people in need – with problems

5. Maintaining the Plant

Floors
Furniture
Cleaning materials – stock keeping
Looking after altar linen
Ordering and care of candles
Ordering and storage of wine and wafers
Caring for silver and communion plate
Keeping the First Aid box up to date

6. Security

Locking up and alarm systems
Policing the building
Action when faced with drunks and violence from the public
When to call the police
How to call the police
How to call other emergency services
Keys – use, custody and control

7. Administration

The church's diary
The church's budget
Handling of petty cash
How to take messages and pass them on

How to fill in registers for baptisms, weddings, confirmations and funerals
Recording and banking monies from collections, boxes etc.
Staff structure and lines of authority
Channels of communication, minutes of staff meetings

8. Emergency Procedures

Fire drills
Position and use of fire extinguishers
How to call Police, Ambulance and Fire Brigade in an emergency
How to make records of incidents
What to do when on duty for a concert

9. Communication

To the general public
Other staff salaried and voluntary
The clergy
Diocesan officers
To parishioners

10. Background knowledge needed to be a verger

Knowledge of church history
Knowledge of English history
Interest in church architecture and art
Pastoral care for people
Knowledge of the Anglican Communion
Knowledge of other denominations
Knowledge of other religions

11. The verger's own faith – his spiritual life

Knowing about Anglican Spirituality
Knowing about other Christian Spirituality

12. The Church of England Guild of Vergers

National officers
Local officers and meetings
The training scheme and opportunity to study for the foundation certificate.

(c)   *The Guild of Vergers*

There is a Guild of Vergers, which offers its own training scheme, and each diocese has its own local organisation for vergers. The general secretary of the Guild of Vergers is

Mr Ian Griffiths,
14 Pennington Court,
245 Rotherhithe Street,
London SE16 1FT

Tel: 0171 231 6888

The welfare officer of the Guild of Vergers is

Mr James Wilson,
1c Colston Parade,
Redcliffe,
Bristol BS1 6RA

Tel: 0117 929 9310

3.   THE ORGANIST AND DIRECTOR OF MUSIC

The Incorporated Society of Musicians publishes two forms of contract suitable for PCCs to use when appointing an organist and director of music. Most churches will want to use the *Agreement for the Appointment of a Director of Music (Self-employed)*. This is designed for part-time organists' posts. The agreement has been endorsed by the Guild of Church Musicians, the Incorporated Association of Organists, the Royal College of Organists, and the Royal School of Church Music. Many dioceses recommend it.

The agreement covers all work likely to be undertaken by a director of music, including playing, conducting a choir, and overseeing other music in the church.

This contract is, strictly, not a contract of employment at all, because it treats the organist as self-employed. That means he should deal with his own income tax and national insurance contributions. It means he is free to take other employment on days of the week when he is not playing for the church. It means that the organist does not have the benefit of the employment rights described in Chapter 6, 'Employees and office holders', such as the right to statutory sick pay, or to bring proceedings for redundancy or unfair dismissal.

There are standard terms for ending the contract, either by one party giving three months' notice, or on a particular date, or in the event of a breach of contract. The parish priest cannot sack the organist without getting the consent of the PCC or, in exceptional circumstances, the consent of the archdeacon instead of the PCC.

Under this contract the organist is entitled to the payment of an additional 50 per cent of his fee where a sound recording is made of his playing. Where a video recording is made, he is entitled to an additional 100 per cent of his fee. As video recordings are frequently made of weddings, it is important that everyone is aware that the organist is entitled to this extra payment.

The other form of contract published by the Incorporated Society of Musicians is for church appointments of at least 16 hours per week. Here the organist becomes a full employee, and the contract is called *Agreement for the Appointment of a Director of Music (Contract of Service (Employed))*. This includes additional clauses covering such matters as the employer's pension scheme and accommodation requirements.

Both forms of contract may be obtained from

THE INCORPORATED SOCIETY OF MUSICIANS
10 Stratford Place,
London W1N 9AE

Tel: 0171 629 4413

The Incorporated Society of Musicians publishes recommended fees for different type of organist's posts, and also recommended fees for playing at weddings and funerals. The Royal School of Church Music also publishes recommended fees.

THE ROYAL SCHOOL OF CHURCH MUSIC
Addington Palace,
Croydon CR9 5AD

Tel: 0181 654 7676

Organists may find it useful to refer to the Incorporated Society of Musicians' *Organists' Guide to Employment* (Incorporated Society of Musicians, 1995). This gives advice on all aspects of organists' work: director of music posts; organist posts; amateur status; weddings, funerals and special services; crematorium services; recitals; accompanying and playing continuo; broadcasts and recordings; tax status; financial planning; copyright; Children Act; booking other musicians; and employment legislation.

For more on musicians and music in church, see Chapter 9, 'Church Services',[2] Chapter 12, 'Computers',[3] Chapter 13, 'Copyright',[4] and Chapter 18, 'Lotteries and other matters'.[5]

4.   THE CHURCH ADMINISTRATOR

A general description of the work done by the church administrator is in Chapter 1, 'Who's who?'.[6] The church administrator's work varies very much from one parish to another. A guide for all churches which employ an administrator is *Appointing and Employing an Administrator* published by Administry. This can be obtained from

ADMINISTRY
PO Box 57,
St Albans,
Herts AL1 3DT

Tel: 01727 856370

Here are the job specifications for three parishes which now employ a church administrator. The names of the parishes in these examples are fictional, but they are based on actual examples. These job specifications should be a help to parishes needing to prepare their own job specification for an administrator.

PART I. CHURCH PEOPLE

(a) Job description for a church administrator (1)

St Paul's Parish Church, Matinstown.

Job description for Church Administrator.

Objective

There are two main objectives in appointing an Administrator at St Paul's. One is the aim of relieving the clergy from much of their administrative work to enable them to be free to concentrate on other areas of their ministry for which they were trained. The second objective is to have someone to co-ordinate and then develop church activities 'behind the scenes' so that the front-line work of the parish can be more effective. The balance of the job is anticipated as being 75 per cent maintaining and co-ordinating existing church activities and 25 per cent innovative work, i.e. taking on responsibilities in areas which St Paul's has not yet tackled, certainly in the first twelve months.

As this is a new post, the areas of work will be reviewed after 6 months.

Accountability

The job holder is employed by the PCC, and is accountable to it through the Parish Priest and Churchwardens.

Attitudes

The Administrator will work closely with the clergy and other church leaders. It is therefore important that he/she is a committed Christian in sympathy with the evangelical Anglican tradition of St Paul's.

Skills

The Administrator will need the skills of basic administration and office management, the ability to initiate and run long-term projects in written or spoken form.

The Administrator will if requested attend Staff meetings, and also those of the PCC.[7]

Duties and Responsibilities.

I.   To be 'clerk of works' responsible for the following areas:

      A.   general maintenance of buildings (including arranging visits of plumbers etc. as needed);

B.   supervision and servicing of equipment (photocopier, video, overhead projector, screen etc.);

C.   liaison with hall bookings manager and hirers of the halls where necessary;

D.   supervision of caretakers;

E.   purchaser of main supplies for the church.

II.   to look after the church office for set hours in the week, to enable this to be the contact point for 'routine' personal callers and telephone calls, rather than the vicarage.

III.   to be responsible for co-ordinating existing activities within the church, such as:

A.   arranging with the Parish Priest a 'programme for the year' listing the main events on the church's calendar and slotting in any new items as they arise;

B.   keeping a record of all committee dates and church rotas;

C.   compiling a directory of 'who's who' within the parish and warning the Parish Priest of any expected changes;

D.   helping to mobilise people as 'jobs' become vacant;

E.   being the central collection point for information for specific projects, e.g. parish weekend, Archdeacon's visitation report etc.

IV.   To ensure efficient communication flow within the parish including updating of notice boards.

V.   To help the Parish Priest review and evaluate existing church activities. With the Parish Priest, to set specific goals for the parish and then to continually review and modify these as necessary.

Line of responsibility

The Administrator will be responsible to the Parish Priest for day-to-day operations, working alongside the Parish Priest's secretary. The Administrator would need some typing support.

Safe from Harm procedures

The parish has adopted a policy to safeguard the welfare of children. The Administrator should follow this policy, and should make sure all members of staff and helpers in the church follow it also.

Faculties

The administrator should be well acquainted with the law on church buildings, and in particular the need to obtain a faculty when necessary. He should be responsible for making sure that a faculty is obtained whenever necessary.

Terms and Conditions of Employment

The number of hours is to be equivalent to five mornings per week (i.e. 20 hours). The post is a paid one. The position is to be for a term of three years.

(b)   Job description for a church administrator (2)

All Saints' Parish Church, Bishopsmitre.

JOB DESCRIPTION FOR THE CHURCH ADMINISTRATOR.

Reports to:

Parish priest and churchwardens.

Responsible for:

Employed staff other than clergy.

Dimensions of Job

Bishopsmitre is the largest parish in the ...... diocese, with a population of over 20,000. The parish church of All Saints is the lead church in the Bishopsmitre grouping with St Michael's, Paddockburn, St Michael and All Angels', Stableton, and St Nicholas', Oatsbran. It was substantially rebuilt following a fire in 1985, when new accommodation was added increasing the opportunities to use the building for a variety of secular and religious purposes.

The parish church has a large congregation, and a large umbrella of supporters throughout the community. There are services daily, with up to four public services on Sundays. It is popular for weddings and baptisms and is in demand for concerts and other musical events.

The new part of the building contains a coffee shop which is open to the public at regular times, a chapel for private prayer, a servers vestry, a parish office and equipped meeting rooms.

The church stands in its own grounds which are maintained by members of the congregation.

All Saints' is now a large operation, and requires managing appropriately. It needs to be kept clean and supplied. It needs to be accessible to church groups and to the larger community. The building is to be used to develop a source of revenue, within clear limits set by the Parochial Church Council. It needs to be kept secure at all times.

Working relations:

Internal

Parish priest, churchwardens, other clergy, assistant verger, cleaners, parish secretary, coffee shop staff, servers, flower arrangers, choirmaster and bell captain. All members of congregation and church groups.

External

Those booking the church building for religious or secular use; visiting clergy; sacristy and stationery suppliers; utilities; security company; local suppliers and craftsmen as appropriate.

Main purpose of Job

The church administrator is responsible to the parish priest and churchwardens for the day-to-day management of the church building and its immediate environs, and for security. Also for paperwork and other arrangements connected with the church's liturgical and secular use.

Key Tasks

1. To make sure that the church building is always secure, by arranging stewards when the church is open outside service times, and arranging the locking of the building and switching on the security system at the end of each day at times to be agreed.

2. To arrange for the alarm system to be neutralised each morning at times to be agreed.

3. Working from the parish office, to be available to those wishing to book the church or church rooms for non-church events. To

133

maintain the bookings diary, making sure the necessary paperwork is completed and fees received.

4. To help develop the use of the building to make money for the church.

5. To supervise staff and to make sure the church is ready for worship, maintaining access, especially in the winter, making sure all the lighting inside and outside is working and the heating system is working.

6. To motivate, encourage and guide lay people involved in church activities such as cleaning and churchyard work, ensuring supplies and equipment are available and in good working order.

7. To maintain and order sacristy supplies and prepare the altars and credence tables for services, returning ornaments and vessels to their right places after each service. To liaise with funeral directors and wedding couples as necessary.

8. To oversee the coffee shop, helping managers as needed.

9. To carry out regular simple inspections of the church fabric and furniture, and its grounds, arranging for repairs to be carried out or reporting them to the parish priest or churchwardens as necessary.

10. To maintain a list of key holders.

11. Make sure that the church is open and ready for church and agreed non-church groups' use; and that it is tidied and locked after use.

12. To ensure routine maintenance schedules are met and agreements maintained in accordance with the PCC's instructions.

13. To check and certify gas, telephone, television and electricity invoices, and others connected with the day-to-day running of the church.

14. To assist the parish priest and churchwardens in any other duties reasonably required.

Working conditions:

Flexible, but around a 40 hour week. This is not a routine job, and hours will vary to suit the pattern of use of the church. Extra hours are required from time to time. Contributory pension scheme and 20 working days holiday. Out of pocket expenses.

Qualifications and Experience:

The position requires a high degree of tact and diplomacy, and a good understanding of the Church of England, its role in Bishopsmitre, and its pattern of worship. The holder should be a practising and communicating member of the Anglican Church or a church in communion with it.

The holder will need to be adept at managing through people, recognising that much of the work will be done by volunteers who need encouragement and guidance rather than instructions.

An orderly business approach is essential: the holder should be familiar with office procedures.

Faculties

The administrator should be well acquainted with the law on church buildings, and in particular the need to obtain a faculty when necessary. He should be responsible for making sure that a faculty is obtained whenever necessary.

Safe from Harm procedures

The parish has adopted a policy to safeguard the welfare of children. The administrator should follow this policy and make sure all members of staff and helpers in the church follow it too.

(c)   *Job description for a church administrator (3)*

St Saviour's Church, Angelsgate.

JOB DESCRIPTION FOR CHURCH ADMINISTRATOR.

I.   GENERAL POLICY

A.   Under the direction of the parish priest, supervise the running of the church office to ensure the most effective use of resources;

B.   Attend a weekly business meeting with the parish priest;

C.   Following discussion with the parish priest, attend other meetings as needed;

D.   Assist communications within the church and with outside organisations and agencies;

E.   Enlist voluntary help from members of the congregation as needed.

II.   SPECIFIC TASKS

A.   Administration of the church diary:

     1.   at the start of each year enter all fixed bookings and service times into the new diary;

     2.   arrange additional bookings as required avoiding double bookings;

     3.   inform relevant people of any outside bookings, and likewise, inform those booking internal events who they need to liaise with;

     4.   rearrange events to accommodate priority bookings e.g. funerals;

     5.   invoice, acknowledge payments for and distribute fees in respect of church lettings;

     6.   book visits of workmen into diary;

     7.   attend diary planning meetings to ensure no clash of dates.

B.   Administration of specific church events

     1.   organise and administer school concerts;

     2.   issue invitations and information for newcomers' parties;

     3.   ensure circulation of: agendas and reports prior to PCC meetings; minutes and reports after PCC meetings;

     4.   ensure completion of all necessary paperwork in relation to the APCM and supervise the production of the final reports.

C.   Post

     1.   internal: deal with requests, information, worship and other returns, memos, minutes, rotas;

     2.   external: deal with payments, requests, orders, invoices.

D.   Phone

Deal with calls as required.

E. Filing

Keep own records in order.

F. People

Deal with day-to-day enquiries, members of the congregation and visitors; and when necessary make referrals to members of the ministerial team or relevant outside agencies.

G. Worship information

1. supervise preparation and production of weekly notice sheets;

2. arrange preparation and printing of special orders of service;

3. advertise special services.

H. Registers and Official Records

1. preparation of all registers and completion and issuing of certificates;

2. referral of enquiries to County Records Office when required;

3. ensure that church records are kept up to date e.g. parish register, book of remembrance.

I. Statutory and Other Licences

1. ensure payment of television, lotteries and other licences as necessary;

2. make contact with the Town Hall and other local authorities in respect of events being held in the church;

3. keep records for, and make returns to, the Performing Rights Society and other copyright companies.

J. Verging and Fabric

1. supervision of the paid cleaning staff;

2. liaise with, and reimburse reasonable expenses to, the voluntary cleaners;

3. ensure notice boards are kept up to date and maintain the general tidiness of the church, dealing with lost property as required;

4. receive goods, and ensure the church is open and available to workmen when needed

5.   make any necessary arrangements for the unlocking and locking of the church for out-of-hours bookings.

K.   Parish magazine

1.   obtain agreement on price;
2.   prepare, print and issue annual subscriptions forms;
3.   keep subscription list up to date;
4.   arrange for collection of circular;
5.   final preparation of masters;
6.   ensure an adequate supply of photocopy paper, including coloured cover paper;
7.   ensure a production team is available;
8.   ensure insertion of circular, labelling and distribution;
9.   empty collecting box on a regular basis and pass the money together with annual subscriptions to the treasurer.

L.   Faculties

The administrator should be well acquainted with the law on church buildings, and in particular the need to obtain a faculty when necessary. He should be responsible for making sure that a faculty is obtained whenever necessary.

M.   Safe from Harm procedures

The parish has adopted a policy to safeguard the welfare of children. Follow the policy, and make sure all members of staff and helpers in the church follow it too.

[1] I have omitted some items which relate solely to cathedrals, and made a few other minor alterations.

[2] See page 174.

[3] See page 216 for the computer program *Sibelius*.

[4] See page 227. Most of the chapter is relevant.

[5] See page 286.

[6] See page 10.

[7] Attendance at staff and PCC meetings should not be a right, but only when requested. The reason is that the staff and the PCC should be free to discuss matters about the employee without his being present.

Chapter 8

CHILDREN

1.   INTRODUCTION

ollowing the Children Act 1989 and two codes of practice published by the Home Office,[1] the church is starting to realise the need for safety and good practice in church youth and children's work.

The House of Bishops issued a policy statement on child protection in July 1995. The House of Bishops is due to issue a revised policy statement later in 1998.[2] Many dioceses have issued guidance to PCCs on the subject. In other dioceses, such guidance is still being prepared. The draft new House of Bishops' policy statement is set out in Appendix 2. The summary at the end of the Home Office report *Safe from Harm* is set out in Appendix 3.

The advice in this chapter is gathered from about twenty-five dioceses. But you should still make sure you have a copy of any guidance issued by your own diocese, and that you follow it.

The PCC and the parish priest are responsible for the safety of all children and young people on church premises and in church-sponsored activities anywhere.

Cases of child abuse have led to court cases against the church in the USA, and it can only be a matter of time before the same happens in the UK. If a parish has carefully followed the guidelines issued by the diocese, a claim for negligence against the parish or the diocese is unlikely to succeed. But if a parish has not followed these guidelines, this is likely to support a claim of negligence, and the claim is unlikely to be covered by the church insurance policy.[3]

2.   DIOCESAN GUIDELINES

The diocesan guidelines are likely to cover a whole range of topics. There will be both general information and very specific points. The main topics likely to be covered are the following.

(a)   *Recruitment of leaders*

There is no system which can provide an absolute guard against appointing people who will abuse children. However every parish should take measures to minimise the risk of this happening. So all leaders of youth and children's groups, crèche helpers and choir leaders should be chosen with care.

- They should be interviewed.
- They should be asked to provide the names and addresses of two people who can provide a personal reference.
- These references should be checked thoroughly.
- They should be asked to sign a declaration whether they have been the subject of criminal or civil court cases, and whether they have caused harm to any child or put them at risk. This includes 'spent' convictions under the Rehabilitation of Offenders Act 1974.[4]

Each diocese has prepared a declaration form for this purpose.[5] The completed forms should be kept in a safe place. They are strictly confidential, and should only be seen by the parish priest and the churchwardens.

Because accusations of abuse are often made many years after the event, these records should be kept for as long as possible. The Ecclesiastical Insurance Group advises that records should be kept indefinitely.[6] The Churches' Child Protection Advisory Service has had to deal with quite a number of cases where allegations have been made very many years after the event – one case in 1996 was *forty years* after the sexual assault, and as a result a retired parish priest was sent to prison.

It is not currently possible for churches to obtain police checks on helpers. However, under the Data Protection Act 1984 an individual can ask the police for a certificate giving details of information held about him or her on computerised police records, and a church considering employing a person can ask that person to obtain this information for the benefit of the church.[7]

If and when sections 112 to 127 of the Police Act 1997 are brought into force, it will be possible for churches to obtain details of criminal records and other relevant information directly from the police, when someone applies for a position involving looking after children. But this is unlikely to be before 1999 at the earliest.[8]

(b)   Leader to child ratios

For the protection of children, young people and leaders, there should always be at least two leaders, no matter how small the group. If this is not possible, small groups with single leaders may meet in a large room or in adjoining rooms with an open door between. If a child or young person is being interviewed alone, there should be another adult nearby, and the door should be kept open wherever possible. Sometimes it would be insensitive to keep the door open if a child was in a very distressed condition and other children were peering around the door to find out what was going on. Essentially, it is important that a worker always lets someone else know where they are in a building with a child and why it might be necessary to see a child in such circumstances.

The Children Act (Guidance and Regulations Vol. II) sets minimum ratios for work with children under 8 years as follows.

> For 0–2 years   1 leader to every 3 children (1:3).
> For 2–3 years   1 leader to every 4 children (1:4).
> For 3–8 years   1 leader to every 8 children (1:8).

(These statutory rules only apply where a group has to be registered with the local authority – for example, a playgroup, a nursery, after-school clubs, summer holiday activities, where such activities last for two hours or more, and are for more than six days a year.)

There are no statutory guidelines for children over eight years. The diocese of Worcester recommends one leader for every eight children. The diocese of St Edmundsbury and Ipswich recommends one leader for the first eight children, followed by one leader for every twelve children thereafter.

These guidelines may well prove impossible in parishes with a low number of leaders. If this is the case, you should discuss the problem with the person who has overall responsibility for children's work in your diocese, and follow his advice.

If there are girls in the group, there should be at least one female leader; likewise if there are boys in the group, there should be at least one male leader.

No person under the age of 16 years should be left in charge of any children of any age.

No child or group of children or young people (under 16) should be left alone at any time.

It is always safer to have *at least* two leaders with every group.

A register of children or young people attending the club or activity should be kept, and a register of the helpers.

A log book with details of unusual events in a club should be kept, with each leader recording what they witnessed. This can be very helpful if leaders have to deal with a difficult young person who may subsequently make accusations of assault. A young person who constantly makes throwaway sexual comments about church workers may later make an allegation of actual abuse. Records of previous examples of this behaviour will enable any allegation to be seen in context. Of course, if a number of young people all make similar comments about one worker, this should warn the leadership that they have a problem with that person. Log books can protect both children and workers.

I suggest that you also record in the log book incidents such as fights, and what action was taken by the leaders. As the information in the log book is likely to be very sensitive, the log book should be kept separate from the accident book which is used to record any accidents or injuries.[9]

(c)   Transport

It may sound obvious, but anyone driving a car should have a current driving licence.

Use only cars fitted with both front and rear seat belts. Make sure that everyone has a seat belt, and uses it. Do not carry more children than the number of available seat belts. If children under 14 are carried without wearing an available seat belt, the driver is breaking the law.

PART I.   CHURCH PEOPLE

If possible, another leader should be with the driver to help with any emergencies.

It is silly for a leader on his own to give a lift to a child, as this can lead to misunderstandings or actual wrong doing. The chance of false allegations being made is almost ruled out if there is another adult with the driver.

Car drivers should ensure they are insured to carry children and young people. Normally this would be covered by 'social/domestic use'.

(d)   *Minibuses*

Churches which use minibuses in connection with Sunday school or youth club activities need to know the driving licence and seat belt rules for minibuses.

(i)   *Driving licence requirements*

Volunteer (unpaid) drivers can drive a minibus with up to 16 passenger seats on church activities without having to obtain a Category D1 driving licence, provided:

- the driver is aged 21 or over.
- he or she has held a full driving licence for at least two years.
- the vehicle does not exceed 3.5 tonnes. An extra 750 kg is allowed for specialist equipment to carry disabled persons.
- the minibus is not towing a trailer.

A fact sheet, *Driving a Minibus in Great Britain*, explains the rules in more detail. This may be obtained from

THE DRIVER AND VEHICLE LICENSING AGENCY
Press Office,
Longview Road,
Morriston,
Swansea SA6 7JL

Tel: 01792 782318

(ii)   *Seat belts*

The rules apply when three or more children are on an *organised trip*. An *organised trip* is a journey which is mainly undertaken to carry children. Each child carried in a minibus or coach should have a forward-facing seat fitted with a seat belt, and should use the seat belt. The rules therefore apply to church youth group trips.[10]

The Department of Transport has produced two documents (VSE 1/96 and VSE 2/96) giving advice about the seat belt rules, and on how to install seat belts correctly. They are available from:

THE DEPARTMENT OF TRANSPORT
VSE 6,
2/06 Great Minster House,
76 Marsham Street,
London SW1P 4DR

Tel: 0171 271 5000

There should be two grown-ups per bus, and one should sit in the back, next to the door.

(e)   *Guidelines on touching*[11]

Keep everything public. A hug in the context of a group is very different from a hug behind closed doors.

Generally, only touch when the child needs it.

Touching should be appropriate for the age of the child, and generally started by the child rather than the worker.

Avoid any physical activity that is, or may be thought to be, sexually stimulating to the adult or child.

Children have a right to decide how much physical contact they have with others except in exceptional circumstances when they need medical attention.

Team members should monitor one another in the area of physical contact. They should be free to help each other by pointing out anything which could be misunderstood.

(f)   *Insurance*

The standard church insurance policy in use in many churches does not provide accident cover for youth and children's work, unless full details of each youth and children's activity is recorded in the minutes of the PCC beforehand. In 1996 the Ecclesiastical Insurance Group produced a new form of policy, known as their Parishguard Policy. The Parishguard Policy provides proper cover both for voluntary workers with children and for the children themselves, without the need for this formality. Under the Parishguard Policy, voluntary workers are treated as employees and covered by employers' liability insurance, and the children are covered for any injury within the British Isles in connection with your church business and activities.

Some dioceses have a youth and children's group insurance scheme for all youth and children's groups linked with churches. Whether you are still using one of the Ecclesiastical Insurance Group's old form of policies or the new Parishguard Policy, you should consider joining your diocesan scheme.

(g)   Safety of premises

Certain basic standards should apply to all premises where work with children and young people is being carried out.

- The church should have proper insurance cover.
- The building should be kept clean and tidy at all times.
- The fixtures, fittings and equipment should meet adequate safety standards.
- Outside areas for play should meet safety standards, and, where appropriate, there should be gates to prevent small children from straying from the premises.
- There should be a direct link between the size and suitability of the premises and the number of children and young people being catered for.

I suggest having an annual safety review, to consider all aspects of safety for children and young people.

Five areas to consider are

- *Hygiene*: There should be an adequate number of toilets and hand basins. Health and Safety regulations for registered activities normally require one toilet and hand basin per 10 children.

- *Lighting*: Lighting should be adequate, particularly on stairs and in halls and entrances. It is important to ensure that children do not have to arrive or leave a church building alone along dark unlit paths.
- *Electrical safety*: Care should be taken where there are heating appliances, cookers, refrigerators and low-level sockets.
- *Furniture*: Furniture should be in good repair, and there should be no high stacks of furniture in a room where young children meet.
- *Food*: Where food is being prepared, at least one worker should hold a Food and Hygiene certificate.[12]

Local councils have a health and safety officer whose job includes giving advice on issues of this sort.

(h)   First aid and medication

At least one of the leaders in a children's or youth group should have attended a recognised First Aid course run either by the St John Ambulance or the British Red Cross. For large groups you should definitely have more than one qualified First Aider.

A properly stocked First Aid kit should be available, and all leaders should know where to find it, and how to use it. It should be kept up to date. The contents should be checked every six months, and after any accident. Medicines and pain-killers should not be kept in the First Aid box. It is usual to have a second box for everyday items such as plasters, tissues, scissors and antiseptic cream.

If the injury is serious, an ambulance should be summoned straight away.

An accident book should be kept, to record the time, place and circumstances of any accident or injury, what action was taken, and by whom. Parents should be told what happened, and they should be asked to sign the record in the accident book. The accident book should also be used to record any accidents to adults. A suitable form of accident book is published by HMSO and available from HMSO bookshops.[13]

No medicines should ever be given to children without the prior permission of parents. Older children should be treated taking into account their age and understanding.

PART I. CHURCH PEOPLE

Parents should be asked whether their children suffer from any particular medical conditions, e.g. asthma, allergies, etc. before the children are taken on any trips, or if they are being left for a long time. Parents should also be asked to sign a consent form before trips.

(i) Registering with the Social Services Department

Under the terms of the Children Act 1989, all provision for children should be registered with the local Social Services Department if it involves under 8s for a period (or total of periods) exceeding two hours in any one day and for more than 6 days a year.

Junior Church, Sunday groups, Sunday morning crèche during worship, after-school clubs and toddlers' groups would not need to register as long as they do not last more than two hours. Nor do you need to register to take children on a church day out, as long as you do not have more than six days out in a year and for two hours or more. All playgroups using the church premises should be registered, as should holiday clubs which run for more than six days a year.

(j) Taking children off the premises

Written permission should always be obtained from the parents or guardians of a child. This permission may be obtained for a given period of time, e.g. a term. Parents should be informed if their children are to be taken in a car or other vehicle.

The church should have a list of names, addresses and telephone numbers for the next of kin of all children, young people and leaders who are away from church premises, and the group leaders should also have such a list.

When a group of children or young people is out or away, there should always be a known contact person in the parish who is available at a phone number in case of emergencies.

(k) What is child abuse?

Not all child abuse is sexual abuse. In Government guidelines, child abuse means physical, sexual, or serious emotional harm.

Working Together refers to four categories of abuse:

- *Neglect*: serious neglect of a child.
    failure to protect a child from danger, including cold or starvation.
- *Physical*: physical injury to a child.
    failure to prevent physical injury to a child.
- *Sexual*: sexual exploitation of a child,
    or where it is likely to occur.
- *Emotional*: serious emotional ill-treatment or rejection of a child.

(l)   *What are the signs of child abuse?*

There are three main signs of child abuse: visual, behavioural, and verbal.

(i)   *Visual*

- A child may be thin and pale, look tired and be poorly cared for.
- There may be repeated signs of bruising or burns.
- Evidence of a severe beating.
- Bruising or soreness round the genital area.

(ii)   *Behavioural*

- A well-adjusted child suddenly becomes withdrawn, depressed, naughty or disruptive.
- A disruptive child. The child may lie, steal and be destructive – breaking things.
- A child who acts out sexual behaviour.
- A child who appears very fearful.
- A child who draws sexually explicit pictures.
- A child who does not want to be left in the care of a particular person.
- Undue favouritism or 'picking on'.

(iii)   *Verbal*

- A child who gives unlikely explanations for bruises or burn marks.
- A child who tells you of actual physical or sexual abuse.

This book is not the place to go into detail on these matters. Some of the signs are obvious and well known. The diocesan guidelines describe the sort of behaviour and other signs which should alert those involved with children that something is wrong.

(m)   *What should be done where abuse is suspected or disclosed?*

The diocesan guidelines also set out what should be done when abuse is suspected or disclosed. Abuse is *suspected* when there are indications of abuse but no direct allegation by the child or a friend. Abuse is *disclosed* when the child or a friend of the child informs you that abuse has allegedly taken place.

If abuse is suspected:

- Inform the parish priest (provided he is not the subject of suspicion) if he is not already aware.
- The parish priest may then seek comments from others who know the child, as part of gathering information together to decide whether further advice should be sought.
- Make notes of what you have seen, and consult with others for what they have seen.
- The parish priest or the observer should seek advice from someone outside the congregation, preferably a professional in child care, or make informal contact with the Social Services Department. The importance of taking such concerns outside the immediate church family is to avoid any suggestions of a cover up. In other words, if the advice is to take no further action, and this is questioned by the authorities, it could look as though there has been some sort of cover up if the whole affair has been dealt with internally. Seeking advice from someone outside the congregation is a protection. Some diocesan guidelines suggest discussing the matter with a person at the bishop's office, but even this may suggest to the outside world that there has been some kind of a cover up.
- If you have suspicions concerning your parish priest you should consult your bishop's advisers on child protection immediately, from whom informal and entirely confidential advice may be sought. People who have suffered abuse from their parish priest often find it very difficult to seek help and advice from people within their own church structure. It may be appropriate for the social services or some independent agency to be involved from the outset.

It is important to be aware of the far-reaching effect of making a referral and naming names. But the welfare of the child is the most important thing.

If abuse is disclosed by the child or a friend making a direct allegation of abuse:

- Always take what the child tells you seriously, even if you find it hard to believe.
- Listen carefully. Write down what you hear, dating and signing the record. Note also whether other people were present.
- Do not promise confidentiality. Make it plain that you may have to tell someone else. The child may feel guilty and not want anyone to be told, but in cases of actual abuse the law requires you to do so.
- Do not ask leading questions or push for unoffered information. Doing so may make it impossible to pursue any criminal charge later.
- Comfort the young person and reassure them that they were right to tell you.
- Explain what you are going to do next.
- For under-18s you are obliged to contact the Social Services Department. If this is impossible, and the child is in danger, contact the police. Do not try to investigate yourself.
- Inform the parish priest (if he is not the person accused of abuse) and the bishop's office as soon as possible.
- In cases of *sexual or physical abuse*, do *not* inform the child's parents unless and until the Social Services tell you that you can. This may sound very harsh, but there are two reasons for this advice. First, you may place the child at risk of further injury. Second, any discussions within the family will reduce the value of any evidence which the child is able to give. In some cases the result is that the police are not able to prosecute the abuser. In cases of *neglect*, you should inform the parents, and encourage them to take the child to see a doctor or the social services.
- If the alleged abuser is a church worker, either paid or voluntary, or the alleged abuse is taking place under the care of the church, you should notify the church's insurers immediately in writing. Failure to do this may prejudice any cover provided by the policy.

- Depending on the circumstances, the parish may also need to take legal advice immediately.

Under no circumstances should the person accused or suspected of abuse be alerted or spoken to. This might lead to the child being frightened, or being put under pressure to take back what he or she said. Crucial evidence may be hidden or destroyed. The alleged abuser may even run away to avoid being arrested.

It is possible to seek advice from the Social Services Department on a hypothetical basis, without identifying the child. But if the Social Services Department are seriously concerned, they will want to know the details. Some older children may not want the Social Services to know what has happened. The rule is, they have to be told. If you are concerned about what to do in a situation, contact your diocese's child protection officer.

3.   HEALING THE WOUNDED

There are specialist support agencies and counsellors available, both within and outside the Christian community. Those who will be in need of support include:

The child or young person. Healing will be a slow process which may be hindered by a lack of self-esteem. Guilt, anger and frustration are some of the feelings they may have towards themselves, their family, and the alleged abuser.

The alleged abuser and his family will also need great support, whether the allegation is true or false. If untrue, the hurt is incalculable. If true, remember that in many cases the abuser may also have been the victim of abuse. However serious their actions, they are still loved by God, and should be supported by the church.

The child's family will need long-term care and support, particularly if the alleged abuser is a member of the family or close relative.

The person receiving the disclosure is also in need of help.

The local congregation and community. Questions will be asked by members of the local church. The members of the congregation should be asked not to talk about the matter to each other. All concerns should be reported to the parish priest or to some other named person. The reason for this is that such discussion within the congregation can ruin the prospect of a successful criminal prosecution.

Confidentiality, long-term care and support are essential for all involved.

4.   WHAT ABOUT KNOWN OFFENDERS?

It is generally accepted that there is a high risk that paedophiles will offend again. If a known offender wants to come to your church, what should the response be of the parish priest and the PCC?

The answer is, you should set clear rules, and enforce them. He (or she) should be welcome into the church, but almost certainly there should be no involvement at all with children. Certain people with responsibility in the church will have to know about the person's history, so that they can keep an eye on him. You should know that paedophiles can be very manipulative in order to gain access to children.

If the offender then breaks any of the boundaries, and especially if he starts behaving wrongly towards children, you should ask him to leave.[14] The churchwardens are entitled to use reasonable force to remove him if he refuses to go. Or they can summon the police to remove him. If he attends another church, inform the leaders.

5.   WHAT SHOULD EACH PCC DO?

The PCC is responsible for:
- the recruitment, training and support of leaders.
- making sure that there is insurance cover for the work that is being carried out among children and young people.
- setting up a safe environment where the risk of the abuse of children is as small as possible.
- adopting a policy statement on safeguarding the welfare of children. That means having a written set of rules, or a written code, and agreeing to follow it.

Your PCC should therefore:

- obtain a copy of the guidelines on child protection issued by your diocese, and consider them.
- realise that the unthinkable can and does happen, and resolve to do its best to prevent it.
- adopt a policy statement on children and young people in the church. Some dioceses publish in their guidelines a model policy statement for its parishes to adopt. If your diocese does not have one of these, I suggest adopting the model policy published by the Churches' Child Protection Advisory Service.
- resolve to put into action the guidelines on child protection issued by your diocese.
- Work out how to put the policy into practice in your parish. This will include ensuring that everyone who is involved with children's work in the church understands the guidelines, and follows them.
- Ensure that the matter is reviewed on a regular basis, say once a year. This should be done by bringing it to the attention of each new PCC.

6.   ORGANISATIONS

THE NSPCC[15]
42 Curtain Road,
London EC2A 3NH.

Tel: 0171 825 2500.

Child Protection Helpline 0800 800500 (open 24 hours).

The NSPCC is a national specialist voluntary agency for the protection of children and young people. Their Helpline gives help and advice to anyone about child abuse issues. The service is confidential, but they can act on information which is given if the caller requests it. They also have excellent publicity information which could be prominently displayed.

CHILDLINE
FreePost 1111,
London N1 0BR,

Tel: 0800 1111 (open 24 hours).

Childline is the national free helpline for children in trouble or worried. 0800 1111 is specifically for children's use. They will offer advice and direct help, and can act if the child requests practical help. Free publicity is available.

Kidscape
152 Buckingham Palace Road,
London SW1W 9TR

Tel: 0171 730 3300.

Kidscape is a national charity teaching children how to keep safe *before* they become victims. It publishes useful information on protecting children from both abuse and bullying.

Churches' Child Protection Advisory Services
PO Box 133,
Swanley,
Kent BR8 7UQ.

Tel: 01322 667207

Helpline: 01322 660011

Fax: 01322 614788

Churches' Child Protection Advisory Services provides support across all Christian denominations, and publishes a range of books and tapes dealing with child care. It works with a number of dioceses across the country, running training programmes, giving advice and support in policy formulation, and helping in individual cases of abuse: I recommend in particular the booklet

David Pearson, *Guidance To Churches: Protecting Children and Appointing Children's Workers*, 5th edn. (Churches' Child Protection Advisory Services, 1995, updated 1996).

Association of Christian Counsellors
173a Wokingham Road,
Reading,
Berks RG6 1LT

Tel: 01734 662207

PART I.   CHURCH PEOPLE

The Association of Christian Counsellors gives advice about training, accreditation and supervision of Christian counsellors.

THE METROPOLITAN POLICE
Crime Policy Unit,
New Scotland Yard,
London SW1H 0BG

The Metropolitan Police produce an excellent booklet, *Advice for Victims of Sexual Assault.*

CHRISTIAN SURVIVORS OF SEXUAL ABUSE
BM-CSSA,
London WC1N 3XX

This *is* the full address. There is no telephone line for general use. Christian Survivors of Sexual Abuse offers support to adults who were sexually abused as children.

7.   FURTHER INFORMATION

(a)   Government guidance

- *Working Together – A guide to arrangements for inter-agency co-operation for the protection of children from abuse* (HMSO, 1991). The Department of Health has announced that *Working Together* is currently being reviewed, and a new guide will be published in 1998.
- *Safe from Harm* HMSO 1993

(b)   Christian publications in the UK

- Diocesan guidelines for each diocese, obtainable from diocesan secretaries.
- *House of Bishops' Policy Document on Child Protection* (Church House Publishing, 1995) (revised document expected 1998).
- David Pearson, *Guidance To Churches: Protecting Children and Appointing Children's Workers* 5th edn. (Churches' Child Protection Advisory Services, 1995, updated 1996). This booklet covers how to respond to abuse, appointing children's workers, supervision and practice issues, dealing with behavioural problems in children's meetings, and model child protection policies.

- *Child Abuse: Pastoral and Procedural Guidelines*, a report from a working party to the Catholic Bishops' Conference of England and Wales on cases of sexual abuse of children involving priests, religious and other church workers, (Catholic Media Office, London, 1994) ISBN 0 905241 13 4.
- *Healing the Wound of Child Sexual Abuse, a Church Response*, (Catholic Bishops' Conference of England and Wales Committee for Social Welfare, 1996) ISBN 0 949005 78 9.
- *Child Protection, Safeguarding the Welfare of Children and Young People within the Church and its Organisations* (Ecclesiastical Insurance Group, 1997).
- *Good Practice,* a pack for local churches to help with safeguarding the welfare of children and young people (United Reformed Church).
- *Safeguarding Children and Young People* (Methodist Church Division of Education and Youth).
- *Safe to Grow* (Baptist Union of Great Britain).

(c)   Books

There are a number of books dealing with information about child abuse, guidance about practical steps churches may want to take to protect children, to support families and to support adults who were abused either as children or as adults. Two excellent ones are:

- *Child Sexual Abuse and the Church* by Patrick Parkinson (Hodder and Stoughton, 1997).
- *Pastoral Care for Young People*, edited by Mark Vernon (Marshall Pickering, 1996). This covers areas such as drugs as well as sex and sexual abuse.

Churches' Child Protection Advisory Services supply a list of books on the subject which they have available.

There are a large number of books written in America on the subject. Here is a sample:

- Jason Berry, *Lead us not into temptation: Catholic Priests and the sexual abuse of children* (New York, Doubleday, 1992).
- Elinor Burkett, *A Gospel of shame: children, sexual abuse and the Church*, (New York, Viking, 1993).

PART I.   CHURCH PEOPLE

- Matthew Colton and Maurice Vanstone, *Betrayal of Trust: sexual abuse by men who work with children* (London, Free Association Press, 1996).
- Tilman Furniss, *Multi-professional handbooks of child sexual abuse, integrated management, therapy and legal intervention* (London, Routledge, 1991).
- John Gonsiorek, *Breach of Trust. Sexual Exploitation by Health Care Professionals and Clergy* (Sage Publications Inc., 1995) ISBN 0 8039 5557 X.
- Philip Jenkins, *Paedophiles and priests: anatomy of a contemporary crisis*, (New York, OUP, 1996).
- Stephen Rossetti, *A tragic grace: the Catholic Church and child sexual abuse* (Collegeville, Minn., Liturgical Press, 1996).
- Stephen Rossetti, *Slayer of the Soul: Child sexual abuse and the Catholic Church* (Mystic, Connecticut, Twenty-Third Publications, 1990).

On more general safety concerns for children, the Ecclesiastical Insurance Group publishes a series of guidance notes for churches. Two in the series are relevant to this chapter.[16]

- *Guidance Notes for Churches. Section 3: Health and Safety* (Ecclesiastical Insurance Group, 1997) includes amongst other topics the use of inflatable bouncy castles.
- *Guidance Notes for Churches. Section 4: General* (Ecclesiastical Insurance Group, 1997) includes amongst other topics the organisation of bonfire and firework displays, organisation of charity walks, and parishes involved in youth work.

---

[1] *Working Together* (HMSO, 1991) and *Safe from Harm* (HMSO, 1993).
[2] Final approval of the new policy statement by the Standing Committee of the House of Bishops is expected in April or May 1998.
[3] The Ecclesiastical Insurance Group's own guidance on child protection, *Child Protection, Safeguarding the Welfare of Children and Young People within the Church and its Organisations* (Ecclesiastical Insurance Group, 1997), page 2 says as follows:

> The observance of 'reasonable care' is a standard insurance condition. Allegations of child abuse and events arising therefrom may or may not be a matter for insurance. ... The policy terms require that all

reasonable steps be taken to prevent injury loss or damage ocurring and failure to take such precautions may prejudice the insurance cover. A duty therefore exists upon Policyholders to adopt 'best practice' based upon current and ongoing guidelines.

[4] You can ask about *all* past convictions for criminal offences of anyone who applies to work with children. The usual rule that you cannot ask about 'spent convictions' does not apply: see the Rehabilitation of Offenders Act 1974 (Exceptions) Order 1975. The draft House of Bishops' revised policy document on child protection (to be published later in 1998 when agreed) contains new forms of declaration, which require 'spent convictions' to be disclosed only if they relate to children. The offences concerned are those listed or treated as listed in Schedule 1 to the Children and Young Persons Act 1933, and the list of offences specified in the Schedule to the Disqualification for Caring with Children Regulations 1991.

[5] When the revised House of Bishops' policy document on child protection is published later in 1998 new declaration forms will be required. See note 4 above.

[6] *Child Protection, Safeguarding the Welfare of Children and Young People within the Church and its Organisations* (Ecclesiastical Insurance Group, 1997), page 4.

[7] The Home Office has expressed disapproval of employers using the Data Protection Act 1984 for this purpose, and it is possible that a law will be introduced to make the practice illegal. However it is the Home Office which in January 1998 introduced the Data Protection Bill 1998, and there is nothing in the Data Protection Bill dealing with the matter.

[8] The Police Act 1997 was one of the last Acts to be passed before the 1997 general election. Contact with the Home Office has revealed that at present no decision has been taken about whether or not these provisions are to be brought into force.

[9] See 'First aid and medication', page 149. Parents of children who are hurt should be asked to sign the accident book, but they should not see what is written in the log book.

[10] The Road Vehicles (Construction and Use) (Amendment) (No. 2) Regulations 1996.

[11] I am grateful to the Churches' Child Protection Advisory Services for these guidelines.

[12] See Chapter 11, 'Food and drink'.

[13] Accident Book, form B1 510, (HMSO).

[14] See Canon E 1 paragraph 4, and Canon F 15 paragraph 3. Canon E 1 requires the churchwardens to maintain order and *decency* in the church. Canon F 15 paragraph 3 provides:

> If any person be guilty of riotous, violent, or *indecent behaviour* in any church, chapel, or churchyard, whether in any time of divine service or not, or of disturbing, vexing, troubling, or mis-using any minister officiating therein, the said churchwardens or their assistants shall take care to restrain the offender and if necessary proceed against him according to law.

[15] The National Society for the Prevention of Cruelty to Children.

[16] For a list of the Ecclesiastical Insurance Group guidance notes, and a summary of their contents, see pages 352–3.

Part II

Church Life

Chapter 9

CHURCH SERVICES

1.   INTRODUCTION

There are many different types of services in the church, and many different styles of worship. They range from the traditional almost to the bizarre, from the very high church to the very low church, and from the legal to the not so legal. At one end of the scale, some churches use the Roman Missal, which is illegal. At the other end, there are informal services with almost no liturgy, where laymen preach without authority to do so, charismatic gifts are exercised, people fall about laughing, the clergy do not wear robes, and the impression is sometimes one of disorder rather than order. This charismatic type of service has elements which are illegal.[1] Somewhere between these two extremes, many churches still use the formal services in the Book of Common Prayer and the Alternative Service Book, which are 100 per cent legal!

I do not wish to be controversial, or to take sides in a debate which goes beyond the limits of this book. I shall try to set out (a) what the law requires, and (b) what it permits. If what is happening in a church goes beyond this, then the PCC should discuss the matter with the parish priest, and with the rural dean or the archdeacon if no agreement is reached with the parish priest. If the PCC supports the parish priest in going beyond what the law allows, then it should be aware that others may complain to the bishop and cause trouble for the parish priest. The PCC should also be aware that the parish priest is treading on dangerous ground, and that abuses can happen *because of (i) doubtful theology and (ii) the lack of accountability*. In the few cases where serious problems have developed, the media have had a field day: as for example in Sheffield in 1995 with the Nine O'Clock Service.

2.   WHAT SERVICES SHOULD BE HELD?

(a)   Normal worship on Sundays and throughout the week

The normal services to take place every Sunday at every parish church are the services of Morning Prayer, Evening Prayer and Holy Communion (commonly known as the statutory services). Strictly, all three services should take place every Sunday unless the bishop has given permission for some other arrangement. In practice, many churches do not hold all three services every Sunday. Indeed, in the country, where a priest is often responsible for several churches, it is impossible for him to fulfil this requirement.

The clergy are also supposed to say the services of Morning Prayer and Evening Prayer throughout the week, together with others who may meet with them in church. Often the parish priest does these services on his own. In many churches Holy Communion is said during the course of the week.

These are the formal services contained in the Book of Common Prayer and the Alternative Service Book (known as the ASB). The Alternative Service Book is authorised until the end of the year 2000, and work is under way on a replacement for it. As part of this process, there is now a new calendar for the Church's year, together with a new lectionary arranged on a three-year cycle, and new collects and post-communion prayers.[2]

A number of churches are using the publication *Celebrating Common Prayer*,[3] a version of the Daily Office prepared by the Society of Saint Francis. Although it is an unofficial form of service, it is very much Anglican in style, and the Foreword is written by the Archbishop of Canterbury. It is increasingly being used by clergy and laity both for private prayer and as the form of daily Morning and Evening Prayer in parish churches.[4]

The growth of informal family services is an important feature of life in the Church of England. In many cases they are a simple form of the services of Holy Communion, or Morning or Evening Prayer, and are no problem. It is when they are not based on any approved form of service that problems can arise. The Sheffield Diocesan Handbook of 1993 shows the tension that existed between the strict requirements for the three formal services, and the growing use of informal worship:

> Where family services, 'Praise Services' and similar forms of worship which are unrelated to the statutory services are to be held, it is suggested that they are planned so as to follow a recognised pattern of service, and also, that provision should be made for people to be led on from these occasions to the statutory services and to full communicant membership of the Church. It is important that family services and the like do not become a substitute for the Church's authorised services.

A new form of service was authorised in 1993, known as *A Service of the Word* (though parishes that use it often do not use that name for it). 'A Service of the Word' may be used instead of Morning or Evening Prayer on any Sunday, and is authorised until the year 2000. It allows great freedom in the way the service is planned, in the use of liturgy, singing, and prayer, and in the choice of Bible reading. But it does have some of each of these elements, and provides a degree of control. In other words, it is flexible enough to allow clergy to plan services which

(a) are authorised, and therefore legal, and (b) minister to the needs of the congregation.

'A Service of the Word' may also be used with Holy Communion according to the rite in the Alternative Service Book.

(b)   Unauthorised services?

The Worship and Doctrine Measure 1974 and the Canons of the Church of England lay down the forms of worship which are to be used in the Church of England. At ordination and afterwards whenever a priest is put in charge of a parish he is required to say:

> in public prayer and administration of the sacraments I will use only the forms of service which are authorised or allowed by Canon.

Canon B 5 allows a parish priest to make minor changes to any form of authorised service. This Canon also says that he may also use any form of service for special occasions which are not mentioned in the Book of Common Prayer or the Alternative Service Book, provided the form of service is honouring to God, in good taste, and sound in doctrine.

What a parish priest cannot do under this Canon is to make up a new form of service for use as the regular Sunday services for the parish. For these services, he should use either the statutory services or the new 'Service of the Word'.

(c)   Holy Communion

In general, only people who have been confirmed are allowed to take Holy Communion. The only other people who may take communion are:

- people who are ready and wanting to be confirmed,
- practising Christians belonging to other denominations who are accustomed to take communion, and
- baptised Christians who are in danger of death.

The law says nothing about permitting children to take communion. The House of Bishops have recently issued guidance on this, for those churches that want to admit children to communion. *Communion before confirmation*, the guidelines agreed by the House of Bishops in 1997, is set out in Appendix 4.

The problem of admitting children to communion before confirmation would disappear if the Church of England were to follow the practice of the Roman Catholic church in encouraging confirmation from the age of seven. There is much to be said both in favour of and against this approach, but it goes beyond the scope of this book.[5]

Some churches permit the Holy Communion to be administered at House Group Meetings. A celebration of the Holy Communion requires the participation of an ordained priest, and should normally be held in a consecrated building.[6] A celebration of the Holy Communion at an informal prayer meeting or House Group is therefore *not* permitted, unless a priest is there to take the service. Lay people can of course assist in distributing the bread and the wine after it has been consecrated by the priest. The names of suitable people who would like to assist in distributing the bread and the wine are given to the bishop of each diocese. Once the bishop has approved these people, they can then distribute the bread and the wine during Holy Communion.

(d)   *Choice of services*

It is up to the parish priest and the PCC to decide which form of service to use on Sundays: the Alternative Service Book form, the services in the Book of Common Prayer, or the new 'Service of the Word'. This can lead to tension amongst the members of the PCC and the congregation. The booklet *Public Worship in the Church of England*[7] gives helpful guidance to churches on how to reach their decision.

> In reaching a decision, parish priest and council will, of course, know that they ought to bear in mind the interests of the whole parish and of all worshippers. The views of the regular congregation are of course to be considered but the needs of those who are not regular worshippers should be considered too. A different style of service may be appropriate for major festivals, though whether this is more traditional or more 'contemporary' than the regular style of worship will depend on an assessment of the needs and preferences of those who will be drawn in. Certainly Christmas, Easter, Pentecost are times

when it is important to try to give satisfaction to all groups within the congregation.   Throughout the year, strongly expressed minority views ought, if possible, to be met in some way within the range of available services. Minority needs will probably only be met satisfactorily if some provision is made for them at Sunday services – a weekday service of Holy Communion or Evening Prayer is rarely an adequate way of meeting the needs of a substantial minority of worshippers.

Many churches have become accustomed to a varied pattern of old and new services on different occasions, some with more Prayer Book services than Alternative Services, others vice versa, and some with Prayer Book and Alternative Services in more or less equal proportions as best suits local circumstances. It is seldom a simple choice between 'the old service' and 'the new service'; there are many possibilities which ought to be carefully explored before decisions are taken.

There is a rule to decide what happens if no agreement can be reached by the parish priest and the PCC. The answer depends on what services have been used in the church over the previous four years. If one particular form of service has been used for at least two continuous years over this four-year period, the PCC can insist that that form is used. Otherwise, the church has to use only the forms of service in the Book of Common Prayer.

But as *Public Worship in the Church of England* states:[8]

It cannot be too strongly emphasised, however, that the intention of the law is that decisions on forms of service to be used at public worship should be taken jointly after full consultation and agreement. This is not achieved if anyone finds it necessary to invoke legal rights. Accordingly, before people become so entrenched in disagreement, a parish would be well advised to seek outside assessment and advice from, say the Rural Dean and Lay Chairman of the Deanery Synod or the Archdeacon.

(e)   Baptisms, marriages and funerals

Where churches aim to evangelise and encourage people in the practice of the Christian faith, it is with these services that they often begin. Many people come to Christian faith through being drawn into the church following one of these services. They include couples who have had their children baptised, or who have been married in church, or who have suffered a bereavement. The church's ministry through these services and through following up the people who come to them, is a gentle and effective form of evangelism. The next few paragraphs explains the legal rules which the PCC should know about, but the church's ministry to these people goes beyond just these services.

No priest may refuse to baptise a child. A parish priest may *delay* baptising a child for the purpose of teaching the parents or guardians or godparents (unless the child is in danger of death, when he should baptise straight away). A parish priest should not baptise a child where the parents come from a different parish without first seeking the agreement of the parish priest of the parish where the parents live. But the Church of England approves of infant baptism, and parish priests and churches should not try to stop parents from having their children baptised.

There is much law on the celebration of marriage, but very little which is of direct concern to the PCC. One important matter is the use of tape recordings and video recordings of weddings. This can lead to copyright problems, and the payment of additional fees to professional musicians and the organist. The copyright aspects are discussed in Chapter 13, 'Copyright'. Fees are dealt with below under the heading 'Music and musicians'.

Again, the law of funerals is of no concern to the PCC. The subject of the maintenance of the churchyard is set out in Chapter 20, 'Repairs and maintenance'.

(f)   Healing services

Services are available, authorised by General Synod, which include Communion of the Sick, the Laying on of Hands and Anointing, a Commendation at the Time of Death, and Prayers and Blessings with the Sick. These are available in the form of a book *Services for the Sick*. The Book of Common Prayer contains 'The Thanksgiving of Women after Child-birth, commonly called the Churching of Women'.

Christ's charge to his disciples was to heal the sick.[9] It is right for all Christians to pray for others when they are sick, that they may be healed. We should encourage each other to do this, and not just rely on the formal services which are authorised for this purpose and taken by the parish priest.

Many churches have a book or notice board for people to write in their prayer requests. Many requests are for healing.

Some churches have ministry teams, where members of the congregation are encouraged and trained to pray for others, for healing and for other personal needs. It is vital that such ministry teams are trained, and that there is *accountability* for what takes place when individuals are prayed for. Accountability involves (at least) the following:

- reporting back (de-briefing) by each member of the team to one of the clergy.
- that member of the clergy following up individual cases, whenever necessary.
- making sure that there is continuing support and prayer for the individual who has been prayed for, by those close to them, over a long period.
- that there should be no emotional pressure placed on the people being ministered to.
- ensuring that the members of the ministry team are properly looked after, so that they are not scarred by what they have heard.

Cases have arisen when ministry has been handled wrongly, with terrible consequences. I personally know one couple whose teenage daughter became seriously mentally ill immediately after a session of ministry. This might have been avoided if a member of the clergy had been informed of what had happened and had acted quickly. The child's parents did not find out for several months what had happened.

Churches wanting to use this form of personal ministry should be accountable for what they do. The Ecclesiastical Insurance Group Parishguard Policy does not cover you for liability arising from any counselling or advice.

Guidelines for the healing ministry have been published jointly by the Methodist Church and the Churches' Council for Health and Healing (CCHH). *Guidelines for Good Practice* is available from:

METHODIST PUBLISHING HOUSE
20 Ivatt Way,
Peterborough PE3 7PG.

(g)   *Exorcism and deliverance*

From time to time clergy are asked to help people who are troubled by what they think are evil powers or spirits. There is no reason why clergy should not say some appropriate prayers with and for these persons.

But appropriate prayers should not extend to deliverance and exorcism without the express permission from the bishop or the archdeacon. Almost all the diocesan regulations I have seen specifically mention this.[10]

To arrange a meeting with a person specifically to deal with 'deliverance', or to suggest to a person that they need 'deliverance', or to carry out deliverance in a noisy and somewhat frightening manner is (i) likely to be misunderstood and lead to adverse publicity, and (ii) breaks every set of diocesan regulations which cover the subject.

It cannot be stated too strongly that exorcism is a specialised ministry. There are very great dangers when inexperienced and unauthorised Christians venture into this field. Diagnosis of possession or oppression in someone requires considerable maturity and experience. So does the assessment of the spiritual health of a disturbed person. Only properly qualified people who have been authorised by the bishop to carry out this important ministry should have anything to do with it.

Churchwardens and PCCs should not permit deliverance and exorcism to take place in their church without the bishop's authority. The Ecclesiastical Insurance Group Parishguard Policy does not cover you for liability arising from any ministry of this nature.[11]

(h)   *Other services*

Various forms of service have been commended by the House of Bishops. These include:

- *Lent, Holy Week, Easter* (Church House Publishing, Cambridge University Press and SPCK, 1986).

- *The Promise of His Glory* (Church House Publishing and Mowbrays, 1991).
- *Services of Prayer and Dedication after Civil Marriage* (Church House Publishing).
- *Night Prayer*, a service based on the ancient office of compline, (Church House Publishing and Mowbrays).

3.   MUSIC AND MUSICIANS

(a)   Choice of music

In 1792 there was a court decision which held that psalms and hymns could be sung during a service even when not specifically authorised by the Book of Common Prayer.[12] To those accustomed to informal services with music led by guitars, the fact that this needed to be decided in court has a sense of unreality about it. Thankfully the Church of England has moved on from those days. The position now is that the parish priest can say the whole service, or sing the whole service, or say part and sing the rest, as he chooses. This is the case for any of the authorised services in the Book of Common Prayer or the Alternative Service Book. He can add hymns and songs whenever he wants.

Two things should be said. The first is that music should be *appropriate* and *reverent*.

Canon B 20 paragraph 3 says:

> It is the duty of the minister to ensure that only such chants, hymns, anthems, and other settings are chosen as are appropriate, both the words and the music, to the solemn act of worship and prayer in the House of God as well as to the congregation assembled for that purpose; and to banish all irreverence in the practice and performance of the same.

The reference to *solemn act of worship and prayer* does not mean that music should be like a dirge. The Psalmist wrote that we should:

> Worship the Lord with gladness; come before him with joyful songs.[13]

Also, it does not mean that we are limited to the great hymn writers of the Victorian age and earlier. Again, from the Psalmist:

> Sing to him a new song; play skilfully, and shout for joy.[14]

The words of many of the great hymns of the past teach some important doctrine of the Christian faith. Many modern songs are based on verses from the Bible, and it is right that they should be. Great care should be taken before permitting songs to be sung which are not based directly on Holy Scripture or some proper Christian doctrine.[15]

The second thing which should be said is that the parish priest has the final word on the choice of music. Where there is an organist, choirmaster or director of music, the parish priest should:[16]

> pay due heed to his advice and assistance in the choosing of chants, hymns, anthems, and other settings, and in the ordering of the music of the Church; but at all times the final responsibility and decision in these matters rests with the minister.

(b)   *Payment to musicians*

The labourer is worthy of his hire.[17]

Some Christians believe that all worship should be given freely to God. They think that no Christian should ask to be paid to sing or play in a church service.

This view is no doubt sincerely held, but it ignores the fact that professional musicians need to earn their living from their music. Although some professional musicians may choose to sing or play in church for nothing, in general, churches who wish to have professional singers and players lead the music for their services should expect to pay them.

Outside London and other large cities, by far the greater number of musicians who sing and play in church are not professional musicians. No doubt they are grateful for any crumbs that fall from the PCC's table, but mostly they sing and play for love.

Both the Royal School of Church Music and the Incorporated Society of Musicians publish recommended salaries and fees for directors of music and organists.[18] They also publish the fees which should be paid for special services such as weddings, funerals and memorial services. Fees payable to the organist and musicians are in addition to the statutory fees which are payable to the church for marriages and funerals.[19] For 1997–8 the Royal School of Church Music recommended fee for a professional organist to play at a wedding is £50 to £78 depending on the size of the church, and £110 if there is a rehearsal as well. These fees should be increased by 50 per cent if a tape recording is made, and by 100 per cent if a video recording is made.[20]

The same increase in fees for sound and video recordings is also due to other professional musicians singing or playing in the service. These fees have been agreed by the Musicians' Union on their behalf.

As it is normally the couple getting married who will have to pay for the music at their wedding, they should be informed before the service how much extra it will cost if a sound or video recording is made.

Organists are often asked to book other musicians – a trumpeter for a wedding, or singers for a special service. If the booking is made on behalf of a church or a wedding couple, this should be made clear at the time of the booking, otherwise the organist may find that he is personally responsible for their fees.

4.   CLERGY DRESS

On Sundays a parish priest taking Morning or Evening prayer should normally wear a cassock, together with a surplice or alb with a scarf or stole.[21]

A word of explanation is perhaps needed.

A *cassock* is a long garment usually black in colour reaching from the neck to the ankles.[22]

A *surplice* is a white cotton or linen garment which goes on top of the cassock. It has wide sleeves and goes down to below the knees. (It has a shorter, simpler, form known as a *cotta*.[23])

An *alb* is a white cotton or linen garment reaching from the neck to the ankles with tight-fitting sleeves. It is either worn loose or held in at the waist by a simple cord known as a girdle. An alb can be worn without a cassock (and often is, in summer).

A *scarf* is a simple black scarf usually made of serge.

A *stole* is a coloured scarf (coloured according to the season of the Church year or the sacrament which is being celebrated), which is worn falling straight down in front by a priest or bishop, or diagonally over the left shoulder by a deacon: it is a sign of the wearer's order. (In the past a priest would wear his stole crossed over in front, and that is how you will see it for instance on monumental brasses.)

Some priests wear a *chasuble*, which is a coloured decorative garment worn on top of the alb for Holy Communion.

Some priests and especially bishops wear a *cope*, which is a semicircular cloak worn in place of the chasuble.

All these are legal.

A parish priest does not need to be robed to take Morning or Evening prayer mid-week. He should be robed whenever he takes a Holy Communion service, and for other services such as baptisms, confirmations, weddings and funerals.[24]

The Canons say nothing about the wearing of robes for 'A Service of the Word', but as this service is an alternative to Morning or Evening Prayer, clergy taking 'A Service of the Word' on Sundays should be robed.

High church priests often wear a lot more than these requirements. Low church parish priests often do not wear robes at all, which is illegal. The Canons say that a parish priest's choice of robes is not important for doctrine,[25] but some parish priests seem to think it is.[26]

A practical reason in favour of wearing robes is that they help children and others to see who the parish priest is, and so recognise him as the parish priest.

Before a parish priest changes the type of robes he wears he should consult the PCC. If they do not agree, the bishop decides the point.[27]

5.   LAY PREACHERS

Sermons may only be preached by the parish priest or by someone with the permission of the bishop to preach.[28] The only exception is in Canon B 43 which deals with visiting lay preachers and ministers from churches other than the Church of England. Such lay preachers and priests can be asked to preach provided the PCC agrees, but if the preaching is to be on a regular basis, the bishop's approval in writing should also be obtained.

What about people being asked to give testimonies, or Bible studies, or lectures in church? There is no difficulty about a testimony being given, as long as there is a proper sermon preached at the same service by the parish priest.[29] There is a problem asking lay people to lead a Bible study or give a lecture in place of the sermon. You should consult the bishop before doing this.

Why is this important? The answer is to make sure that 'sound doctrine' is being preached.

6.   GOOD ORDER

The parish priest should ensure that all worship is 'reverent and seemly'. *Reverent* means honouring to God, and *seemly* means attractive and suitable. The churchwardens are under a duty to maintain 'order' and 'decency' in church. The opposite of *order* is *disorder*. Indecency is not just to do with sex, it is any form of bad behaviour. If need be the churchwardens can use reasonable force to remove anyone causing disorder or behaving badly.

How does this apply to the exercise of charismatic gifts in church, and to the controversial 'Toronto Blessing'?[30] There are three points to make.

The first point is Scriptural. St Paul gave instructions on the use of charismatic gifts in church, and we should try to understand and follow them.[31]

The second is that the parish priest should be in control. If he is not convinced that these activities are the work of the Holy Spirit, it is his right and his duty to stop them. If he believes they are the work of the Holy Spirit, then he should not stop what is going on, but should guide the congregation on how to use these gifts properly.

The third is that if and when these manifestations occur, the parish priest should explain what is going on to the congregation. It should be clear that the parish priest is in control and still leading the service.

7.   WHAT TO DO WHEN THERE IS NO PRIEST TO TAKE THE SERVICE

Churchwardens are sometimes faced with the problem of what to do when the person responsible for the Sunday service either fails to arrive, or sends a message saying he or she will not be able to take the service. The answer is, they should lead the service themselves or invite a reader who happens to be present to lead it.

Here is some guidance on how to proceed.

Remember that everyone has come to worship God, and will support you in what you are doing.

Talk with your fellow warden briefly, and with the organist, to plan the service you will take.

Find the lectionary and the service book, and choose people to read the lessons, and perhaps someone to lead the prayers. Make sure all the readings and collects are found and marked.

The following forms of service can be led by the churchwardens or any lay person. If the churchwardens are there, they should take authority, and either lead a service themselves, with help from others if required, or ask someone else to lead. The instructions for the form of service set out below come from the diocese of Truro. Other dioceses have similar liturgies for use in such circumstances.

Proceed slowly and calmly. Remember, you are not trying to produce the perfect service, but to worship God with the rest of the congregation.

(a)   *Morning and evening prayer*

You may lead either Matins or Evensong as it would have been led by the clergy or readers who normally officiate at your church.

Only priests and bishops have the authority to declare the forgiveness of sins.[32]   Therefore when you say the 'Absolution' after the 'General Confession' you should substitute the words *us* and *our sins* for *you* and *your sins*. Or, if you prefer, instead of the Absolution read the collect for the 21st Sunday after Trinity in the Book of Common Prayer.

The service should follow on after the third collect as usual. Strictly there should be no sermon or address, as no one can legally preach in church without the bishop's permission. But no one should object if you read an appropriate sermon or extract from a devotional book as an alternative to a sermon. Continue with an anthem or hymn, followed by the Intercessions and Grace, and a final hymn.

If you prefer, the whole of the service may be said, without music.

Notices and Banns of Marriage should be read after the third collect.

(b)   Holy Communion or Eucharist.

If you normally use the service from the Book of Common Prayer, you should switch to Morning or Evening prayer as appropriate. The Book of Common Prayer does not allow anyone other than a priest to conduct any part of the Holy Communion service.

If instead you normally use the form of service in the Alternative Service Book, you may conduct the first part of this service (the Ante-Communion), but you should not do the part of the service where the bread and wine are blessed and distributed (the actual celebration of the Lord's Supper). So, take the service as far as the Absolution, using 'us' instead of 'you' in that particular prayer. After the Absolution, use the Intercessions, the Lord's Prayer and the General Thanksgiving, and close with the Grace. All hymns can be used in their usual place.

(c)   A Service of the Word

If you are used to having 'A Service of the Word' as your regular Sunday service, you should follow your normal form of this Service. But, as with Morning Prayer and Evening Prayer, when you say the 'Absolution' you should use the words us and our sins instead of you and your sins. Or, if you prefer, instead of the Absolution read the collect for the 21st Sunday after Trinity in the Book of Common Prayer.

(d)   Short Informal Service

If the congregation is small and you do not wish to conduct a full service, or cannot find anyone else to do so, it will be in order to:

- Sing a hymn.

- Read the collect for the day.
- Read the Bible readings for the day.
- Lead the congregation in prayer.
- Sing a hymn.

Or you may do all or any part of the above without any hymn.

8.   FURTHER INFORMATION

Public Worship in the Church of England. A guide to the law governing worship and doctrine in the Church of England, 6th edn. (Church House Publishing, 1994).

Richard Hines, *Dressing for Worship: A fresh look at what Christians wear in church* (Grove Books, 1996).[33]

Eucharistic Presidency (Church House Publishing, 1997) is a report about whether lay people should preside at the Holy Communion.

The Toronto Experience (Church House Publishing, 1997). A report about the 'Toronto blessing'.

The Christian Year: Calendar, Lectionary and Collects (Church House Publishing, 1997).

---

[1] Specifically, the lack of clergy dress, and laymen preaching without authority to do so. The law is neutral about the 'Toronto Blessing'. Speaking in tongues, prophecy and other charismatic gifts are legal so long as they do not substantially disrupt the service, and provided they glorify God and edify the people. See Rupert Bursell, *Liturgy, Order and the Law* (Oxford University Press, 1996), page 68, and 1 Cor. 14:13–19.

[2] See *The Christian Year: Calendar, Lectionary and Collects* (Church House Publishing, 1997).

[3] *Celebrating Common Prayer – The Daily Office SSF* (Mowbray, 1992).

[4] Churches should be cautious about using *Celebrating Common Prayer* for their regular Sunday worship, as it is not one of the officially authorised services.

[5] See James Behrens, *Confirmation, Sacrament of Grace* (Gracewing Fowler Wright, 1995); and James Behrens' letter in *The Times*, 3 May 1997.

[6] Canon B 12 states that no person other than an ordained priest shall consecrate and administer the Holy Communion. Canon B 40 says that no priest shall celebrate the Holy Communion elsewhere than in a consecrated building without the bishop's permission. Canon B 40 does allow Holy Communion to be given to the sick in their own homes.

[7] *Public Worship in the Church of England. A guide to the law governing worship and doctrine in the Church of England*, 6th edn. (Church House Publishing, 1994). The extract quoted is from paragraphs 15 and 16.

[8] Paragraph 31.

[9] Matt. 10:8; Luke 9:2; Luke 10:9.

[10] The diocesan handbooks for Blackburn, Bradford, Carlisle, Lichfield, London, Oxford, Sheffield and Worcester forbid any form of deliverance and exorcism without the bishop's permission beforehand. The dioceses of Winchester and Worcester distinguish exorcism from 'minor' deliverance. The handbooks for Salisbury and Truro and for the diocese in Europe do not mention the subject. See *The Blackburn File* (Diocese of Blackburn, 1997), *The Bradford Diocesan Manual* (Bradford Diocesan Office, 1995), *The Carlisle Diocesan Handbook* (Carlisle Diocesan Office, 1990), *The Derby Diocesan Handbook* (Diocese of Derby, 1997), *The Diocesan Handbook and Bishop's Regulations* (Diocese in Europe, 1987), *The Lichfield Diocesan Handbook* (Diocese of Lichfield, 1991), *The Diocesan Handbook for Churchwardens* (Diocese of Lincoln, 1995), *The Bishop's Regulations for the Diocese of London* (London Diocesan Office, 1987), *The Oxford Diocesan Year Book* (Diocese of Oxford, 1996), *The Portsmouth Diocesan Handbook* (Diocese of Portsmouth, 1993), *The Salisbury Diocesan Handbook* (Diocese of Salisbury, 1991), *The Sheffield Diocesan Handbook* (Diocese of Sheffield, 1993), *The Truro Diocesan Handbook* (Diocese of Truro, 1995), *The Bishop's Regulations and Guidelines for the Diocese of Winchester* (Diocese of Winchester, 1993), *The Worcester Diocesan Handbook* (Diocese of Worcester, 1995).

[11] The policy excludes liability for counselling.

[12] *Hutchins v Denziloe and Loveland* (1792) 1 Hag Con 170 at pp. 175–180.

[13] Ps. 100: 2.

[14] Ps. 33:3.

[15] It is not only modern songs which should be checked for sound doctrine. The theology of the well known hymn *Jerusalem* (words by William Blake) is surely doubtful, much as one would like to believe the legend that Jesus literally walked in England.

[16] Canon B 20, paragraph 2.

[17] Luke 10:7 (Authorised Version), also 1 Tim. 5:18.

[18] For the addresses of the the Incorporated Society of Musicians and the Royal School of Church Music see page 128.

[19] See the Parochial Fees Order 1997. The main statutory fees are set out on page 275. A notice showing these fees is normally on the church notice board.

[20] See in particular clause 11 of the standard contract between a PCC and an organist, *An agreement for the Appointment of a Director of Music*, published by the Incorporated Society of Musicians.

[21] Canon B 8, para. 4.

[22] Royal chaplains wear scarlet cassocks.

[23] I am told that if you are conducting a baptism a cotta is much more practical to wear than a full surplice!

[24] Canon B 8, paras. 3 and 5.

[25] Canon B 8, para. 1.

[26] Those who do not wear robes want to emphasise the priesthood of all believers, see 1 Peter 2:4–10.

[27] Canon B 8, para. 2.

[28] Act of Uniformity 1662, section 15.

[29] Rupert Bursell states the contrary view in his book *Liturgy, Order and the Law* (Oxford University Press, 1996) at page 26.

[30] The 'Toronto Blessing' is an extraordinary thing to watch. Members of the church (sometimes quite respectable members of the church!) suddenly find themselves laughing or weeping uncontrollably during the service. They may fall down on the floor, move their limbs about wildly, and make odd noises. Those who speak in favour of it say that this is the work of the Holy Spirit. Those who speak against it give all sorts of other explanations as to what is going on.

[31] 1 Cor. 14.

[32] Deacons are not so authorised.

[33] See also the article by Richard Hines, 'Dressing down instead of up', *Church Times*, 30 May 1997, page 13.

Chapter 10

THE ANNUAL PAROCHIAL CHURCH MEETING

1.   INTRODUCTION

T he annual parochial church meeting (or, simply, the annual meeting) is an important meeting for the whole church. It is the opportunity for the members of the congregation to elect the people they want to be on the PCC. The congregation can ask questions and comment about the finances of the church, the state of the church building, or about any matter of concern to the parish. The PCC has to take account of any views expressed at the annual parochial church meeting. The annual parochial church meeting is unfortunately also an occasion when people who are on the electoral roll but who rarely if ever come to the church's services turn up and cause trouble for the parish priest and the regular members of the congregation.

The annual parochial church meeting usually follows immediately after the meeting to choose the new churchwardens. That meeting has a number of names easily confused with the annual parochial church meeting. Sometimes it is known as the annual parish meeting, sometimes the meeting of the parishioners. The important thing is that the two meetings are separate. A description of how the new churchwardens are chosen is in Chapter 2, 'The Churchwardens', and so is not repeated here.

The rules dealing with the annual parochial church meeting are contained in the *Church Representation Rules* (Church House Publishing, 1996). They are also set out in *A Handbook for Churchwardens and Parochial Church Councillors* by Kenneth MacMorran and Timothy Briden (Mowbray, 1996). Make sure that there is a copy of the rules to hand in case there are any queries as to what should take place, or trouble-makers. I refer to various rule numbers below, so you can find the topics easily.

2.   THE AGENDA

The word *agenda* means *the things to be done*. The agenda for a meeting is a list of the things which are going to be done at that meeting. To get an overview of everything which is supposed to happen at the annual parochial church meeting, let us look at the agenda.

(i)   Opening prayers

As in the case of PCC meetings, the annual parochial church meeting often begins with prayers or a hymn. The annual parochial church meeting is an important meeting, and it is right that we should commit the meeting and the decisions to be made to God, and ask Him to be with us as we report and discuss things together.

(ii)   Apologies for absence

This is simply to note the names of those who have said they are unable to be at the meeting.

(iii)   Minutes of the previous annual parochial church meeting

The people present are asked to approve the minutes of the previous annual parochial church meeting. The previous annual parochial church meeting took place a year ago, and people may not remember it very clearly. But it is important that the minutes of that meeting are approved, with corrections if necessary. Until they are approved they are merely a record of the secretary's views as to what passed at the meeting; once they are approved they become the official record of the meeting.

(iv)   Matters arising

Most matters arising will be covered elsewhere in the agenda (for example, in the annual report of the proceedings of the PCC). But there may be a few items which should be noted here, which would not otherwise be mentioned.

Then we come to the two main items on the agenda: the reports, and the elections.

(v)   The reports

The PCC has to present the following items to the meeting:

- a report on changes in membership of the electoral roll since the last annual parochial church meeting.
- a report on what the PCC has done over the year, and the activities of the parish generally.
- the financial statements of the PCC for the previous year ending 31 December, independently examined or audited.
- a report on the fabric, goods and ornaments of the church. This report is usually presented by the churchwardens, but it will have been considered by the PCC.
- a report on the proceedings of the deanery synod.

These reports are discussed below.

The meeting can discuss each of these reports, and make recommendations to the PCC. Some of the items may need to be discussed at some length.

(vi)   The elections and appointments

The following elections take place:

- members for the deanery synod (only every third year).
- members for the PCC.

The meeting should also appoint:

- sidemen, and
- the independent examiner or auditor to the PCC, who should be someone not on the PCC.[1]

These are not strictly elections, but the meeting needs to approve the choice put forward by the parish priest and the PCC.

The elections and appointments should be done in this order.

(vii)   Any other business

Any person can ask any question about parochial church matters, or bring up a topic concerning general church matters for discussion. The parish priest can stop the discussion on any item when he thinks it has gone on for long enough. If the item is important and needs more time, he may decide to adjourn the discussion so that it can be continued some other time. Or he may suggest that the matter should be looked at by the PCC at one of its meetings.

This is the time when the parish priest can set out his vision for the future. After all the formal reports and the elections, the meeting can now come alive! The parish priest may have some grand new plan for the parish. The annual parochial church meeting is an excellent time to explain it to the whole congregation. Or there may be a visiting speaker who can give a talk about some Christian work outside the parish. The annual parochial church meeting is not just a dull meeting tied up with the past, but a time to interest and excite people with both what is happening now, and what is about to happen.

(viii)   Closing prayers

I suggest these should include the following:

- committing to God the decisions that have been made.
- asking Him to guide the new members of the PCC in their work over the coming year.

Now let us look at things in more detail. First, there is quite a lot to do before the meeting.

3.   PREPARATION FOR THE MEETING

Here is a check list of the things which need to be done before the meeting.

- Agree on a date for the meeting.
- The electoral roll should be revised or a new roll prepared.
- The reports which are needed for the meeting should be written, and approved by the PCC.
- Candidates should be proposed for the new PCC.
- A notice advertising the meeting should be put up on the church door or notice board.
- A copy of the financial statements should be displayed on a notice board either inside or outside the church for at least seven days before the meeting, including at least one Sunday when the church is used for worship.
- A notice should be put on or near the church door advertising the first meeting of the new PCC.

Each of these needs a separate heading.

(a)   *The date for the meeting*

Rule 6 (1).

The annual parochial church meeting should be held not later than 30 April. (Guild churches in the City of London should hold their meeting not later than the week following Easter.)

The actual date should be settled about two months in advance, to allow sufficient time for the electoral roll to be revised in time for the meeting.

(b)   *The electoral roll*

Rules 1 to 4.

The electoral roll is a list of the names and addresses of every person who can vote in the annual parochial church meeting. Every six years a completely new roll is prepared in the two months leading up to the annual parochial church meeting, and those on the previous roll are informed so that they can re-apply. In all other years the existing list is simply amended, with new names being added and some names taken off. New rolls were prepared in 1996, so the next year for new rolls will be 2002. The person responsible for dealing with the electoral roll is called the *electoral roll officer.*

(i)   *Who can be on the electoral roll?*

To be on the electoral roll of a parish you should be baptised, and at least 16 years old. You should either live in the parish or have worshipped at the church regularly for at least six months. You should be a lay person (not ordained).[2] You should be a member of the Church of England, or of certain other churches. These other churches are

- any church which is 'in communion' with the Church of England. That means other churches belonging to the Anglican Communion, and certain foreign churches.[3]
- any church which believes in the Holy Trinity, provided you are prepared to declare that you are a member of the Church of England as well as belonging to that church.

You can be on the electoral roll of more than one parish (for example, if you live in one parish, but worship in another), but if you are a member of more than one parish, you should choose which parish you want to vote in, because you can only vote in one.

(ii)   Application forms

To apply for your name to be added to the roll you have to fill out a form. You can have your name added to the roll at any stage in the year, but most people have their names added in the few weeks before the annual parochial church meeting, when notices are given out about this in the church services.

(iii)   Taking names off the roll

A person's name is removed from the roll:

- when he dies.
- if he becomes ordained.
- if he asks to have his name taken off the roll. This usually happens if a person moves out of one parish to another, or from one church to another.
- if he does not live in the parish, and has not regularly worshipped at the church for six months.

People who live in the parish can have their names on the electoral roll even if they never come to church. People who do not live in the parish should come to church in order to stay on the electoral roll (unless the reason they have not come to church is because they have been ill).

(iv)   The revision of the roll

About 5–6 weeks before the annual parochial church meeting, put a printed notice up on or near the church door announcing that the electoral roll is to be revised. (Your diocesan office will have copies of the notice for you.) The notice says the date when the list is to be revised. It says that people should have their name on the roll if they want to come to the annual parochial church meeting, and it says that to have their name added to the roll they need to fill in an application form and hand it in before the date when the list is to be revised.

People who already have their name on the roll do not need to fill in any form or do anything else. The only people who need to fill in an application form are those who in the last year have moved into the parish, joined the church, or reached the age of 16.

The notice has to remain up for at least 14 days. On each of the Sundays during this time a notice is usually given in the Sunday services reminding people to fill in a form for their names to be added to the roll if they are not already on it.

When the notice has been up on the church door for this time, the electoral roll officer makes any changes which are needed to the roll, adding the names of all those who have handed in application forms, and taking off any names of those who have died or left the church. He should finish this revision between 15 and 28 days before the annual parochial church meeting.

When the list has been revised, the new list should be put up on the church door, and also a list of any names removed from the roll since the last revision. These lists should stay up on the church door up to the date of the annual parochial church meeting. During this time, any errors on the list can be corrected, but no new names can be added if people forgot to fill in their forms on time.

The electoral roll does not contain telephone numbers. The church may have this information, but the only details to be published are the names and addresses. The list should state every person's address, but a person does not have to give his address if he does not want to.

A short summary may help.

- 5–6 weeks before the annual parochial church meeting put up the notice on the church door.
- The notice should be up for at least 14 days.
- Make announcements in the church services.
- Take down the notice and revise the list. This should be finished between 15 and 28 days before the meeting.
- Put up the revised list on the church door, and leave it there until the annual parochial church meeting.

(v)   Making a new roll

Much the same will happen in the year 2002 when a new roll will be prepared, and every sixth year afterwards. The main difference is that *everyone* has to fill in a form to be on the new roll, even if they were on the old roll.

When a new roll is being prepared, the notice should be put up on the church door not less than two months before the date of the annual parochial church meeting.

At every service on the two Sundays after the notice is put on the church door, the person leading the service should tell the congregation that a new roll is being prepared.

The PCC should remind everyone whose name was on the old roll that they need to fill in a form if they want to have their names on the new roll.

Here is the summary for the preparation of the new roll.

- At least two months before the annual parochial church meeting put up the notice on the church door.
- The notice should be up for at least 14 days.
- Make announcements in the church services.
- The PCC should remind everyone whose names were on the old roll to fill in a form to have their names on the new roll.
- Write up the new roll. This should be finished between 15 and 28 days before the meeting.
- Put up the new roll on the church door, and leave it there until the annual parochial church meeting.

(vi)   Inform the diocese

Not later than 1 June each year you should fill in a form and return it to the diocesan secretary. You fill in on the form the number of people on the electoral roll at the date of the annual parochial church meeting. A copy of the form should be put on the church door after it has been sent to the diocesan secretary, and left up for at least 14 days.

(c)   The reports

Rule 9.

The PCC has to present the following items to the meeting:

- a report on changes in membership of the electoral roll since the last annual parochial church meeting.
- a report on what the PCC has done over the year, and the activities of the parish generally.
- the financial statements of the PCC for the previous year ending 31 December, independently examined or audited.
- a report on the fabric, goods and ornaments of the church. This report is usually presented by the churchwardens, but it will have been considered by the PCC.
- a report on the proceedings of the deanery synod.

(i)   Electoral roll report

This is a report on the numbers who have left the church and joined the church over the previous year.

(ii)   The annual report

The report is a summary of what the PCC has done, and what the church as a whole has done, over the year. Under the Charities Act 1993, all charities have to prepare their annual reports in a set form. A PCC is a charity, and is therefore subject to the Charities Act 1993. The Church Accounting Regulations 1997 set out in detail what PCCs need to include in their annual reports, and this is explained in Chapter 26, 'Church Accounts'.

The paragraph above describes the annual report in rather formal terms. PCCs should see the annual report as an opportunity to publicise to the congregation and to the parish all the events and excitements of the previous year. The minutes of PCC meetings are confidential to the members of the PCC, so many members of the congregation may be unaware of much that has been going on. Now is the chance to tell everyone what God has been doing in the church.

(iii)   Financial statements

The financial statements are usually presented by the church treasurer. The Church Accounting Regulations 1997 lay down what needs to be said in these statements, and this is covered in Chapter 26, 'Church Accounts'. The Church Accounting Regulations 1997 requires that the financial statements should have been independently examined or audited before the meeting. They should be *audited* if the income or expenditure was £250,000 or more in the year of the accounts or either of the two preceding years. If they were under this figure, they should have been *independently examined* by someone who is qualified to do this. An independent examination is not as strict nor as expensive as an audit.

(iv)   Fabric report

This is a report on the state of the building. The report says what repairs and alterations have been carried out over the past year, and what changes to the contents of the church have taken place. Every year the churchwardens should discuss the state of the building with the parish priest, and should:

- inspect the building and articles belonging to it, or arrange for them to be inspected.
- make an annual fabric report to the PCC on the state of the building and its contents. So, for example, the purchase of a computer system and photocopier are items for the fabric report. The report should include a list of all repairs carried out or proposed in the previous year, and particularly any repairs carried out or proposed which were recommended in the quinquennial report.

The fabric report is presented to the PCC at the meeting before the annual parochial church meeting. The PCC can amend the report, and it is then presented to the annual parochial church meeting.

(v)   Deanery synod report

This simply reports what the deanery synod has been doing over the year.

(d)   Candidates for the new PCC

The parish priest should discuss with the PCC and with other members of the congregation who might wish to stand for election to the PCC and deanery synod. In some churches there are more candidates than there are places, and so there will be a contested election. In many other churches it is not easy to find enough people to fill the PCC.

The membership of the PCC is covered in Chapter 3, 'The PCC'.[4] Briefly, candidates for the PCC:

- should be on the electoral roll.
- should be over 16.
- should agree to being appointed.
- should normally have been confirmed, and have received communion at least three times in the previous year.[5]

Many churches try to ensure that there is a balance on the PCC of all the different type of people in the church: male and female, young and old, different races and backgrounds. If too many people of the same type are on the PCC together, there is a danger of cliques forming. This can lead to people in the congregation feeling that there is no one who can represent them properly.

Naturally it is right to consider a person's Christian commitment and character before suggesting that they should stand for election.

There is no rule against paid employees of the church being on the PCC, but it can lead to obvious problems if their positions need to be discussed.

Some people think that the parish priest should play the major part in choosing the people who should stand for election for the PCC. They think that because Jesus chose his own disciples, so the parish priest should choose the members of his PCC. But there is a danger that the parish priest will only choose people who he knows will agree with everything he says, and never stand up against him. It is important that the PCC should be able to work with the parish priest, but it is also important that it should fairly represent the congregation, and not consist just of the parish priest's 'henchmen'.

(e)   The notice advertising the meeting

Rule 7.

A notice in the proper form should be put up on the main door of the church. The latest day it can be put up is two Sundays before the day of the annual parochial church meeting. The notice should be signed by the parish priest. A copy of the form to be used is sent to the church by the diocesan secretary well in time.

In fact three notices should be put up at the same time. The first is the notice advertising the annual parochial church meeting. The second notice is one advertising the joint meeting of parishioners, which is the separate meeting for the election of the churchwardens. The third notice is one advertising the first meeting of the newly elected PCC. This takes place immediately after the annual parochial church meeting, and all that happens at it is the election of the officers of the PCC. These are the vice-chairman, the PCC secretary, the treasurer, the electoral roll officer, and the auditor if he has not been appointed by the annual parochial church meeting: see Appendix II, paragraph 1 of the Rules.

Remember too that the new or revised electoral roll is put up on the church door when it has been revised, and the church accounts also, when they are ready. The church door or notice board gets covered with paper in the weeks leading up to the annual parochial church meeting.

4.   THE MEETING ITSELF

(a)   Who can attend?

Rule 6 (2).

Only people whose names are on the electoral roll can be at the annual parochial church meeting. It is not a public meeting. So once the churchwardens have been selected by the meeting of the parishioners, any lay person whose name is not on the electoral roll should politely be asked to leave.

(b)   The chairman

Rule 8.

The parish priest is the chairman of the annual parochial church meeting. If the parish priest is not present, the vice-chairman of the PCC (usually, one of the churchwardens) chairs the meeting.

The chairman has a very important role. He is in overall control of the meeting. This means it is up to him to introduce the items, and to decide when to move on from one item to the next. This may be difficult when an important issue is being discussed, and many questions are being asked. He should strike a balance between on the one hand not allowing proper questions to be put, and on the other hand letting trouble-makers speak for too long and disrupt the meeting. There is a skill in controlling a meeting, but people generally want to see fair play, and will support the chairman if he encounters any difficulties. If the chairman thinks there is a risk of a disturbance, he can ask the police to send a constable to be present.

The chairman also has a second, or casting, vote, if any matter is put to the vote, and the votes for and against are equal. This does not apply to the election of PCC members: if there is an equal division of votes between two or more candidates, the final choice is made by lot.

(c)   The reports

Once the accounts and financial statement have been discussed by the meeting and approved, the parish priest should sign them.

(d)   Elections and appointments

Rules 9 (4), 10, 11, 16 and 17.

The meeting should:

- every third year elect members for the deanery synod.
- elect members for the PCC.
- appoint sidesmen.
- appoint the independent examiner or auditor to the PCC, who should be someone not on the PCC.

The elections should be done in this order.

The number of elected members of the PCC is decided by the annual parochial church meeting, but if the meeting alters the existing number, the alteration only takes effect from the next meeting. So, if the 1998 meeting alters the number from 18 to 16, it remains 18 for the 1998 year and becomes 16 for the election in 1999.

To be elected on the PCC, a person should:

- be on the electoral roll.
- be over 16.
- consent to being appointed.

- have been confirmed (or ready and wanting to be confirmed), and should have received communion at least three times in the previous year.

Normally PCC members are elected for one year, from the conclusion of one annual parochial church meeting until the conclusion of the next. Some parishes prefer that members of the PCC should serve for three years. The annual parochial church meeting can decide to adopt this course, in which case a third of the elected members of the PCC retire each year, being those who have served the longest.

The annual parochial church meeting can decide to put a limit on the number of years a person can serve on the PCC without a break. The annual parochial church meeting can also decide how many years such a person should remain off the PCC after serving this number of years, before he or she stands for election once again.

Anyone wanting to stand for election should be proposed by someone else on the electoral roll. If the number of candidates is no more than the number of places to be filled, the parish priest simply declares that all the candidates are elected. If there are more candidates than there are places to be filled, the normal way to conduct the election is to have voting papers, which should be signed by the voter on the back.[6]

The result of the election should be announced to the annual parochial church meeting as soon as it is known. A notice announcing the names of the new PCC members, the new members of the deanery synod, and the new churchwardens should be put on the church door and left there for at least 14 days.

5.   AFTER THE MEETING

After the meeting:
- the new PCC should hold its first meeting.
- a notice giving the names of the new churchwardens and the names of all the members of the new PCC should be put on the church door.
- the annual report of the PCC and the parish and the financial statements should be published and displayed in the parish.
- various forms have to be sent back to the diocesan secretary showing the number on the new electoral roll, the results of the elections for

churchwardens, and the names of the members of the PCC. A copy of the annual report and the financial statements should also be sent to the diocesan secretary.

(a)   First meeting of the new PCC

Rule 15 and Appendix II.

At the first meeting of the new PCC, the PCC should appoint its officers:

- a vice-chairman, who should be a lay member of the PCC.
- a secretary, who need not be a member of the PCC.
- a treasurer, or joint treasurers, who should be a member or members of the PCC. If no one is willing to be appointed, the churchwardens become responsible for the accounts.
- an electoral roll officer. The electoral roll officer need not be a member of the PCC. In some churches the PCC secretary is also the electoral roll officer.
- members of the standing committee of the PCC.
- an auditor or independent examiner to the PCC, if the annual parochial church meeting has not appointed one.

Many dioceses recommend holding the first meeting of the PCC immediately after the annual parochial church meeting. In order to do this, notice of the meeting should be put up on the church door at the same time as the announcement of the annual parochial church meeting.

(b)   Notices on the church door

After the meeting, the following notices should be put on the church door, and left there for 14 days:

- a notice announcing the names of the new PCC members, the new members of the deanery synod, and the new churchwardens.
- a copy of the accounts and financial statement once they have been approved by the annual parochial church meeting and signed by the parish priest.
- a copy of the notice sent to the diocesan secretary giving the number of names on the electoral roll.

(c)   *The minutes of the meeting*

The secretary of the PCC takes notes of the annual parochial church meeting, and writes up the minutes. Although they will not be seen by the PCC until the meeting before the next year's annual parochial church meeting, the minutes should be written up by the secretary while the events are still fresh in his or her mind.

6.   TEAM AND GROUP MINISTRIES

The annual parochial church meeting has special powers in the case of a team or group ministry. The annual parochial church meeting can set up a group council or a team council. It can also set up a district church council if there is more than one church or place of worship in the parish. These topics are covered in Chapter 16, 'Team Ministries'.

---

[1] For more on the choice of the independent examiner, see Chapter 26, 'Church Accounts'.

[2] This regrettably means that retired clergy who may be living in the parish have no vote on the election of the laity to the PCC. Retired clergy can however be co-opted onto the PCC, they can attend and speak at the annual parochial church meeting, and they can vote on other matters.

[3] There is a list of churches which belong to the Anglican Communion published each year in the Church of England Year Book. The Anglican Communion includes the Church of Ireland, the Scottish Episcopal Church, the Church in Wales, the Anglican Church of Australia, the Episcopal Church in the United States of America, the Anglican Church of Canada, the Anglican Church in New Zealand, and many other churches. If you need to know whether a particular foreign church which is not part of the Anglican Communion is in communion with the Church of England, contact your diocesan secretary.

[4] See page 41.

[5] People who want to be confirmed and are ready to be confirmed can also be appointed, even though they may well not have received communion.

[6] The annual meeting can decide to allow postal votes, but unless it does so, only people present at the meeting are allowed to vote. The annual meeting can also decide to hold the elections using the method known as the single transferable vote. Very few churches use this procedure.

Chapter 11

FOOD AND DRINK

1.   INTRODUCTION

This chapter is not about how to make Coronation Chicken for 100: it is about food safety and hygiene, and the licensing laws for alcohol.

2.   FOOD SAFETY

The Food Safety Act 1990 is a wide-ranging law which applies to almost everyone who makes and sells food. The only food which is not covered by the Act is food prepared at home for domestic use. The Act makes it an offence to sell any food which fails to meet safety standards. It applies to major retailers such as supermarkets, to small restaurants and cafes, and to food sales at charity fund-raising events. The regulations made under the Food Safety Act 1990 apply whether or not the food is sold for profit.

3.   REGISTRATION

One of the regulations made under the Food Safety Act 1990 Act is the Food Premises (Registration) Regulations 1991. These regulations state that the owners of food businesses have to register their premises with the local authority. Once you are registered, the local environmental health officers will come and inspect your premises from time to time. If you are not registered when you should be, you can be prosecuted for committing a criminal offence.

The term *food businesses* used in the regulation covers the sale or supply of food, whether for profit or not. It therefore includes giving the food away free, and it covers charitable and voluntary organisations such as churches.

Under the Food Premises (Registration) Regulations 1991, you should register your premises if they are used for the sale or supply of food on five or more days within a period of five weeks.

Many churches sometimes offer food after their Sunday services. Some churches run midweek evening courses where a meal is provided. One very popular course is known as *Alpha*, which runs for ten weeks on one evening a week. A meal is almost always provided before the study time on an *Alpha* course.

It is clear that if your church runs an *Alpha* course, and you provide food every week throughout the course, you should be registered with the local authority. Likewise, if you provide food for the weekly church youth group, or any other group involved with the church, and you supply food on more than five days within a period of five weeks, you should be registered.

To register your premises contact your local environmental health officer, via the local authority. Registration is a one-off event. If you plan to offer any form of catering services through your church, you should register your premises, so you are covered for any eventuality.

4.   FOOD PREPARATION AND STORAGE

Even if your church is not registered with the local authority, it should still heed the basic hygiene principles set by the Food Safety (General Food Hygiene) Regulations 1995. Any good cookery course covers food safety and hygiene, and it is essential that everybody who is involved with preparing food for church functions knows these principles.

You may think that these regulations are not necessary for the church, and that they should only apply for 'proper' food businesses. But think how important food is to the life of the church. Food and fellowship go hand in hand together. Eating meals with other members of the church is an important and enjoyable part of church life. Food is a service we can provide to elderly or needy people who would not otherwise have a proper meal. Food is very popular at events such as youth groups, and it encourages visitors to come to church events. Food helps to draw people into the church family. If we want to do things properly, we should take the trouble to ensure that the food we supply is wholesome and properly prepared. Controls over food hygiene do not have to be complicated, but they should be in place. Better that than 30 people suffering from food poisoning after a Harvest Supper because one of the dishes was contaminated with bacteria.

If a church has failed to follow these basic food regulations, its insurance policy may not cover a claim against the church by someone who becomes sick as a result.

(a)   *Food premises – the church kitchen*

Your kitchen should:

- be clean, and maintained in good repair.
- be properly designed so that you can prepare and keep food hygienically.
- have a supply of drinking water.
- have suitable controls against pests.
- be properly lighted.
- be properly vented.
- be properly drained.

- have sufficient hand basins for hand washing.
- have surface and wall finishes which are easy to clean. Tiled walls are best.
- have a place for storing and removing food waste.

You should have clean lavatories which do not lead directly into the kitchen.

After you have registered your premises, the environmental health officer will visit the church to ensure that your kitchen meets the required standard.

If the PCC is proposing to make any improvements to your catering premises it is advisable to involve the environmental health officer during the planning stage. You will then be able to take the officer's recommendations on board before the work is carried out.

(b)   Preventing food contamination

You should take proper steps to store food at safe temperatures. All food should be covered or wrapped. Raw food should be kept separate from cooked foods: for example, keep cooked food at the top of the fridge, and raw food at the bottom. Where possible, use fresh food. Rotate your stock of tinned and frozen food – that means, use the oldest food first, provided it is still safe. Make sure meat is properly cooked.

All cooked food should be labelled with a name and date of preparation. This is especially important in a church when different people are often involved in the catering. It will also assist careful stock rotation, and help to make sure you do not serve food which is out of date.

(i)   Food temperature

Under the Food Safety (Temperature Control) Regulations 1995 all types of food which can develop harmful bacteria or poisons if not stored at the right temperature should be kept either:

- hot, at or above 63°C (145 °F), or
- cold, at or below 8°C (46°F).

Such foods are likely to fall into a number of categories:

- dairy products,
  such as soft or semi-hard cheeses ripened by mould and/or bacteria,
  and dairy-based desserts.
- cooked products,
  all foods containing eggs, meat, fish, milk, cereals, rice, pulses and
  vegetables, and sandwiches containing these ingredients.
- smoked or cured ready-to-eat meat or fish,
  such as sliced cured meats like ham, smoked fish and salami.
- prepared ready-to-eat foods,
  such as prepared vegetables, vegetable salads like coleslaw, or
  prepared products containing mayonnaise.
- uncooked or partly cooked pastry and dough products,
  such as pizzas or fresh pasta containing meat, fish or vegetables.

Under the regulations any prepared food not kept below 8°C or above 63°C for longer than 90 minutes must be thrown away. This is most likely to affect buffets. Whilst this may seem very wasteful, the law is there to prevent the growth of harmful bacteria, which can lead to people falling ill with food poisoning.

It is a criminal offence to serve or to sell food which is harmful or unfit to eat. There is a defence if the church proves that it *took all reasonable precautions and exercised all due diligence* to avoid committing the offence. This means that at your church you should be able to prove that you have adhered to the temperature regulations. The easiest way to achieve this is to use a temperature probe, and to take the temperature of all food you serve. You should record this on a sheet of paper, showing the menu item, the date, the time, and the temperature, with the signature of the person taking the temperature.

(ii)   Food storage

Get chilled and frozen food into a fridge or freezer as fast as possible after buying it. All freezers have a thermometer to check the temperature of the contents.

Ideally the coldest part of the fridge should be between 0°C and 5°C. A freezer should not be above -18°C. Use a fridge thermometer to check.

To keep the fridge cold all the time, don't overload it. Don't leave the door open longer than necessary.

Uncovered or dripping raw meat or defrosting food can contaminate other food with bacteria. So, keep raw meat or defrosting food at the bottom of the fridge, or in a separate fridge from other food. Keep all food covered. Avoid foods dripping onto vegetables and salads.

Remember – food poisoning from cooked foods often occurs as a result of cross-contamination from raw foods.

Don't keep frozen food longer than the instructions on food labels.

(iii)   Cooking meat

Wash your hands before and after handling raw meat.

To cook meat safely so that Salmonella and Listeria are killed, the centre of the meat should reach a core temperature of at least 70°C (158°F) for at least two minutes. Check it with a meat thermometer.

Make sure your cooking equipment can achieve this consistently. Use an oven thermometer to check the reliability of your oven temperatures.

Monitor your cooking. You should make a written record of the core temperature of at least one item from every cookery session, using a probe thermometer. Wash the probe thermometer after each use.

If the food is cooked for eating later, it should be cooled as quickly as possible. But putting it in the fridge straight away would raise the fridge temperature. So cool food in the coldest place available. As soon as it is cool, put it in the fridge or freezer. Cooked meat should be left to cool for no longer than 90 minutes before being put in the fridge. If the joint is large, cut it in half to speed up the cooling-down process. Do not forget to wrap and label the meat, including the date that it was cooked.

When re-heating food, ensure that a temperature of at least 63°C is reached for at least two minutes. This will ensure that the harmful bacteria are killed off.

(c)   Personal hygiene for food handlers

Anyone involved with food should maintain a high degree of personal cleanliness. This means:

- wearing clean clothes and a clean apron.
- observing good personal hygiene. Long hair should be tied back or worn under a cap or hat.
- washing your hands regularly when handling food. You should always wash your hands on entering the kitchen, using anti-bacterial soap. To prevent cross-contamination, wash your hands between preparation of cooked and uncooked foods.
- not smoking in the kitchen.
- not cooking or helping if you are ill (in particular if you have infected wounds, skin infections, diarrhoea or vomiting, or even a cold).
- wearing a plaster over any cuts.

(d)   Training and supervising food handlers

People handling food should be properly supervised, instructed and trained in food hygiene. A one-day basic food hygiene course is available, often free of charge, from the environmental health department of local authorities. I strongly recommend that whoever holds the responsibility for catering within your church should attend this course, preferably with other members of the church who are frequently involved in the catering.

Professional cooking and catering courses also cover food hygiene.

(e)   Home-made food

It is a criminal offence to serve or to sell food which is harmful or unfit to eat. This applies whether the food was prepared in the church kitchen, or was cooked by members of the congregation in their own homes. As mentioned, there is a defence if the church proves that it *took all reasonable precautions and exercised all due diligence* to avoid committing the offence.

What does that mean as regards home-made food? No church can be expected to supervise all the kitchens of the members of the congregation who regularly bake cakes, make sandwiches and cook dishes for church lunches and fetes. Are we to refuse their cooking because of the risk of prosecution if something is unsafe?

In a word, No. But we should be aware of the danger, and take appropriate action. That means we should:

- keep a list of who is cooking what, if they are bringing it from home.
- do our best to make sure that all the people who cook and prepare dishes are aware of food hazards.
- encourage people to learn more about food hygiene. This can be done informally by members of the church teaching one another, and in some cases by encouraging people to go on a food hygiene course.
- have someone responsible to make sure that this is done on a regular basis.

If churches take these steps, they are unlikely to be taken to court.

(f) *Food hazards*

Under the Food Safety Act all large catering organisations must complete a hazard analysis, known as a Hazard Analysis Critical Control Point (HACCP). Whilst this may seem an unnecessary task for a small church catering operation, it is a worthwhile thing to do as it will help you to eliminate potential accidents. Do keep a record of your findings, to show to the environmental health officer if he should wish to see it. The following example may be suitable.[1]

Step	Hazard	Control	Monitoring
Purchase and delivery	• Harmful bacteria, mould or foreign bodies present in/on food	• Use reputable suppliers. • Check goods on receipt	• Check delivery vehicles, date marks, temperatures and condition of food
Storage	• Bacterial growth or further contamination by micro-organisms or chemicals • mice, ants, cockroaches etc.	• Store at safe temperatures • Cover/wrap foods. • Keep foods dry • Separate raw/cooked foods • Stock rotation	• Check temperatures and date marks • Check storage conditions
Preparation	• Bacterial growth or further contamination	• Limit handling times • Use clean equipment • Good personal hygiene • Hygienic premises	• Visual checks • Cleaning schedules
Cooking	• Survival of harmful bacteria	• Adequate cooking e.g. cook to a safe centre temperature	• Cooking times • Routine temperature checks
Further storage	• Growth of bacteria • Further contamination	• Store at safe temperatures • Cover/wrap foods • Separate raw/cooked foods	• Check temperatures • Visual checks

211

5.   SUMMARY

Under the Food Safety (General Food Hygiene) Regulations 1995 the PCC is responsible:

- for making sure that your food is supplied or sold in a hygienic way.
- for identifying food safety hazards – such as those shown above.
- for knowing which steps in the way you prepare and serve food are critical for food safety.
- for making sure that safety controls are in place, that they are maintained, and that they are reviewed.

If you fail to comply with these regulations you are committing a criminal offence, and can be prosecuted. More importantly, if one of your meals contains something which is infected with bacteria, you could endanger someone's life.

6.   ALCOHOL AT CHURCH EVENTS

If alcohol is to be sold at a church function, the PCC should get a form of licence known as an *occasional permission* from the licensing justices.[2] This applies for example:

- if the function has a raffle or tombola, and the prizes include bottles of whiskey or other spirits.
- if there is a stall with wine or other alcohol for sale.
- if wine is included with a supper for which tickets are sold.

If you are going to have a function and want to sell alcohol, contact the clerk of the licensing justices in good time, find out when they are going to meet, and ask for the necessary forms and what the procedure is.

The application to the licensing justices should be made at least one month before the date of the function, and at least 15 days before the meeting of the licensing justices.

You will need to contact the licensing justices to find out when your application will be heard. The clerk of the licensing justices will tell you the date, and whether you will need to attend to answer any questions.

The licensing justices will have to be satisfied that the function being held is in connection with church activities, that the place of the function is suitable for sale of alcohol, that it is within the licensing district of the justices, and that the sale of alcohol at the function is not likely to lead to disturbance or disorderly conduct, or to annoy people living in the neighbourhood.

If the licensing justices give permission, the licence will state the place, the date and the hours during which alcohol can be sold, and there may be conditions attached. You should make sure that you do not break any of the conditions, and you should keep to the time allowed. Alcohol can then be sold at the function to any person who has been invited or has paid to be there, and who is over 18.

You can only obtain four of these occasional permissions a year. If you want to sell alcohol more than four times a year, you will need to apply for a full *on-licence*, in other words, an ordinary licence to sell alcohol on the premises.

If you sell alcohol without having a licence, you are committing a criminal offence under the Licensing Act 1964.

You do not need a licence if you do not charge for the alcohol. So, for example, you do not need a licence to serve wine at a free church lunch. But if you charge for a meal and supply wine with the meal, that is treated as selling alcohol, even though you may not charge for the wine separately.[3] You should therefore have a licence to do this. You can not get round the rule by asking for a donation instead of charging for the meal.

7.   FURTHER INFORMATION

A number of booklets on food hygiene are available free from the Department of Health, the Ministry of Agriculture, Fisheries and Food (MAFF), and from local authorities. I recommend the following:

Food Safety Act 1990 and you, The: a guide for the food industry from HM Government (MAFF Publications, 1994).

Food Sense booklet: Food Safety (MAFF Publications, 1993).

Guide to food hazards and your business (Department of Health, 1996).

Guide to the general temperature control regulations (Department of Health, 1996).

Guide to the general food hygiene regulations (Department of Health, 1995).

THE DEPARTMENT OF HEALTH
PO Box 410,
Wetherby,
LS23 7LN

Tel: 01937 840 250

MAFF PUBLICATIONS
Admail 6000,
London SW1A 2XX.

Tel: 0645 556000

The Ecclesiastical Insurance Group publishes a series of guidance notes for churches. *Guidance Notes for Churches. Section 3: Health and Safety* includes a section on the preparation and sale of food on church premises.[4]

---

[1] This table of food hazards is taken from the Department of Health's booklet *A guide to food hazards and your business*. It is Crown copyright, and is reproduced with permission.

[2] See the Licensing (Occasional Permissions) Act 1983.

[3] See *Doak v Bedford* [1964] 2 QB 587, and the commentary to section 160 of the Licensing Act 1964 in *Paterson's Licensing Acts* 1998 (Butterworths, 1997).

[4] For a list of the Ecclesiastical Insurance Group guidance notes, and a summary of their contents, see page 352.

Chapter 12

COMPUTERS

1.   INTRODUCTION

Most churches use computers. In addition to word-processing, computers can be used for membership and pastoral records, church finance, writing music, preparing teaching materials for children's work, desktop publishing, theological study, and electronic mail, just to give a few examples.

For ordinary correspondence any of the standard computer programs are suitable. The two current market leaders are *Microsoft Word*® and

WordPerfect®, which are both Windows programs. Some churches are still using very good older software such as the DOS program *WordPerfect*® *5.1*. For church accounts and dealing with covenanting, there are suitable programs specially written for church use. These are described in the Chapter 4, 'The Treasurer', Chapter 25, 'Covenants and Gift Aid', and Chapter 26, 'Church Accounts'. The music program *Sibelius* is outstanding. For details, contact:

SIBELIUS SOFTWARE
75 Burleigh Street,
Cambridge CB1 1DJ

Tel: 01223 302765

For Christian software, contact:

SUNRISE SOFTWARE
Scorrier Park,
Scorrier,
Cornwall TR16 5AU.

Tel: 01209 821821

For desktop publishing, graphical design, electronic mail and other programs, computer magazines such as *Personal Computer World* carry reviews of the leading products, and give the names and addresses of suppliers.

Three areas need to be managed properly:

- software licensing.
- data protection.
- computer security.

These are the subject of this chapter.

2.   SOFTWARE LICENSING

When you buy a computer program, you do not become the owner of the software on the disks. You purchase the right to use the software, but that does not mean that you can copy it onto as many computers as you want. The program itself is still owned by the software developer – *Microsoft Corporation*, for example. The software developer will usually only allow you to use the software on one machine, or on a set number of machines if you purchase more than one copy of the program.

If you have software specially written for you, you may be required to sign a software licensing agreement before the software is supplied. This agreement will usually say how many machines you may use the software on. The licence agreement for standard programs is often printed on the package containing the software. If you open the package, you agree to accept these terms. If you do not want to accept the terms of the licence agreement, you can usually return the package for a refund, provided you have not opened it.

For most standard programs you will need to buy one copy for every computer which is to run the program. So, for example, if the parish priest has one computer in the vicarage and another in the church office, and wants to run the same software on both computers, you will need to buy two copies of each program. For some products (*Microsoft Word*®, for example), you can purchase what are known as *additional licences*, which work out slightly cheaper than purchasing complete copies of the program. Or you may be able to purchase a *site licence* which will allow you to use the program on any number of computers at one address.

People who have a program on their home computer may think they are saving the church money by installing it onto the church computer without buying a new copy. But by doing this both they and the church are committing a *breach of copyright*.[1] Organisations such as the *Federation Against Software Theft (FAST)* may seize the church computer, and bring legal proceedings against the church.

Churches should be scrupulously honest about software licensing, as about all aspects of their finance. PCCs should take steps to ensure that all software on the church computer is properly licensed.

3.   DATA PROTECTION

In almost all cases computers have stored on them data or facts about living people. This data may be as simple as their names, addresses and telephone numbers, or there may be a lot more information about them stored on the computer. Under the Data Protection Act 1984, subject to a few exceptions, *anybody who is responsible for holding personal data on a computer should be registered with the Data Protection Registrar.* This means that every PCC which uses a computer should be registered under the Data Protection Act 1984. In some cases the parish priest should be registered as well as the PCC. The Act also sets out certain standards of good computer practice to be followed by everyone who is registered.

During 1998 the Data Protection Act 1984 will be replaced by a new Act. The Data Protection Bill was published in January 1998. It gives effect to the requirements of Directive 95/46/EC of the European Parliament. When the new rules come into force the data protection principles described in this chapter will apply not only to computer records but also to most filing systems containing manual records.[2]

4.   WHAT IS PERSONAL DATA?

A key term in the Data Protection Act and the new Data Protection Bill is the expression *personal data*. The word *data* is familiar to most people who use computers. It means any facts or figures, any information or details. The data may be records in a database, letters, computer files, in short, almost anything apart from the actual software you buy to run on your computer. *Personal data* means any data about a living person, such as their name, address and telephone number, any letters written to them, and any facts or opinions about them. The following are examples of personal information likely to be held on a church computer:

- a list of names, addresses and telephone numbers of members of the congregation.
- additional information such as birthdays, family status, the names of their children.
- a list of the children attending the children's church.
- a list of home group leaders.
- a list of youth work leaders.
- a list of choir members.
- any letters kept on the computer after they have been sent.
- a list of people who have given money to the church in the past, kept on the computer so that you know who to ask and who can can be encouraged to make further gifts.

The parish priest who uses his computer merely to type up his sermons is not using his computer to hold personal data, and so does not need to register. Similarly, the organist who uses a Christian software package such as WorshipMaster® to help make up the service sheets does not need to register, as long as he does not also use his computer for letters or as an address list for church business.

5. REGISTRATION[3]

(a) Who needs to register?

If personal data is stored on a computer which is used for church business, the PCC should be registered. If the parish priest has personal data about his parishioners on his own computer, and the PCC does not have access to this computer, then the parish priest needs to be registered as well as the PCC.

People who use their computer only to organise their personal, family or household affairs, or for fun, do not need to register under the Data Protection Act. If a person uses his home computer to do work for the church, that person does not need to register under the Data Protection Act, but the PCC does. So where a secretary types letters for the parish priest and keeps a church address list on her home computer, the secretary does not need to be registered, but the PCC or the parish priest does.

A team ministry is not a legal person, and therefore can not register under the Data Protection Act. Each PCC of the group of churches needs to register if it has personal data held on computer. So do any of the priests in the team ministry who have personal data on their computers.[4]

In short, in almost all cases where a church uses a computer, the PCC needs to be registered. If the parish priest keeps personal data on his own computer which the PCC does not have access to, the parish priest needs to be registered too.

(b) Special cases where you do not need to register

A church does not need to register if it only keeps personal data on computer for the following purposes. I stress that in most cases churches keep personal data for other purposes as well as these special cases, and in such cases churches do need to register.

(i)   Mailing lists

If a church keeps a list of names and addresses on a computer just for use as a parish mailing list, the church does not need to be registered. But if it holds any other data, for example telephone numbers, the church does need to be registered.

(ii)   Accounts

If a church has personal data on a computer just for doing the church accounts, the church does not need to be registered. This covers personal data used for PAYE returns, invoices, tax returns and covenant administration.

Many churches keep on computer the names and addresses of people who have given money to the church. If this is used only for tax purposes, then the church does not need to be registered. But if it is kept on computer in order to know who to ask when more money is needed, then the data is being used for fund-raising as well as for accounts.

(iii)   Church electoral roll

You do not need to register if the personal data you have on your computer is already available in a public document. The church electoral roll is a public document, and so you do not need to register if you have the church electoral roll on computer. However the church electoral roll is a list of names and addresses only. If you keep on the computer any other personal data such as telephone numbers, you do need to register, because this additional data is not public.

(iv)   Word-processing.

Under the Data Protection Act 1984 a person who merely used a computer as a word-processor – in other words, as a typewriter which can correct mistakes – does not need to register.[5] The Data Protection Bill 1998 has no similar provision. So under the new Bill you will have to register even if you only use your computer for word-processing.[6]

220

(v)   *Contact lists*

You do not need to register if you use a computer merely to hold the names of people who are simply contacts for other churches or church related organisations. The reason is that the interest is in the organisations the people belong to, not in the people themselves.

(c)   **How to register**

Telephone the Data Protection Registrar's office on 01625 545740. You will be asked some questions on the telephone. You have to decide what purposes you will be using the personal data for. The Data Protection Registrar suggests that churches should register that they will be using personal data for church administration, for personnel/employee administration, and for fund-raising. The Data Protection Registrar suggests that priests register that they will be using personal data for pastoral care. The Data Protection Registrar's office then send you a form which they have filled in from the facts you told them in your phone call, for you to check and return to them.

Registration lasts for three years, and costs £75. There is no reduced fee for churches.

6.   **GOOD COMPUTER PRACTICE**

The Data Protection Act 1984 is not just about registration; it is also about how you use your computers and how you look after the personal data contained in them. This applies to all computer users, churches and others. These rules for good computer practice are known as the eight Data Protection Principles. They are as follows:

- You should obtain and process personal data fairly and lawfully.

So, be careful about recording any personal data if the source of the information is a third party.

- You should only hold the personal data for the purposes which you are registered for under the Data Protection Act.

So, if a church does not include fund-raising as one of the purposes of registration, it would be illegal for the church to use its computer for fund-raising, e.g. by sending a letter to members of the congregation who have previously made gifts to the church.

- You should not use the personal data or tell it to anyone for any other purpose.

Consider the common situation of a person inquiring from the parish priest if he knows the address and telephone number of a member of his parish. If the address is held on computer, the proper course for the parish priest is not to give this information to anyone who asks for it, but to ask the member whether he minds his address being given to the inquirer.

- The personal data should be adequate, relevant, and no more than you need.

You should aim to ensure that the personal data you hold are sufficient for the purposes you are registered for. You should also aim to ensure that you do not hold additional data which you do not need for those purposes.

In some cases parish priests keep computer records of couples coming to be married. Cases have arisen where the parish priest has entered a code onto the record showing whether or not the couples have been sleeping together.[7] It is not necessary to keep this information on computer for administration or for pastoral care, and so it should *not* be recorded.

- The personal data should be accurate and kept up to date.

If you discover that a mistake, you should correct it without delay.

- Do not keep personal data longer than you need it.

Once a member of your congregation has moved to another church, any personal data about him or her should normally be deleted from your computer. The only information it is proper to keep is a record of the person's new address, as there may be persons wishing to contact them; but before giving anyone this information, you should first contact the person to ask whether they mind their address being given to the inquirer.[8]

- In general, people are entitled to know what data you have about them on your computer.

You are entitled to charge a fee of up to £10 before giving this information. You should provide the answer within 40 days of the request.

222

You do not need to tell someone the name of the person who told you information about them. If you record on your computer a complaint which has been made about a person, that person has a right to be told the nature of the complaint, but he is not entitled to be told who made the complaint, unless the person who made the complaint agrees to his name being disclosed.

- You should take proper security measures to make sure that only the people who you intend to see the data can do so, and to protect the data against accidental loss.

This last data protection principle deserves a section of its own.

7. COMPUTER SECURITY

Many churches do not take enough care about computer security. You should consider the following matters.

(a) Access to computer records by staff

In many churches all personal information is held on a single computer to which all staff have access. This may be what you want, but there will be many cases where only some staff should have access to all records, and only some of these staff should be allowed to change or remove personal data on computer.

- Use passwords. These should be changed fairly often.
- Do all the staff need the same rights of access? Decide who can use the computer, whether they can look at everything on the computer, or only certain parts of it, and whether they are allowed to change any records on the computer.

(b) Access to records by people other than staff

Decide who can be told personal data. In a church setting, many people will consent to their address and telephone number being given to other members of the fellowship. But not all people will agree to this: some women will not want their address and telephone number to be given to anyone they do not know, even if they are part of the same church.

(c)   *Prevention of the accidental loss or theft of personal data*

You should think of the possibility of theft of computer equipment, fire or even power failure. I suggest:

- keep back-up copies of files somewhere well away from the computer, for example in someone's home. Make a practice of doing back-ups of the main files every day, or at least once a week. For £200 a computer can be fitted with a tape drive which makes it simple to back up the whole of a computer's hard disk.[9]
- buy a security kit to stop a computer being stolen. They cost about £20 – £25, and contain a steel cable and a lock, to attach the computer to a piece of furniture. Computers left unguarded in an office area in a church are an easy target for a walk-in thief.

(d)   *Sensitive data*

The Act sets out four type of personal data which are thought to be most sensitive. These are facts about:

- race.
- political opinions, religious and other beliefs.
- physical and mental health, and sexual life.
- criminal convictions.

If a parish priest holds such sensitive data on computer, or even if he has been given facts 'in confidence', then he should take extra security measures. For example, he should not keep such data on a computer to which all members of staff have access; for even passwords can be broken by people who know how.

(e)   *Viruses*

Computer viruses can wreck havoc on a computer. No system is completely secure against them, but a very good start is to use one of the standard anti-virus programs available from any good computer shop.[10] These programs run in the background the whole time the computer is on, and sound a warning if a disk containing a virus is used. Large churches should consider having a system under which all floppy disks have first to be tested by a special computer before being used in other computers.

8.   FURTHER INFORMATION

Registration under the Data Protection Act 1984: Guidelines for parishes (issued by the Secretary General of the General Synod, July 1997). This circular enclosed a copy of the Data Protection Registrar's guidance *Registration under the Data Protection Act 1984 for the Church of England* (Office of the Data Protection Registrar, April 1996).

The Registrar's staff are happy to help with any questions about registration and the data protection principles. The person to contact at the Data Protection Office about church registration is (at the time of writing) Philip Jones.

The Data Protection Office publishes a free booklet called *Data Protection Act 1984, The Guidelines* (Data Protection Office, 1994).

THE OFFICE OF THE DATA PROTECTION REGISTRAR
Wycliffe House,
Water Lane,
Wilmslow,
Cheshire SK9 5AF.

Tel: 01625 545700.

Fax: 01625 524510.

Information is also available on the Internet at http://www.open.gov.uk/dpr/dprhome.htm.

There is also an article I wrote in the Ecclesiastical Law Journal: 'Data Protection and the Church of England' (1996) 4 Ecc LJ 470.

---

[1] Copyright is discussed more generally in Chapter 13, 'Copyright'. The Copyright, Designs and Patents Act 1988 section 3 (1) (b) treats a computer program as a type of literary work protected by copyright.

[2] Strictly, the new rules will only apply to a filing system structured so that you can identify particular information relating to a particular individual. A correspondence file kept in alphabetical order, or a set of cards kept in an alphabetical index, will both be caught by the new rules. The Bill gives special protection to sensitive information about racial or ethnic origin, political opinions, religious or other beliefs, health, sexual life, and the commission of

criminal offences. Churches will be able to keep certain sensitive information under Schedule 3 paragraph 4 of the Bill. The Data Protection Registrar will be known as the Data Protection Commissioner.

[3] Under the Data Protection Bill, 'registration' is being replaced by 'notification'. There is no practical difference for computer users. Churches still have to notify the Data Protection Commissioner of their intention to process personal data before they do so, and the Data Protection Commissioner maintains a register of the information supplied.

[4] See Chapter 16, 'Team ministries'.

[5] Section 1 (8) of the 1984 Act.

[6] Probably the reason for the change is that almost everybody now uses their computer for more than merely word-processing. If you keep a copy of your letters on your computer after the letters have been sent, this goes beyond word-processing. If you keep an address list or any other kind of personal data on your computer then you need to register anyway. In short, to keep the word-processing exemption might mislead people who should register into thinking that they need not do so.

[7] My source for this information is Douglas Fryer, the Data Protection Co-ordinator for the Central Board of Finance at Church House.

[8] There are circumstances where a new address could be sensitive information.

[9] Section 50A of the Copyright, Designs and Patents Act 1988 says that it is not a breach of copyright to make a copy of a computer program to use as a backup.

[10] I use Dr Solomon's Anti-Virus Toolkit, but there are many others.

Chapter 13

COPYRIGHT

1.   INTRODUCTION

Copyright is the legal right of an author or composer to control the use of what he has written or created. You can make *single* copies of short extracts from complete works for your own research or for your private study. But otherwise, you risk civil and possibly criminal proceedings under the Copyright, Designs and Patents Act 1988 if you copy without permission anything protected by copyright.

If a work is still in copyright, then in general no-one can copy it, or record it, or perform it in public, without the copyright owner's permission. The copyright owner is entitled to refuse permission, or to ask for a fee, known as a *royalty*, as the price for his permission.

If a person makes a copy of a work which is in copyright without getting this permission, this is known as a *breach of copyright* or an *infringement of copyright* (the phrases have the same meaning), and can

227

lead to legal proceedings. The copyright owner is likely to seek an injunction to stop you doing it again, damages[1] equal to the royalty he should have received if you had asked permission, and the payment of his legal costs. The sums of money involved can be very large.[2] Some copyright infringements can also lead to a criminal prosecution.[3]

Copyright also applies to computer programs.[4] If you install a computer program onto the church computer without permission to do so, you are committing a breach of copyright. Copyright in computer programs has been covered in Chapter 12, 'Computers', and so will not be repeated here.

2.   HOW LONG DOES COPYRIGHT LAST?

Before 1 January 1996, copyright lasted 50 years from the end of the calendar year when the author died.[5] In order to bring our laws into line with the laws of other European Community countries, from 1 January 1996 this 50 year period has been extended to 70 years, where the author of the work comes from an EEC country, or where the work was written in an EEC country.[6] In other cases, the 50 year period still applies.

After this time, anyone can use the material. The work is said to be *in the public domain*, which means that the rules about copyright no longer apply.

The change in the law in 1996 has had the effect of bringing back copyright for some music which had become in the public domain. Take for example the case of Elgar, who died in 1934. Copyright in his work expired 50 years later, on 1 January 1985. But under the new rule, his music is once again protected by copyright, and will remain so until 31 December 2004. Other European composers similarly affected are Berg (died 1935), Delius (died 1934), Dukas (died 1935), Holst (died 1934), Warlock (died 1930), and Webern (died 1945). In the case of such composers, copies made before 1996 when their work was in the public domain may still be used even though the music is now once again copyright.

Copyright also covers the typography (the layout of the printed page) of any book for a period of 25 years from publication.[7] So you cannot photocopy a book first published less than 25 years ago, even if the words and music are in the public domain. If you want to copy a hymn from a hymnbook in 1998, you need to check that the author of the words and the composer of the music both died before 1928, and that the hymnbook was published before 1973.

3.   WHAT IS A BREACH OF COPYRIGHT?

Where a work is still copyright you should not do any of the following acts without permission:[8]

- copy it. An obvious example is copying music for the choir using a photocopier. But so is copying the words of a hymn or chorus on an overhead projector, or on a service sheet.
- make any arrangement or transcription of the music.[9] This means that if you want to adapt or arrange a piece of music for different instruments, write a descant, write new harmonies, or even improvise harmonies, you should obtain the copyright owner's permission first. The organist who improvises new harmonies for the last verse of a hymn is infringing the composer's copyright, unless the composer died more than 70 years ago.
- play or perform it in public.[10]
- broadcast it.[11]
- issue copies to the public.[12]

4.   AM I ALLOWED TO COPY JUST A FEW PAGES FROM A BOOK?

It is a breach of copyright to copy a *substantial part* of a work. But *substantial* does not just refer to *how much* you copy, but also to *how important* it is. Even a few bars of music may be a substantial part of a musical work if they are easily recognisable.[13] The usual case of a choir being supplied with photocopies of one anthem or song taken from a whole collection is plainly a breach of copyright.

There is a defence known as *fair dealing*, which applies to cases such as copying for the purposes of private study or research.[14] This would not permit copying for the choir or the congregation of a church.

5.   USE DURING CHURCH SERVICES

(a)   Copying

The fact that the unauthorised copies are to be used in a church service or by the church choir is no defence to a claim for breach of copyright.

(b)   Performing

Where a work is still copyright, it should not be played or performed in public without permission. Singing an anthem during a church service is performing it in public. Do you therefore need to get permission whenever you want to include an anthem which is still in copyright in your church services?

The answer is, No. Almost all composers have signed an agreement with the Performing Rights Society (or one of its affiliated organisations abroad). As part of the agreement, the Performing Rights Society deals with all copyright matters covering public performances of the composers' works. The Performing Rights Society gives permission for performances, and pays the composers a share of the royalties it receives. The Performing Rights Society has agreed not to charge any fee for performances during ordinary church services. But the Performing Rights Society will charge a fee if it considers that the performance is not part of a proper service; so, for example, just adding opening and closing prayers to an organ recital does not turn it into a service.

If no service is taking place, a licence is required for any public concert or recital of a copyright musical work in a church or church hall.

(c)   Playing tapes and records

It is not a breach of copyright to play a tape or record in a church service.[15]

6.   CHRISTIAN COPYRIGHT LICENSING

An organisation called Christian Copyright Licensing has entered into copyright agreements with a large number of Christian music publishers. This enables churches to obtain permission to use these publishers' material by purchasing a licence from Christian Copyright Licensing, instead of having to deal with all the publishers one by one.

The *church copyright licence* from Christian Copyright Licensing permits a church to copy the words of thousands of worship songs and hymns for use in church services, in bulletins, liturgies, programmes, song sheets, posters, in bound or unbound song books compiled by the church, and to make transparencies for overhead projectors. The annual licence fee payable depends on the size of the church; it starts at £50 for small congregations and goes up to £300 for very large congregations.

Christian Copyright Licensing also offer a *music reproduction licence* to any church that has a church copyright licence.[16] The music reproduction licence allows a church to photocopy the music of songs and hymns published by a wide range of music book publishers. The fee for the music reproduction licence is an additional one half of the church copyright licence for the church.

For words or music not covered by the church copyright licence or the music reproduction licence, a church should ensure that it purchases proper copies, and if necessary contacts the copyright owner directly.

More than 27,000 churches, schools and Christian organisations have a church copyright licence.

7. VIDEO AND AUDIO RECORDINGS OF WEDDINGS AND CHRISTENINGS

Couples getting married or having their children christened are allowed to record the service without paying any copyright charges provided three conditions are met:[17]

- the rights in the recording and copies of the recording are not to be sold for profit, apart from to the couple or parents who ordered it.
- no more than three copies of the recording are made.
- no part of the recording is to be shown in public.

As I said in Chapter 9, 'Church Services', an organist can ask for an extra 50 per cent of his fee for playing at a service if a sound recording is made, and an extra 100 per cent of his fee if a video recording is made. Professional musicians taking part in the service can ask for the same increases in their fees. Couples wanting to have music at their wedding or at the christening of their children should be told of the extra charge when the arrangements are being made for the service, so that there is no embarrassment afterwards.

8.   THE BIBLE AND LITURGICAL BOOKS

Some churches like to use their own printed version of the normal Sunday Services, and the services for baptisms, marriages and funerals. Special arrangements have been made to allow this without having to apply for specific permission, provided certain conditions are met:

- The copies are not to be sold.
- The name of the church is to be shown on the front cover or first page.
- The number of copies is limited to 500.
- The following copyright acknowledgement is included:
  The Alternative Service Book 1980
  Alternative Services, First Series: Solemnisation of Matrimony /Burial Services
  Alternative Services, Second Series: Baptism and Confirmation
  Ministry to the Sick
  Lent, Holy Week, Easter: Services and Prayers
  The Promise of His Glory
  Services of Prayer and Dedication after Civil Marriage

  material from which is included in this service, is/are copyright © The Central Board of Finance of the Church of England.

(Include only the relevant title or titles from this list.)

Some churches like to print in the service sheet or on a separate slip of paper the passage or text from the Bible or the Liturgical Psalter that is set to be read for that day. You are allowed to do this as long as the service sheet or the slip of paper is to be used only on that day.

Some churches like to include a passage from the Bible in a parish magazine or news sheet. You can do this, provided that no more than 500 copies are printed, and provided the copies are not being sold.

Permission is not required to copy short extracts from the Bible and the Psalter in other books or articles, as long as you print the right copyright acknowledgement. The publishers of the various editions of the Bible have each set their own limits for what may be done without permission, and the words they want printed in the copyright acknowledgement. For example, in the case of the New International Bible, up to 1,000 verses or less than 50 per cent of a full book may be copied, as long as:

- not more than 500 copies are made.
- they are not for sale.
- the NIV text adds up to less than 50 per cent of the whole text.
- the following copyright acknowledgement is printed:
    From the New International Version, copyright © 1973, 1978, 1984 by the International Bible Society. Published by Hodder and Stoughton.

If you are thinking of doing this for other editions of the Bible, or from the Psalter, obtain a copy of *Liturgical Texts for Local Use: Guidelines and Copyright Information* (Church House Publishing). This sets out:

- the names and addresses of the copyright owners of the most usual editions of the Bible and the Psalter.
- how much may be copied free of charge.
- the form of the copyright notice required in each case.

9. LOCAL MUSICAL SETTINGS

Organists and other musicians sometimes compose musical settings of texts taken from the Alternative Service Book for use in a local church.[18] The composer does not need to obtain copyright permission to do this, provided three conditions are met:[19]

- The words should be exactly as they are in the Alternative Service Book.
- The copies should carry the name of the parish, and should not be offered for sale or for use by others.
- The following copyright acknowledgement should be included:
    The Alternative Service Book 1980, extracts from which are reproduced in this setting, is copyright © The Central Board of Finance of the Church of England.

10. FURTHER INFORMATION

THE PERFORMING RIGHTS SOCIETY
29–33 Berners Street,
London W1P 4AA

Tel: 0171 580 5544

CHRISTIAN COPYRIGHT LICENSING
P.O. Box 1339,
Eastbourne BN21 4YF

Tel: 01323 417711

Liturgical Texts for Local Use: Guidelines and Copyright Information, (Church House Publishing).

Administry publishes a guide *Let's play fair on copyright*.

ADMINISTRY
PO Box 57,
St Albans,
Herts AL1 3DT

Tel: 01727 856370

---

[1] Damages is a sum of money which a court orders you to pay to make up for the wrong you have caused.

[2] *Legal Opinions concerning the Church of England* (Church House Publishing, 1994 plus 1997 supplement) page 72 gives an example in 1983 where £5,000 damages inclusive of costs was ordered.

[3] Copyright, Designs and Patents Act 1988, section 107.

[4] Copyright, Designs and Patents Act 1988 section 3 (1) (b) treats a computer program as a type of literary work protected by copyright.

[5] Copyright, Designs and Patents Act 1988, section 12, as originally enacted.

---

[6] Copyright, Designs and Patents Act 1988, section 12, as substituted by the Duration of Copyright and Rights in Performances Regulations 1995, SI 1995 No. 3297.

[7] Copyright, Designs and Patents Act 1988, section 15.

[8] Copyright, Designs and Patents Act 1988, section 16 (1).

[9] Copyright, Designs and Patents Act 1988, section 21 (1), and 21 (3) (b).

[10] Copyright, Designs and Patents Act 1988, section 19.

[11] Copyright, Designs and Patents Act 1988, section 20.

[12] Copyright, Designs and Patents Act 1988, section 18.

Copinger and Skone James on Copyright, 13th edn. (Sweet & Maxwell, 1991) section 8–28.

[14] Copyright, Designs and Patents Act 1988, section 29.

[15] Copyright, Designs and Patents Act 1988, section 67.

[16] This has only been available since 1 April 1998.

[17] See *Liturgical Texts for Local Use: Guidelines and Copyright Information*, pages 17 and 18.

[18] The author composed his own setting of the Holy Communion service for the church where he was churchwarden.

[19] *Liturgical Texts for Local Use: Guidelines and Copyright Information*, page 20.

Chapter 14

HANDLING THE PRESS

1.   A PARISH PRESS PLAN

E very parish should have a clear plan for dealing with press enquiries. This plan should be in place, and people should know about it, before anything happens which excites the press. This is especially important if what happens is something difficult or embarrassing for the church.

There are four points in the parish press plan:

- Have a single spokesman for the parish.
- Be in control of what is said to the press.
- Set up good communications within the parish.
- Get help when you need it.

(a)   *Have a single spokesman for the parish*

In many parishes, there is no clear idea whose job it is to speak to the press. The press will telephone the parish priest, the churchwardens, the treasurer, members of the congregation, and anyone who is willing to speak to them. If there is no agreed plan, each of these people may well offer their own views, and things will be said to the press which may be mistaken, hurtful, or even malicious. The result is that you have no control over what is said in the press.

The way to prevent this happening is:

- One person should be chosen to act as the press spokesman.
- All leaders in the parish should be clear about their own role in the event of press interest.

In many cases the parish priest will be the press spokesman. But quite a number of parishes have some other person who can take on this role, for example a person with some experience in journalism or public relations.

Once a press spokesman has been appointed, that person should be the one to publicise church events. He should also be the first to receive a full briefing about anything embarrassing or sensitive which might attract press interest. The leaders need to be able to contact him during the working day and in the evenings.

Once a parish has appointed its press spokesman, all leaders and parish workers should politely but firmly direct press enquiries to that person. In this way, the parish can control what information is given to the press, and reduce the chance of harmful or thoughtless comments being published. The press also get to know who to contact for news about the parish.

(b)   *Be in control of what is said to the press*

This means being in control of both *what* information is given, and *when* it is given.

If the parish priest is the press spokesman, he should be careful not to comment on matters which have been said or confessed to him privately as a priest, whilst giving pastoral care.

238

If the police are involved, the press spokesman should be careful not to say anything which could influence the criminal investigation or trial. Do not suggest your view on whether the person concerned is guilty or not. Nor should you say anything about the person or the event if you might have to give evidence later in court. The same thing applies if there are civil proceedings. Do not say anything which could influence the court action. Once the trial is finished, you are much more free to comment.

The diocesan registrar and the diocesan communications officer will assist you and advise you on what you can properly say about any matter.

The press spokesman should prepare a statement which can be given to the press. Do not be drawn to expand on it.

Sometimes, the first you may hear about something serious is when a reporter phones you about it. If this happens, follow these guidelines:

- Write down the reporter's questions.
- Do not say 'No comment', or make any kind of statement.
- Inform the reporter that the press spokesman for the parish will return his call as soon as possible.
- Contact the press spokesman.
- Make sure the diocesan communications officer knows what you are doing.
- If you cannot contact these people, and you need to reply quickly, write out as short a statement as possible, and check it with a member of the Bishop's staff before phoning back. If there are legal implications – e.g. if a court case is pending, consult the diocesan registrar.
- Be careful how you answer any extra questions you may be asked when you phone back.

  A few general points:

- You do not have to answer every question. Keep control of what you say.
- Beware of answering 'yes' or 'no' to questions which you feel are in some way 'tricky' or 'loaded'. Use your own words instead.
- Don't say anything flippant or silly.

- Nothing can be safely said 'off the record'. Anything you say may be published.

The diocesan communications officer will need to form a full picture of the story and to check the facts. It is often possible to correct mistakes or a misunderstanding before a story is printed.

Please do not comment on an incident in another parish.

(c)   Set up good communications within the parish

All written statements to the press should be circulated to all parish staff and leaders, and to other diocesan staff immediately. Everybody should be clear about who speaks to the press, and what has been said.

The press spokesman should make sure that he knows where and how to contact all the key persons involved. If the story runs for more than a few days, a progress meeting should be called. In larger parishes and if the matter is still newsworthy, regular progress meetings should be held.

It may be necessary to explain what is happening to the congregation. How this is done is up to the leaders, but if the police are involved make sure that you clear with them what you want to say before you say it. Remember that anything you say to the congregation becomes public, and may be passed on to the press.

(d)   Get help when you need it

If something comes to your notice which you suspect could lead to a major story, inform the diocesan communications officer at once. He will discuss with you what action needs to be taken, and consult senior staff if needed. This will give you time to prepare a plan before the story breaks.

The diocesan registrar and the diocesan communications officer will assist you and advise you on what you can properly say about any matter. They can help you to prepare a statement to be issued to the press. In some circumstances it may be best for the diocesan communications officer to run the story, rather than leave it in the hands of the parish. If it is agreed to do this, refer all reporters to the diocesan communications officer.

2.   ANNOUNCEMENTS

(a)   *Getting publicity*

Good communications are an essential part of the church's task of mission, proclaiming the gospel, and teaching. Often the church misses the chance to tell the media about a newsworthy story.

(i)   *Advance notice*

If you want to give publicity to an event, give the press as much notice as possible – at least two weeks. Some papers need more notice than that. Send details to the local press and local free newspapers, and also for inclusion in the 'What's On' spot on local radio.

(ii)   *Follow up*

It can pay to follow up a press release with a phone call. Offer the press a time when they can take photographs.

(iii)   *Build up a relationship with the press*

Remember that there can be nothing to beat building up a personal relationship with the local press. Arrange a meeting, and follow it up. Make sure that they know the press spokesman for your church.

(b)   *The press release*

Well-written press releases are the best way of giving information to the media. They let you present your facts and ideas in the way and in the order that you wish. You control the timing, you have a record of what you said, and you know that what you have told the press is correct.

Be prepared for the reporter to contact you for more information.

The first two sentences make or break a press release. Tell them *who*, *what*, *why*, *when*, *how*, *where*, and *how much it cost*!

- Always type your press releases with double spacing.
- Leave a two inch margin at either side.
- Use only one side of the paper.
- Make sure that the name of the church is clearly printed at the top of the first page.

- Always give a contact name and telephone number.
- Don't use Christian expressions or abbreviations which people may not understand.
- Write in short sentences, one idea to a sentence.
- Give names and titles in full.
- Avoid saying that the news may only be published after a particular time and day.
- At the end write END.

3.   RADIO AND TELEVISION INTERVIEWS

Remember, an interview is not an argument. The interviewer simply wants to have information or opinions from you as clearly and fully as possible.

(a)   Who should be interviewed?

- If you have a press spokesman, use him or her.
- If the subject is good news, there is no reason why others should not add their bit as well to what the press spokesman says. If the news is on a difficult or embarrassing subject, you *have to* keep control of the situation, and this probably means that only the press spokesman should be interviewed.

(b)   Before being interviewed

- Find out what the interview is about. What are the main points you want to get across?
- Tell the interviewer if there are subjects you will not discuss.
- Check your facts, and have them at your fingertips.
- Discover whether the interview is to obtain facts and figures, or whether you are going to be asked your views.
- Consider the effect of refusing to be interviewed. What would a 'no comment' suggest to the listener?
- Have you got long enough to prepare? Do not feel pushed by an interviewer into giving an interview without warning. Most will give you plenty of notice. If you feel you are not ready, tell your interviewer that you will ring him back in half an hour, and do so.

(c)   *During the interview*

- Be clear and concise. Make immediate contact with the listener.
- Be sincere and friendly. Use an ordinary tone of voice. Don't use jargon and technical language. Be polite to people who have different points of view from your own.
- Sometimes you should avoid answering a question. Do this politely but firmly, giving a reason: for example, 'It would be wrong for me to comment while the police are investigating the matter'.

4.   FUNERALS AND MEMORIAL SERVICES

The funerals and memorial services for the victims of large-scale disasters or personal violence can often attract a great deal of media attention. If this happens, you should be in contact with the diocesan communications officer, who will arrange for a key person to be available for the media to contact, and so protect people involved with the incident as much as possible. Practical matters such as the placing of reporters, photographers, television and radio crews will need to be organised.

5.   FURTHER INFORMATION

Andy Radford, *Working with the media – a handbook for every church office* (Church House Publishing).

How to promote your church (Church House Publishing).

Peter Crumper, *Keep in Touch* (Scripture Union).

The Guardian Media Guide (Guardian Newspapers).

Press Management: Guidelines for parishes (St Albans Diocese Communications Unit, 1997).

News for the world (the use of the media) (Administry).

ADMINISTRY
PO Box 57,
St Albans,
Herts AL1 3DT
Tel: 01727 856370

Chapter 15

RESOLVING CONFLICTS

1.   TRUST AND CO-OPERATION

Two of the most important ingredients in any church are trust, and being able to work together. The churchwardens, the PCC, the parish priest, and the rest of the congregation need to trust and co-operate with each other. They should be able to 'get on' with each other, and work together.

So, in Chapter 2, 'The Churchwardens', I explained that a churchwarden needs to care for his parish priest and be able to work with him. This does not mean agreeing with everything he says, but it does mean having a close working relationship with him. I said that this is best developed where there are regular meetings for prayer and for sharing a vision of the parish's life and mission.

The relationship between the churchwarden and the members of the congregation is also important. As Canon E 1 says, the churchwarden is to be an example to the congregation, and is to 'promote unity and peace among them'.

In Chapter 3, 'The PCC', I said that the key-note in the relationship between the PCC and the parish priest is that they should work together and support each other. Decisions should be taken jointly, and yet each should discuss ideas and initiatives with the other.

This can be difficult in a team or group ministry.[1] The churchwardens often have to do much of the parish priest's work for him in terms of pastoral care. Trust, and being able to depend on each other, is vital.

2.   AREAS LEADING TO TENSION

(a)   Public worship

It is clear that decisions have to be taken which are not likely to please everybody. In Chapter 9, 'Church Services', I said that the decision as to what form of service to use on Sunday can lead to tension amongst the members of the PCC and the congregation. I quoted the helpful guidance given in the booklet *Public Worship in the Church of England*[2] on how this particular decision should be reached so as to avoid upsetting people.

Indeed, anything to do with the form of public worship seems to stir up strong tensions among Christians. Many people are used to only one style of worship, and do not like any other form. The Church of England allows a great range of churchmanship, from the very high with much ritual and 'smells and bells', to the very low evangelical style of worship where almost any ritual is thought to be bad doctrine, and a step on the road to disaster. Such matters as the exercise of charismatic gifts and the 'Toronto blessing' are hotly debated, with some saying they are of God, others that they are of the devil, and still others saying that they are some kind of psychological nonsense.

(b)   Alterations to buildings

Another area which frequently leads to conflict is a major alteration to the church building. A typical example is removing the existing pews and replacing them with chairs. Those in favour of such a change may believe that the existing layout no longer serves the needs of the congregation, and that chairs will give a more flexible arrangement. Those against a change may believe that the proposed alterations would spoil the architectural design of the church; they may consider that pews are more comfortable and more convenient than modern chairs; or they may simply have sentimental reasons for wanting to keep the church as they have always known it.

(c)   Personality clashes

It is not only decisions which lead to such disagreements. Personality clashes happen even in Christian circles. Differences in culture, class, status, and race can all lead to mistakes and unhappiness. Some people are very conscious of distinctions of this sort, and find it hard to change where this is called for. Or the church may have been under the control of a group of people in the congregation, and the parish priest tries to take control by making many changes perhaps a little too quickly. The result can be a group of people who lose confidence in their parish priest, and who feel they no longer support or trust him.

(d)   Small incidents blown up

A parishioner may have been refused a memorial stone by the parish priest, and people who hear about it start to take sides. A decision not to hold a church summer fete one year can upset those who like to assist. In one church a member of the congregation threatened to take the parish priest and PCC to court for defamation over something she thought had been said about her.

People can become unreasonable in their attitudes to such incidents. Views can become entrenched, and emotions aroused. A person starts to see the dispute as a challenge to himself as an individual, rather than simply a minor disagreement within a congregation. The result is that what should be a small incident can grow into a major disaster.

(e)   *Serious wrongs*

Lastly there are cases where a serious wrong may have been taken place. Someone may be suspected of having stolen money from the church, or the parish priest or a churchwarden is suspected of having an affair. If a crime has taken place the police may need to be involved, and the church has its own formal procedure to discipline clergy and churchwardens for very serious matters. But most wrongs can be sorted out within this wide range.

3.   MEANS OF RESOLVING DISPUTES

Disharmony in the Christian community is a serious matter. In the New Testament, Euodia and Syntyche are urged to agree with each other.[3] But there is also realism in the urge to agree:

> If it is possible, as far as it depends on you, live at peace with everyone.[4]

Many Christians believe that conflict should never happen, and that the fact that there is a disagreement means that the parties involved have in some sense failed. They are right in realising that conflict which is unresolved is a wound which will fester and get worse; but conflict which is resolved *increases* the strength of the parties. Marriages which have survived conflict are often stronger than those which have not suffered from it. The important thing is not to avoid conflict, but to know how to resolve it when it occurs.

Where there is disharmony the desired solution is reconciliation. There is a need to work towards a mutually acceptable resolution of the disagreement or dispute. This often involves four steps:

(a)   *Four steps in dispute resolution*

(i)   *Recognising that there is a conflict*

Do not sweep the problem under the carpet, and pretend it is not there. To do so only causes it to fester.

(ii)   Discussing the conflict

By discussing the problem, you show that you respect and value the other person, and that you accept that his point of view is genuine, even though you do not agree with it. You should be prepared to listen to his point of view.

(iii)   Understand the conflict

Understanding another person's point of view does not mean having to agree with it or having to give up your own point of view. It *may* have that effect – but it *may* just be that God wants to change your view, and you should not be afraid of that.

(iv)   Co-operating in resolving the problem

Understanding the other person's point of view should lead to being willing to co-operate in finding a solution to the problem.

(b)   Resolution provided for in church rules

In some cases the canons provide a means to resolve, or at least decide, particular issues. So, for example, the rules provide a means to determine what form of service should take place if the parish priest cannot agree with the PCC. It is worth quoting again what is said in *Public Worship in the Church of England* about this procedure:[5]

> It cannot be too strongly emphasised, however, that the intention of the law is that decisions on forms of service to be used at public worship should be taken jointly after full consultation and agreement. This is not achieved if anyone finds it necessary to invoke legal rights.

(c)   The role of the churchwarden

There is an obligation on the churchwarden to try to heal any rifts. Generally he should try and support the parish priest in the way the parish priest wants to run the parish, but that does not mean being the parish priest's 'toady' if a dispute arises. Nor should he be, as it were, the leader of the opposition. *He should attempt to remain neutral in any dispute, and approachable by all sides.* Those members of the congregation who disagree with what the parish priest is doing should feel able to voice their concerns to the churchwardens, and to know that when they do so they will receive a sympathetic ear, even if the churchwardens support what the parish priest is doing.

A churchwarden can often find himself in difficulty on the issue of confidentiality. A good rule of thumb if someone wants to tell you something 'in confidence' is to make it clear before the information is given that you may have to pass on the information, and to obtain their consent to do so if you think it appropriate.

(d)   The role of the rural dean and the archdeacon

Sometimes help is needed from outside the parish. Various people are available to do this, in particular, the rural dean and the archdeacon. There is no clear division of roles between these two offices on this matter but, as the archdeacon is an officer of the bishop, contacting the archdeacon is a lot more significant than a quiet word with the rural dean.

If the dispute concerns the church building, it may be more appropriate to ask the archdeacon for advice, as he is directly involved with church buildings; for other types of dispute it may be more appropriate to go to the rural dean in the first instance.

(e)   Leaving the parish

Ultimately, an individual member of the congregation who does not approve of the way something is being done in the church has the option of voting with his feet, in other words, of leaving the church and finding some where else to worship. That is comparatively easy for persons who live in a large city with many churches; it is not so easy for someone living in a rural community where there is only one local church for him to attend. This should not always be regarded as a failure: it may actually be the best thing both for the individual and for the rest of the church if that person does find somewhere else to worship. The tragedy is only in those cases where the person leaves the church, and does not find somewhere else to go to. It is also far better for the person who does decide to leave, if he does so with goodwill. That means that he should go with the blessing and love of his former church, and that he in turn should hold no grudge against that church, even though they have decided to go their separate ways.

(f)   *The role of the bishop*

Sometimes the rules provide that the bishop shall decide particular issues. If for example, a parish priest refuses to baptise a child, or unduly delays the baptism, the parents can take the matter straight to the bishop who, after consulting the parish priest, gives such directions as he thinks fit.

Another example is where there is a genuine disagreement between the PCC and the parish priest which cannot be resolved. The rules provide that the bishop should decide how to determine the matter. In practice, either party should feel free to contact the rural dean or the archdeacon for advice, before the bishop needs to be consulted.

Other cases can be referred by the rural dean or the archdeacon to the bishop if they consider it appropriate. The rural dean and the archdeacon are well placed to judge whether a problem is a one-off incident which can be resolved by the exercise of a certain amount of goodwill on all sides, or whether it is symptomatic of a more serious problem, which needs the bishop's intervention.

The most serious case is known as *serious pastoral breakdown*, in other words a complete breakdown of the relationship which should exist between the parish priest and his congregation. If the case appears to be one of serious pastoral breakdown, the bishop will almost certainly become involved. He may write to the parties or ask to see them. If the parish priest and the churchwardens together visit the bishop, listen to his counsel, and resolve to put it into practice, that may well be an end of the problem.

The bishop may decide to conduct what is called a *visitation*. This is a formal procedure, almost like a trial, when the bishop goes to the parish, and conducts an inquiry as to what has gone wrong. He may rebuke whoever he considers to be in the wrong, and offer advice to help restore good relations.

As a last resort, the bishop may decide to issue proceedings under the Incumbents (Vacation of Benefices) Measure 1977. These proceedings take a long time. This is deliberately so, so that every effort can be made by all parties to heal the dispute, and restore confidence within the parish. Once the procedure starts there is an obligatory delay of six months to try to restore order.   There is then a report by the archdeacon, a hearing in front of a tribunal when the parties can be legally represented.   If the tribunal recommends the bishop to do so, the bishop can remove the parish priest from his position as parish priest.   The tribunal may on the other hand consider that the fault lay on the side of some members of the PCC or the parishioners, in which case the bishop can rebuke them, and disqualify them from serving on the PCC.

The House of Bishops has issued rules of guidance, for proceedings under the Incumbents (Vacation of Benefices) Measure 1977.   These focus on the steps to promote reconciliation where there has been a pastoral breakdown in a parish.   They are published as *The Incumbents (Vacation of Benefices) Measures 1977 and 1993: Code of Practice* (Church House Publishing).

(g)   *Conciliation and mediation*

ADR, short for Alternative Dispute Resolution, is a means of resolving family, community, commercial and industrial disputes, and is growing in popularity.   Instead of taking the case to court, the parties agree to use a neutral person called a mediator or conciliator to assist in resolving the dispute.   The terms *conciliation* and *mediation* are very similar in meaning, and it does not really matter which one is used. They both refer to a voluntary process in which an independent third party assists the parties through a confidential series of both joint and private meetings to achieve their own solution.   The process is *voluntary*: either party can walk away if he feels it is not helping.   It is *confidential*: things said to the mediator will not be disclosed either to the other party or to the outside world.   The mediator helps the parties to explore options.   He may suggest possible solutions, but he does not impose them on the parties.

Conciliation is about *reconciliation*: the restoring of a relationship.   It may involve saying sorry; it certainly involves understanding.   It is a very positive approach to the Christian faith.   The parties should stop looking back on the history of a dispute, stop blaming each other, and start looking at the way forward.   Reconciliation is fundamental to the Christian life.

The same approach works in the commercial world. Two examples I come across as a barrister are property disputes and computer contract disputes. Going to court over these disputes can be extremely expensive, and it can take months or even years for the case to be finished. It will almost certainly put an end to any goodwill between the parties. If instead the parties agree to use mediation, the mediator will speak to both sides, he will advise, listen, help each side to see the strengths and weaknesses of its own and the other side's case, he will suggest common ground between the parties, and in many cases can lead the parties towards a compromise. The extraordinary thing is that it does often work, and that disputes are resolved in days, weeks or, at worst, months, but not years – and at a fraction of the cost that would be involved in bringing them to court.

Mediation and conciliation only work if both parties genuinely want to resolve the dispute if possible. It will not work if one party has no genuine interest in settlement. But mediation is at the heart of the Christian gospel,[6] and if there is a breakdown in a relationship, we should look to see how the relationship can be restored, and the parties reconciled to one another, rather than seeking to bring the relationship to an end. The Christian community has a lesson to learn from the commercial world, that mediation and conciliation do work.

The report on clergy discipline *Under Authority* sets out a suggested procedure to resolve disputes using mediation or conciliation. The report suggests[7] that bishops should have a number of people in each diocese available to be called upon to fulfil the role of conciliator.

Many commercial mediators are accredited or registered with CEDR, the Centre for Dispute Resolution. CEDR is a registered charity, and is widely regarded as the leading provider of ADR services in Europe. Most of its work is related to commercial disputes, but the United Reformed Church commissioned from CEDR a two-day training course entitled *Managing Conflict in the Church*. The course costs (in 1998) £175 + VAT per person including accommodation, food, and course materials. It is suitable for all members of the Christian Church regardless of denomination, whether they be ordained priests, lay preachers, leaders or non-office holders. The course includes a series of case studies of typical conflicts arising in a church setting, and teaches the skills involved in being a good mediator.

(h)   Unbecoming conduct

There is of course also the possibility of a trial against the parish priest for *unbecoming conduct*. This is usually, though not always, because the parish priest is accused of some sexual scandal. Beyond being aware of its existence, church members do not need to know any more about this form of procedure unless it actually affects their church. This is especially so as the procedure is in the process of being completely changed following the report *Under Authority*.

4.   FURTHER INFORMATION

Under Authority: Report on Clergy Discipline (Church House Publishing, 1996). See especially chapter 3, 'basic principles', Chapter 9, 'the core procedures' and Appendix C, 'other changes needed' – especially the new complaints resolution procedures.

Incumbents (Vacation of Benefices) Measures 1977 and 1993: Code of Practice (Church House Publishing).

Brian Wales-Smith, *Resolving your dispute by mediation* (The Academy of Experts, 1995).

THE ACADEMY OF EXPERTS
2 South Square,
Gray's Inn,
London WC1R 5HP.

Tel: 0171 637 0333.

CENTRE FOR DISPUTE RESOLUTION (CEDR)
Princes House,
95 Gresham Street,
London EC2V 7NA

Tel: 0171 481 4441

Dealing with conflict, published by Administry. Administry also runs a part day training course for parish priests, managers and church leadership teams, called *Managing change and conflict*.

ADMINISTRY
PO Box 57,
St Albans,
Herts AL1 3DT
Tel: 01727 856370

---

[1] See Chapter 16, 'Team ministries'.
[2] *Public Worship in the Church of England. A guide to the law governing worship and doctrine in the Church of England* (Church House Publishing, 1994).
[3] Phil. 4: 2–3.
[4] Rom. 12:18.
[5] Paragraph 31.
[6] See e.g. 1 Tim. 2:5.
[7] Paragraph 8.33.

Chapter 16

TEAM MINISTRIES

1.   INTRODUCTION

team ministry is where a parish or a group of parishes is under the pastoral care of a team of vicars and other clergy, rather than just one parish priest. A team ministry may have a number of parish churches.

A group ministry is a looser arrangement than a team ministry. Each vicar in the area has his own parish to look after, but as well as doing this, all the vicars in the group assist each other to look after the whole area of the group.[1]

2.   TEAM MINISTRY

(a)   How it is formed

Team ministries and group ministries are formed by a *pastoral scheme* made under the Pastoral Measure 1983.[2] The details of the scheme for an area are set out in a legal document, which sets out how the parishes are going to be organised under the scheme.

The leader of the team is called the *team rector*. The other clergy members of the team are called *team vicars*. These are their formal titles for official documents: in everyday use they are normally all called *vicar*. In addition there may be curates, lay workers, retired clergy and readers. The team rector and the other clergy in the team are together known as the *team chapter*.

(b)   How long rectors and team vicars hold office

Under some schemes the team rector has a freehold, which means that he can stay until he retires. In other schemes the team rector has a fixed term of years. Team vicars have a fixed term of years, as laid down by the scheme, or as settled by the bishop who appoints them.

Where a team rector or team vicar has a fixed term of years, the bishop can extend it for up to the same period again.

(c)   How they are appointed

The names of the first rector and the first team vicars in a team ministry are often set out in the pastoral scheme which sets up the team ministry.

When a new team rector is needed, he may be appointed by the bishop or by a patronage board. When a new team vicar is needed, he may be appointed by the bishop and the team rector jointly, or by a patronage board. Before appointing a team vicar, the bishop or the patronage board should consult:

- the other members of the team.
- the PCC of every parish in the team ministry.
- any district church council that is involved. District church councils are described below.

(d)   Their duties

The team rector has overall care for the people in the area covered by the team ministry. He is also the leader of the team. The scheme may set out how the team ministry is to be organised, but otherwise it is up to the team rector. The team rector should consult the team vicars and the other team members before appointing any new members of the team.

(e)   District church councils, team councils, and deputy churchwardens

Where the team ministry is in one parish, there may be more than one church or place of worship in the parish. Where this is the case, the bishop, or the scheme itself, may set up a *district church council* for each separate church. A district church councils is often referred to as a DCC, in the same way as a parochial church council is referred to as the PCC. The arrangements vary from one scheme to another, but are likely to cover the following areas:

- how many people should be on each DCC.
- who is to act as chairman.
- what rules should govern it.
- which of the PCC's jobs should be given to it.
- the election of deputy churchwardens for each district church.
- making sure that each district church is properly represented on the PCC.

The PCC for the parish still remains, but the DCC carries out some of the jobs of the PCC relating to the district church.

If the team ministry covers more than one parish, the scheme or the bishop may set up a *team council*. A team council covers the whole area of all the parishes. Again, the scheme or the bishop needs to decide:

- who is to be the chairman.
- how many members it is to have.
- what it is to do.

Where there is a team council there are no extra churchwardens or deputy churchwardens. Each parish within the team ministry still has its own PCC and its own churchwardens.

The arrangements set out in the scheme or by the bishop for team councils and district church councils can only run for the first five years of the team ministry. After this time, the churches have to agree to continue these councils by voting to do so at their annual parochial church meetings. This is explained below.[3]

3.   GROUP MINISTRY

(a)   How it is formed

A group ministry is also formed by a pastoral scheme. Under a team ministry all the parishes are under the care of all members of the team. In contrast, under a group ministry, each vicar of a parish in the group continues to be in charge of his own parish, and each parish remains distinct and separate from the other parishes in the group.

(b)   Appointments

When a new vicar needs to be appointed as part of a group ministry, the patron[4] should obtain the bishop's approval of the person to be appointed before presenting him for appointment. The bishop consults the other vicars and priests-in-charge in the group before reaching his decision.

(c)   Their duties

Each vicar decides what duties in his parish may be carried out by the other members of the group ministry. All the vicars should assist each other to provide the best possible care for the people living in the area of the group.

A vicar cannot withdraw his parish from the group or refuse to take part in the group ministry without resigning his position as vicar.

The vicars meet together as a chapter to discuss and decide all matters of concern or interest to the group.

You can have a team ministry forming part of a group ministry. Where this happens, only the team rector (not the team vicars) can give directions to the vicars in the other parishes in the group.

(d)   Group councils

In a group ministry each PCC remains independent from all the others, but in addition there may be a group council covering all the parishes in the group ministry. As in the case of district church councils, the arrangements setting up the group council need to cover:

- how many people should be on the group council.
- who is to be chairman.
- what rules should govern it.
- which of each PCC's jobs should be given to it.

These arrangements are often made as part of the scheme setting up the group ministry. After the first five years of the scheme, if the churches in the group ministry want the group council to continue, they need to vote to do so at their annual parochial church meetings. This is explained below.

4.   THE CHURCH REPRESENTATION RULES

The Church Representation Rules allow parishes to set up district church councils, joint parochial church councils, team councils and group councils. Here is a short reminder of what each of these councils are.

- District church councils are appointed where a parish has more than one church, and each church wants its own separate council.
- Joint parochial church councils are appointed where a vicar is in charge of more than one parish.
- A team council is a council covering all the parishes in a team ministry.
- A group council is a council covering all the parishes in a group ministry.

The general pattern is the same for all of them. At their annual parochial church meetings, the churches which are to be part of the scheme have to vote in favour of a scheme to put in place one of these types of council. The vote in favour of the scheme has to be passed by a two-thirds majority of the people who are present and voting at the meeting. The bishop's council and a committee of the diocesan synod also need to agree to the scheme.

The scheme needs to set out how the new council is to be run, and what it is to do. Some things have to be done by the PCC, and cannot be given to one of these other types of council to do. These are:

- voting on any new scheme under the Pastoral Measure.
- appointing parish representatives when a new vicar needs to be chosen.[5]
- passing a resolution saying that the church would not accept a woman priest.

As I have explained, a pastoral scheme can set up one of these councils, but not for longer than five years. After five years, if the church or churches want to continue the council, they need to set up their own scheme by using this procedure.

(a)   District church councils

Rule 18.

Where a parish has two or more churches or places of worship, the annual parochial church meeting may make a scheme so that each congregation is properly represented on the PCC. Or a scheme may set up a DCC for one of the churches in the parish.

A scheme setting up a DCC needs to deal with the election of DCC members, who is to chair its meetings, and who are to be members because they hold some position in the church. The scheme may provide for the district church to have deputy churchwardens, and if so, what their duties are to be.[6]

(b)   Joint parochial church councils

Rule 19.

Joint councils meets from time to time to discuss matters which affect all the parishes represented on the joint council.

(c)   Team councils

Rule 20.

The team council consists of:

- the team rector.

- all other members of the team.
- all assistant curates, deaconesses and lay workers licensed to a parish within the team.
- a number of lay representatives to be chosen by each PCC.

Each PCC elects some of its own members to serve on the team council. Apart from the team rector, the total number of clergy and lay assistants should not amount to more than one-third of the team council. If necessary, some of the clergy and lay assistants should agree not to serve on the team council, to keep the balance down to this level.

The team council meets from time to time to discuss matters which affect all the churches in the team.

(d)   Group councils

Rule 21.

The group council consists of:

- all the members of the group ministry.
- all assistant curates, deaconesses and lay workers licensed to one of the parishes within the group.
- a number of lay representatives to be chosen by each PCC.

There is no rule on how many lay representatives need to be on the group council. It is up to the churches setting up the scheme to decide this.

The group council meets from time to time to discuss matters which affect all the churches in the group.

5.   CONVENTIONAL DISTRICTS

A *church plant* is the name used to describe what happens when an established church sets up a new church. The established church hopes that the new church will 'take off' on its own, that it will soon grow up to be free of any ties with the old church, and be big enough to start planting other churches itself.

Church planting is sometimes done by using what is known as a *conventional district*. A conventional district is not a parish, but it is usually formed in the hope that it will in due course be made into a parish. The district or area is placed under the care of a *curate-in-charge* with the agreement of the vicar of the parish. A conventional district has an organisation similar to a parish. It has its own churchwardens, electoral roll and parochial church council.

If a conventional district is set up for the new church plant, the new church can be given the feel of being a parish, with churchwardens, an electoral roll and a PCC, while it is growing. In time, if the new church is a success, the conventional district can be made into a proper parish if the bishop and everybody else agrees.

6.   FURTHER INFORMATION

Good Practice in Group and Team Ministry, ACCM Occasional Papers No. 39 (Church House Publishing, 1991).

Team and Group Ministries Measure 1995: Code of Recommended Practice (Church House Publishing, 1995).

Breaking New Ground – Church Planting in the Church of England (Church House Publishing, 1994).

---

[1] Except where one or more parishes have passed resolutions A and B under the Priests (Ordination of Women) Measure 1993. When this happens, a woman priest in the group would be unable to act as a priest in those parishes.

[2] For background information on setting up a scheme, see *The Pastoral Measure 1983 Code of Practice* (Church House Publishing, 1983). Many people need to be involved: the bishop, the pastoral committee for the diocese, the Church Commissioners, all PCCs and parish priests in the area, all patrons affected by the scheme, and finally the Privy Council, who make an order bringing the scheme into effect.

[3] See the heading *The Church Representation Rules*, page 261.

[4] The role of the patron is explained in Chapter 17, 'When the parish priest leaves'.

[5] See Chapter 17, 'When the parish priest leaves'.

[6] As from March 1998, with the permission of the bishop's council a DCC is allowed to produce its own accounts instead of consolidating them in the accounts of the whole parish: see the Church Representation Rules (Amendment) Resolution 1998, SI 1998 No. 319.

Chapter 17

WHEN THE PARISH PRIEST LEAVES

1.   INTRODUCTION

W hen the parish priest leaves, there is what is known as a vacancy or an interregnum. Some vacancies are filled very quickly, others can take years to fill. Life has to go on in the parish. This chapter describes what happens, both how a new parish priest is chosen, and how to keep the show on the road, so to speak, during the waiting period.

The term *vacancy* is misleading. Only the vicarage[1] is empty; the church itself continues. The term *interregnum* comes from the Latin for *between two rulers*. This, too, is misleading, because a minister comes to serve, not to rule.[2] But the terms have stuck.

During a vacancy the churchwardens and the rural dean are in charge of the parish. Advice can be obtained from the diocesan secretary or the archdeacon on any particular difficulties.

2.   PRACTICAL MATTERS BEFORE THE PARISH PRIEST LEAVES

There are some practical matters to sort out. Churchwardens should make sure they know:

- where all the parish records are, and the contents of all files and correspondence.
- practical arrangements about the vicarage – where the keys and the meters are, and what needs repair.

Lists and rotas should be prepared to deal with various routine chores in the church previously done by or organised by the parish priest.

The churchwardens should discuss with the rural dean (and with the readers in the parish if there are any) the pattern of services, bearing in mind:

- the needs of the parish.
- the availability of clergy and readers.
- the cost of providing the services.
- the pastoral considerations.

3.   HOW IS THE NEW PARISH PRIEST CHOSEN?

The new parish priest is chosen by a person called the patron, acting together with the bishop and two parish representatives appointed by the PCC. In some cases the bishop himself is the patron. Where the Crown is the patron, the procedure is slightly different,[3] but in the normal case what happens is as follows.

(a)   Notices to the PCC

The process starts by various notices being sent by the bishop to the patron and to the secretary of the PCC.[4]

(b)   The PCC meets

Within four weeks, the PCC should meet and do the following:

- prepare a written summary or profile,[5] describing the conditions, needs and traditions of the parish, and the kind of parish priest the PCC feels the parish needs.
- appoint the two parish representatives (who should be laymen) to contact the patron and the bishop. They are not necessarily the churchwardens.
- decide whether to ask the patron to consider advertising the vacancy. The final decision on advertising rests with the patron.
- decide whether to ask for a joint meeting with the bishop and the patron.
- decide whether to ask the bishop how the parish relates to the needs of the diocese and the wider interests of the church.
- decide whether or not to pass a resolution saying that the PCC would not accept a woman as the new parish priest, or as a priest to lead Holy Communion or say the absolution in the parish.[6]

Usually the two churchwardens are appointed as the representatives of the parish. But this does not have to be the case.

The PCC can suggest the name of the individual they would like the patron to appoint, but they cannot insist on their choice.

(c)   The patron, the bishop and the parish representatives meet

If the PCC has asked for a meeting with the bishop and the patron, this takes place within six weeks. The rural dean and the lay chairman of the local deanery synod should be invited to the meeting.[7] The purpose of the meeting is to exchange views on the PCC's wishes, and on the bishop's views on how the parish relates to the needs of the diocese.

(d)   The parties attempt to agree who shall be appointed

When the patron finds a person whom he would like to appoint, he sends notices to the bishop and to the parish representatives naming the person he proposes to offer the position to. The bishop has four weeks to make up his mind whether or not to accept this person, the parish representatives have two weeks. In other words, both have a power of veto over the candidate put forward by the patron. If the parish representatives wish to veto a candidate they should be prepared to justify their reason for doing so. A good reason would be that the candidate does not meet a significant requirement mentioned in the parish profile.

If either the bishop or the parish representatives refuse to accept the person proposed by the patron, the patron may request the archbishop to review the matter. The archbishop may overrule the bishop and the parish representatives, and authorise the patron to make an offer to the person he proposes.[8]

Usually however the patron will try to find somebody else acceptable to the bishop and the parish representatives.

(e)   If the position remains vacant for nine months

This process may go on for some time, with the patron suggesting other names to the bishop and the parish representatives. After nine months the right to choose the new parish priest passes from the patron to the archbishop.[9]

If the bishop refuses to approve the patron's choice, and the patron appeals to the archbishop, the time while the archbishop is considering the matter does not count as part of the nine months. But if the patron's appeal is against the decision of the parish representatives, the nine months' time limit is not extended.

The archbishop writes to the parish asking for a copy of the written summary of the conditions, needs and traditions of the parish, and any other matters which the parish would like the archbishop to consider.

The archbishop consults the bishop, the parish representatives, and any other persons who in his opinion can also represent the views of the parishioners, and then decides who should be appointed.

4.   SUSPENSION OF PRESENTATION

Where a bishop is considering reorganising the parishes in his diocese, he may not wish to appoint a new parish priest to a parish when a position becomes vacant. If the bishop appoints a new parish priest, the parish priest could be in the parish until he retires, which could hinder the bishop's ideas for reorganising his diocese. The bishop may prefer to appoint instead a *priest-in-charge*, which is like a fixed-term contract, meaning that the bishop can bring the priest's appointment to an end if he wants to.

If the bishop wants to appoint a priest-in-charge rather than a new parish priest, he can *suspend the right of presentation*[10] No new parish priest can be appointed to the parish when the right of presentation is suspended. The bishop can suspend the right of presentation for up to five years, and he can renew the suspension for up to five more years. After ten years, if the parish has not been reorganised as part of some pastoral scheme, a new parish priest should be appointed. In practice, if this stage is reached, the bishop will ask the patron to confirm that the priest-in-charge may now be appointed as parish priest. If the patron and the PCC were involved in the selection of the priest-in-charge, there is usually no problem about this. But if the diocese has appointed someone without consulting the patron, this could lead to a serious embarrassment for the diocese. So it is as well for the diocese to work with the patron and with the parish in selecting a suitable person to be priest-in-charge.

The bishop should inform the PCC why he is considering exercising his right of suspension. The PCC can ask to see the bishop to discuss the matter. This will give the PCC an opportunity of explaining to the bishop the sort of person they would like to be appointed as priest-in-charge, if that is what the bishop decides to do.

Suspension of presentation gives the church a chance to change the way a parish or a group of parishes is organised. In legal terms it is very different from the freehold, but it has no impact on the everyday life of the priest and the parishioners. So it is quite all right to refer to a priest-in-charge as 'the vicar' when speaking about him or her. The only time it really matters is in formal legal documents.

5.   TAKING THE INITIATIVE

When a parish knows that its parish priest is about to retire, there is much to be said for starting work on the task of finding a successor before the formal procedure begins. Contact should be made with the patron and with the bishop, for advice and suggestions as to possible candidates, and to establish good relations. Soundings can be taken from the congregation and from all contacts available to the members of the church. Discreet visits can be made to a church where a possible candidate is currently serving, to obtain a 'feel' of the church. Work can begin on the preparation of the parish profile. Your object should be to find the best-qualified candidate, and to obtain a match between his gifts, skills and talents and the needs and requirements of your particular parish. The more time and effort you put into this, the more likely you are to find the right person.

6.   HOW TO PREPARE THE PARISH PROFILE

The diocese of Guildford suggests the following headings to include in the parish profile.[11]

(a)   the benefice/parish

Describe its location, geography, social mix, age-groups, development, provision for work, shops, sense of community, focal points, housing development. Mention schools, colleges, rest/nursing homes, day centres, and hospitals.

(b) churches and halls

Briefly describe the churches in the parish, when built, outstanding features, state of repair, halls, any other church properties.

(c) church services

State the times and types of services, the rite used (Book of Common Prayer, Evensong, informal family service), and average attendance. Weekday services. Mention clergy dress, churchmanship, traditions, styles of music, degree of formality.

(d) other members of the team

Mention curates, non-stipendiary ministers, readers, retired clergy, lay people. What do they all do? Do you employ anybody?

(e) parish organisations

Fellowships, clubs, study groups, social activities, parish days, retreats, choir and musical activities.

(f) work with other parishes

Shared work with neighbouring parishes.

(g) ecumenical links

Your Christian neighbours, relationships and meetings with them.

(h) parish support

Secretarial, office, payment of parish expenses etc.

(i) financial state

Are you meeting the quota, stewardship renewal, building appeals etc.?

(j) the rectory/vicarage

A brief description.

(k) vision/mission statement

If your parish has produced such a statement, it should be included.

(1)   *the parish's needs and the person you are looking for*

- Review the ministry of your outgoing parish priest, and list the strengths and weaknesses of that ministry.
- Review and list the strengths and weaknesses of your church's life and ministry. Include all the activities of the church, and its policies such as outreach, relations with secular organisations, ecumenical relations, marriage and baptism.
- Identify what your church needs to address.
- Identify whom you have available involved in this work, and those who might be.
- List in order of priority what particular parts of that work will need the active participation of your new priest.
- List the spiritual gifts, the personal characteristics, the skills and abilities your new priest will need to do the work that you believe lies ahead.

The profile may be quite lengthy if it includes all this material. Select the most important facts and produce a shorter version that can be given to initial enquirers. The full statement of needs will be sent to all firm applicants.

7.   AN EXAMPLE

The parish priest of St John's decided to accept an offer to move to a new parish. The bishop wrote to the secretary of the St John's PCC, inviting the parish to prepare a written summary setting out the conditions, needs and traditions of the parish, and asking the PCC to appoint its two representatives. The PCC met, and agreed the following statement.

The Parish of St John's, [Address]

St John's is a small parish of less than 4,000 inhabitants, just to the south of .... road. Its boundaries are ... to the north, ... to the south, ... to the east, and .... to the west. It is in the ...... deanery.

Much of it is bed-sit territory, thus attracting the lonely, and all the problems inherent with the anonymity of a crowded area. It is a renowned area for homosexual and heterosexual prostitution, and there is a great deal of drug trafficking. However, owner-occupation is increasing and there are a number of people in our congregation who have lived in the locality for years. Because our church building is in a prominent position we attract passers-by of every nationality, and we feel we have a particular mission to these people.

We are looking for:

1.   A God-centred man of prayer, with a deep regard for the sacraments and a sense of occasion when taking services.

2.   Middle-of-the-road churchmanship, with sound theology and doctrine (i.e. believes in the resurrection), awareness of our liturgical heritage, preaches the gospel, able to encourage and direct spiritual awareness.

3.   Preferably married, with children, able to encourage and expand Junior Church.

4.   A good communicator, discreet listener and efficient administrator, with pastoral skills and a sense of mission to the people of this area whether regular worshippers or not.

5.   Finally, it would help if he had a sense of humour and a diversity of interests.

Many parish profiles could only be filled by the Archangel Gabriel. To seek all the qualities listed in the profile of St John's was probably unrealistic. It is important to describe the parish, its churchmanship, and its specific needs, but to seek additional qualities which every parish wants – some of the ones listed in paragraph 4 of the profile – is unnecessary and may even be unhelpful. One wonders too whether the requirement for a family man was suitable in an area full of both heterosexual and homosexual prostitution, and drug trafficking.

The churchwardens were chosen to be the parish representatives. A meeting between the churchwardens, the bishop and the patron took place, and several names were discussed. Correspondence continued over several months. No agreement was reached on the person to be appointed.

Nine months later a formal letter arrived from Lambeth Palace addressed to the secretary of the PCC. The letter said that the right to appoint an incumbent had now passed to the Archbishop of Canterbury. The letter asked the PCC to send to Lambeth Palace a copy of the PCC's statement describing the conditions, needs and traditions of the parish, and to mention any other matters which the PCC wished the Archbishop to consider.

The PCC sent its statement to the archbishop, and discussions took place between the archbishop's office and the parish representatives. Within three months the archbishop's office had found a suitable person to fill the vacancy, and the parish representatives agreed to his appointment. The archbishop then offered him the position, and he accepted.

8.   RUNNING THE CHURCH DURING THE VACANCY

The churchwardens with the PCC are responsible for maintaining the life of the church. The churchwardens have the responsibility:

- to provide for the services of worship and the continuation of the pastoral care of the church.
- to pay all the costs involved in these church services.
- to take care of the vicarage and any other property of the parish.
- to collect certain fees payable by law, and account for them to the diocesan office.

(a)   Collecting fees

The churchwardens and the rural dean are appointed *sequestrators*. This means they have to account to the bishop for any money which would normally have been received by the parish priest. This covers fees for marriages, funerals, burials, erection of monuments in the churchyard, certificates of baptism and searches in parochial registers. It also covers any income from trusts. Dioceses normally permit retired priests to keep the fees for any marriage or funeral service they take, but all other income should be paid to the diocesan board of finance.

The main fees payable by law as from 1 January 1998 are set out below:[12]

MARRIAGES	£	FUNERALS	£
Publication of banns	13.00	Service (in church, cemetery or crematorium)	61.00
Certificate of banns, if required	8.00	Burial in churchyard following on from service in church	111.00
Marriage service	122.00	Burial in churchyard on a separate occasion or without service in church	133.00
		Burial certificate, if required	8.00

BAPTISMS	£	MONUMENTS	£
There is no fee for a service of baptism		These normally range from £11.00 to £94.00 depending on the type and size of the monument required	
Certificate of baptism, if required	8.00		

SEARCHES IN REGISTERS, ETC.	£
For the first hour (inclusive of one copy of an entry in certain registers)	12.00
For each subsequent hour or part of an hour	10.00
Additional copies of entries	12.00

(b) Church services

The churchwardens and the rural dean arrange for visiting clergy to conduct Sunday services, baptisms, weddings and funerals, and pastoral visits as necessary. It is not always necessary to continue all the midweek services, particularly if similar services are available in neighbouring parishes.

In theory, three services should take place in every parish church every Sunday: Holy Communion, Morning Prayer and Evening Prayer.

An informal 'Service of the Word' or family service may be used instead of Morning Prayer or Evening Prayer, and this may be combined with the Holy Communion service. As explained in Chapter 9, 'Church Services', in practice many churches do not hold all three services every Sunday. Indeed, in the country, where a priest is often responsible for several churches, it is impossible for him to fulfil this requirement.

Even if your church does normally have three services on a Sunday, during a vacancy it may be impossible to continue to do this. Churchwardens should discuss with the rural dean what number of services should be held. A priest is essential for a Holy Communion service, but if no priest is available a reader or the churchwardens may lead the congregation in Morning or Evening Prayer. Further details on how to do this are in Chapter 9, 'Church Services'.

Churchwardens should decide who is to be responsible for locking and unlocking the church, and preparing it for services. This will include preparing the order of service, selecting the hymns and lessons, and appointing the lesson readers. When there are visiting clergy someone should be responsible for meeting and welcoming them, introducing them to the congregation, and where appropriate ensuring that they are offered hospitality. Especially in rural areas, where a small church may not have a lavatory or washing facilities, and the visiting priest may have had to travel some distance, some thought should be given to his or her needs in this respect. It is especially important for visiting clergy that a prepared order of service is available. These matters also apply for weddings, funerals and baptisms.

(c)   Payment for church services

Visiting clergy are entitled to be reimbursed their travelling expenses. Usually fees are only payable to retired clergy and to members of religious orders. Careful records should be kept of all these expenses and fees, so that the sums can be reclaimed from the diocese in due course.

(d)   PCC meetings

It is important that these continue throughout the interregnum in the normal way. In normal life the chairman of the PCC is the parish priest, and a lay member of the PCC acts as vice-chairman. In a vacancy, the vice-chairman of the PCC chairs the PCC meetings. The rural dean may be invited to attend meetings of the PCC.

(e)   The annual parochial church meeting

If the interregnum continues during the time of the annual parish meeting, the vice-chairman of the PCC chairs the annual parochial church meeting. The PCC should invite the rural dean or the archdeacon to attend. If a new churchwarden is appointed the vice-chairman of the PCC should inform the archdeacon and the diocesan secretary of the change without delay.

(f)   Care of the vicarage

In winter months, the churchwardens should ensure that water services are turned off, and all systems drained down professionally. The churchwardens are responsible for security, and for protecting the house from vandalism and squatting. On no account should any temporary occupation of the house be allowed or offered.

Minor repair expenses should be borne by the PCC. If more substantial work is needed, the churchwardens should obtain the permission of the secretary to the diocesan parsonages committee before having anything done.

The Ecclesiastical Insurance Group Parishguard Policy says that when a vicarage is empty, the Ecclesiastical Insurance Group should be informed within 30 days, the property should be fully locked, and it should be checked inside and out by someone responsible at least once a week.[13]

Some dioceses issue more detailed instructions as to what should be done about the vicarage, for example:

- whether or not electricity, gas and telephone services should be disconnected.
- what should be done about internal decorations or improvements.
- what expenses should be incurred for looking after trees and the garden.

- what should be done about regular maintenance such as checking gutters and drain pipes.

You should therefore contact your diocesan office for further information.

(g)   *Letting the vicarage*

Most types of property can be let on what are called *assured shorthold tenancies*, or, simply, *shorthold tenancies*.[14] There is no minimum fixed term for a shorthold tenancy, but the court cannot order a tenant to give up possession before the end of six months from the start of the tenancy.

For several reasons, this straightforward arrangement is not usually suitable for a vicarage during an ordinary interregnum.

First, it is not possible accurately to predict the length of an interregnum. If a priest is appointed it would be normal for him to give three months' notice to his existing parish, but there are occasions when he would like to move more quickly. In some cases he may be under pressure to vacate his existing house as quickly as possible.

Second, although a landlord is entitled to possession when the shorthold tenancy comes to an end, the tenant may not actually leave on the required date. If this happens, the diocese can only recover possession by getting a court order. Even booking a hearing at the county court can take a couple of months, and it usually takes at least another month after the hearing before the diocese recovers possession.

Third, there is the six months' minimum period. You can start your proceedings as soon as the lease has come to an end, but if a possession order is made, it cannot take effect before the end of the six months' period.

Fourth, you will probably need at least a month to get the property up to scratch so that it can be let, and then to find a suitable tenant.

Fifth, it is quite useful for the property to be vacant for a certain period, so that the parish can carry out any internal redecoration that it may feel able to do, and for the diocese to carry out internal repairs and improvements.

Sixth, there are technical legal difficulties under an ecclesiastical act of 1838[15] which need to be checked before any letting is made.

In short, letting the vicarage can cause a long delay in a new clergy appointment, add several months to an interregnum, and be a major nuisance. Some dioceses therefore have a policy of not letting the vicarage during an ordinary interregnum.

(h)   Confidential documents

The rural dean will normally take possession of any confidential documents relating to the parish or the parishioners held previously by the outgoing parish priest.

(i)   Weddings, banns, baptisms etc.

Put up a notice on the main notice board saying when and where arrangements can be made for weddings, banns and baptisms.

(j)   Funerals

Contact the local undertaker and tell him who to contact. Contact the rural dean if clergy are needed to assist.

(k)   Church registers

The church registers should be maintained during the interregnum. This includes entering in the register after each Holy Communion service the number who took communion. The priest taking each service should sign the service register.

(l)   Paying the quota

The quota is the parish's contribution to the cost of ministry in the diocese, and the parish should continue to pay it during a vacancy. The quota helps pay for the maintenance of the vicarage, for the stipends of visiting clergy, for the training of clergy and readers, and for a wide range of diocesan resources.

9.   THE INSTITUTION OF THE NEW PARISH PRIEST

The institution and induction service is a big event, and is usually followed by a party! The bishop conducts the service, and all the local dignitaries and senior clergy should be invited. After consultation with the bishop, invitations should be sent to:

- the bishop, the archdeacon, the rural dean.
- the lay chairman of the deanery synod, the diocesan secretary, and other diocesan and deanery officials.
- local authority representatives.
- local community leaders.
- and local leaders of other Christian denominations.

Notify the local press and radio, and arrange for a friendly welcome for reporters and press representatives.

10.   FURTHER INFORMATION

For general guidance on interviewing, see the section on the subject in Chapter 6, 'Employees and office holders'.

Hugh Balfour's *Whose Church is it anyway?* (Reform/St Matthias Press, 1997) ISBN 1 873166 31 1, contains several chapters describing the selection process for new parish priests. It is written from an evangelical standpoint, but there is much for people of other churchmanships. The chapter 'Searching Questions' contains suggestions for possible lines of questioning when the churchwardens are interviewing a candidate. The chapter 'Filling the gap – the legal position' contains many practical hints to help a parish find the best person for its needs.

Vacancy/Interregnum Pack (Diocese of Guildford, July 1996) gives advice on the conduct of interviews and suggests possible interview questions.

Tony Bradley, *Understanding the interregnum: Making judgements when kings move* (Grove Books, 1997) discusses the *potential* an interregnum offers a church. It is not a time to 'batten down the hatches', but a time to be used *constructively* until the new parish priest arrives.

Table of parochial fees (Church Commissioners, 1998).

THE CHURCH COMMISSIONERS
1 Millbank,
London SW1P 3JZ

Administry publishes two guides:

- *Choosing a new minister.*
- *Any questions?* (techniques for interviewing)

ADMINISTRY
PO Box 57,
St Albans,
Herts AL1 3DT

Tel: 01727 856370

---

[1] Strictly, the parsonage.

[2] The word *minister* also comes from Latin. *Ministrare* means *to serve.*

[3] Patronage (Benefices) Measure 1986, section 35.

[4] Patronage (Benefices) Measure 1986, section 7.

[5] The measure calls this a *statement.* An example is given on page 272.

[6] Patronage (Benefices) Measure 1986, section 11. If the PCC has previously passed a resolution saying it would not accept a woman priest, it can now pass a resolution saying that the earlier resolution shall no longer have effect, and that a woman priest would now be acceptable. For details concerning resolutions A and B under the the the Priests (Ordination of Women) Measure 1993, see Chapter 3, 'The PCC'.

[7] Patronage (Benefices) Measure 1986, section 12.

[8] Patronage (Benefices) Measure 1986, section 13.

[9] Patronage (Benefices) Measure 1986, section 16.

[10] See Section 67 of the Pastoral Measure Act 1983, and the Pastoral Measure 1983 Code of Practice.

[11] *Vacancy/Interregnum Pack* (Diocese of Guildford, July 1996).

[12] See the Parochial Fees Order 1997, and the *Table of parochial fees*, prepared by the Church Commissioners. This sets out what part of the fee goes to the parish priest, and what part to the PCC. There is a new Parochial Fees Order each year.

[13] Parishguard Policy, page 7 (special provision – unused property extension).

[14] See the Housing Act 1988 section 19A (inserted by the Housing Act 1996 section 96).

[15] The Pluralities Act 1838. An incumbent or the bishop can recover possession of a non-shorthold letting only if the property is actually required for a clergy appointment, and that appointment is then made. If the interregnum arises during the process of pastoral reorganisation, there may be no appointment. *If no appointment is made, the court can grant possession back to the evicted tenant.* Another technical difficulty under the 1838 Act is that it is essential that the ownership of the property is transferred from the benefice into diocesan glebe, before the letting is made. This process takes six to eight weeks.

Chapter 18

LOTTERIES AND OTHER MATTERS

1. INTRODUCTION

This chapter covers a number of important topics. They are all quite short, which is why they are together in this chapter.

2. LOTTERIES

I am not going to write about whether or not a church should run a lottery. I am just going to draw attention to the law on lotteries, so that churches know the rules which govern them if they decide to hold one.

A lottery is a scheme for giving out prizes by lot or chance. They are governed by the Lotteries and Amusements Act 1976 and the National Lottery Act 1993.

PART II.   CHURCH LIFE

(a)   Small lotteries held as part of a fete or similar event

You can hold a lottery as part of a bazaar, a sale of work, a fete, a dinner, a dance, a sporting or athletic event, or some other entertainment. The following rules apply to such lotteries.[1]

- All money taken at the event after deducting expenses should go to charity. (The church, of course, is a charity.)
- You can claim up to £250 for the cost of the prizes.[2]
- You are not allowed to give money as a prize.
- You should only sell tickets at the event itself, not elsewhere.
- You should not sell tickets before the event.
- The name of the winner should be declared during the course of the event, and only at the event, not elsewhere.
- The lottery should not be the main attraction at the event.

So you can hold a raffle or a tombola as part of the church annual fete, as long as you keep to these rules.

(b)   Other types of lottery

A church wanting to hold any other form of lottery needs to be registered with the local authority to hold what is known as a *society's lottery*. If you are going to sell more than £20,000 worth of tickets for one lottery, or if you are going to sell more than £250,000 worth of tickets over a year, the church will also need to be registered with the Gaming Board. There are detailed rules for society's lotteries.[3] Before running a society's lottery, you should discuss with the diocesan secretary the policy issues. If you decide to go ahead, you will also need to take legal advice from the diocesan registrar.

3.   BOOKING OF CHURCHES AND CHURCH HALLS BY OTHER ORGANISATIONS

Sometimes a church or church hall is booked for a concert or jumble sale, and later it is needed for a service or some other church event. This could lead to a claim being made against the church by the disappointed organisers of the event which has had to be cancelled. The claim could be the cost of hiring another place at short notice. It could be much more than this, with additional expenses being claimed, or the profits which the organiser hoped to make.

There should be a proper booking system in place to try to prevent a clash of this nature happening. But there is a further precaution which churches should take, and that is to make sure that the terms of any booking state clearly that the church may cancel the booking if it needs the church or church hall itself, subject only to returning any booking fee which has been paid. If the booking agreement says this, then there is no chance of any other claim being made against the church if the booking has to be cancelled.

A properly drawn up booking agreement should also permit the hirer of the church or church hall to cancel the booking for any reason. The agreement should say what notice has to be given if the booking fee (or a proportion of the booking fee) is to be returned.

The Ecclesiastical Insurance Group Parishguard Policy gives you the option of taking insurance cover for errors and omissions leading to legal liability.[4] The example the policy gives is the 'double booking' of two wedding ceremonies. You do not need to pay for this if you take the precautions I describe.

4.   PLAYS, CONCERTS, AND EXHIBITIONS OF FILMS AND PICTURES IN CHURCHES

Where any church is to be used for a play, a concert, or an exhibition of films or pictures, Canon F 16 says that the parish priest has to take care that the words, music and pictures are suitable for showing in a church.

The canon also reminds parish priests that they should consult the local authority before allowing such events to take place, to check that fire escape arrangements and any other health and safety requirements are satisfactory. This includes having public liability insurance to cover the event.

A public entertainment licence may be required for a function in a church hall, but is not required for a musical event in a church. If a public entertainment licence is required, you have to give at least 28 days' notice to the local authority in order to get one.

A licence from the licensing justices will be needed if alcohol is to be sold at the event.

5. MUSIC AND DANCING AT CHURCH FUNCTIONS

If there is going to be music and dancing at the function, and the public are to be admitted, then you may need a public entertainment licence from the local authority. You do not need a public entertainment licence for music in a place of worship or at religious meetings. You might for an event in the church hall. You should contact the local authority to find out whether they consider you need a public entertainment licence for the event you want to hold. If they say you do need a licence, they will tell you how to obtain one. You will need to give the local authority at least 28 days' notice.

6. ANIMALS

(a) Cattle and sheep

The parish priest has a right to graze his sheep or cattle or any other farmyard animal in the churchyard. In rural areas this can be a major help to the problem of maintaining churchyards.[5]

(b) Dogs

Parishioners have a right to attend their parish church for public worship, so long as there is room. But they have no right to bring a dog with them into church, unless it is a guide dog for the blind. PCCs and parish priests can therefore choose whether or not to allow dogs to be brought to church.

If someone comes to church with a dangerous-looking dog, and the sidesman is worried about the safety of the other members of the congregation, the right thing to do is to refuse permission for the dog to be brought into the church. If this leads to a disturbance, the churchwardens should either escort the dog and its owner out of the church, or summon the police to do so.

(c)   *Bats and other protected species*

Bats are a protected species under the Wildlife and Countryside Act 1981.[6] You are not allowed to kill, injure, disturb or move protected species; and you should not damage or destroy, or obstruct access to, a place they are using for shelter without permission to do so.[7]

This rule does not apply to bats found in the living area of a house,[8] but it does apply to bats and other protected species found in churches. Despite the saying *bats in the belfry*, bats generally prefer areas which are more sheltered, less noisy, and less affected by the weather. They are usually found in small cracks and crevices, or hanging upside down in the open, under the roof, or in the eaves. If you have a problem with bats you should contact English Nature, who will inspect the church, and give you advice and permission to do whatever should be done.[9]

The headquarters of English Nature is

ENGLISH NATURE
Northminster House,
Peterborough PE1 1AU

Tel: 01733 455000

There are also regional offices. In London, the address is

ENGLISH NATURE
Ormond House,
26–27 Boswell Street,
London WC1N 3JZ

Tel: 0171 831 6922

The Council for the Care of Churches publishes a free leaflet on bats which gives useful information on the subject: *Bats in Churches* by Tony Mitchell-Jones (Council for the Care of Churches, 1987).

7.   SANCTUARY

From early Anglo-Saxon times, criminals and debtors could seek refuge in a church. When they were there, they were not allowed to be arrested and taken from the church against their will.

The right of sanctuary was swept away in 1624 by a statute which said:

> by the authority of this present parliament, That no Sanctuary or Privilege of Sanctuary shall be hereafter admitted or allowed in any case.[10]

Sanctuary does not appear in England again until this century.[11]

The modern sanctuary movement originated in America in the 1970s. By the mid 1980s hundreds of churches had declared themselves to be public sanctuaries for Central American refugees who were fleeing from violence and torture at home. The first public church sanctuary in Britain was in 1985, and there have been over a dozen cases since. The most famous is that of Viraj Mendis who took sanctuary in a church in Manchester from December 1986 until January 1989, when police officers and immigration officials used sledgehammers and hydraulic equipment to enter the church and remove him. More recently, the Ogunwobi family lived in Downs Baptist Church in Hackney, East London for three years, to avoid deportation to Nigeria. After a campaign involving the church congregation, the local council and various civil rights leaders, in July 1997 the family was allowed to remain here.[12]

Although some churches continue to offer sanctuary to illegal immigrants, they may be committing a crime by doing so. Under the Immigration Act 1971[13]

> a person knowingly harbouring anyone whom he knows or has reasonable cause for believing to be either an illegal immigrant or a person who has committed an offence under section 24 (1) (b) or (c) above,[14] shall be guilty of an offence, punishable on summary conviction with a fine … or with imprisonment for not more than six months, or with both.

'Harbouring' means giving shelter to someone. No church has yet been prosecuted for this offence. Churches should only think of offering sanctuary while attempts are made to change a decision of the Home Office refusing the family concerned the right to stay. Sanctuary should be offered only as a last resort, in cases where:

- there is a well-grounded fear of persecution, or
- there is a serious threat to family life, or

- there has been some basic denial of justice or compassion to the person or family wanting to stay in this country.

The risk of prosecution is increased if churches offer employment to asylum seekers while also giving them sanctuary. As I explained in Chapter 6, 'Employees and office holders', it is a criminal offence to employ a person who is not entitled to live or work in the United Kingdom.[15]

---

[1] See the Lotteries and Amusements Act 1976, section 3.

[2] See the Exempt Entertainments (Variation of Money Limit) Order 1993, SI 1993 No. 3222, article 2.

[3] The Lotteries Regulations 1993, SI 1993 No. 3223.

[4] Parishguard Policy, page 25.

[5] Timothy Briden and Brian Hanson, *Moore's Introduction to English Canon Law*, 3rd edn. (Mowbray, 1992). pages 88 and 93 (note 10).

[6] See the Wildlife and Countryside Act 1981 Schedules 5 and 6.

[7] See the Wildlife and Countryside Act 1981 section 9.

[8] See the Wildlife and Countryside Act 1981 section 10 (2) and 10 (5).

[9] The Wildlife and Countryside Act 1981 section 16 refers to the Agriculture Minister and the Nature Conservancy Council as the appropriate authority to deal with protected species. The Nature Conservancy Council is now known as English Nature, and it is English Nature that deals with bats in churches.

[10] 1 Jac. I c. 28, s.7 (1623–4).

[11] For a full description of the early law of sanctuary, see Baker, J.H. 'The English law of sanctuary' (1990) 2 Ecc LJ 8, and Teresa Field. 'Biblical influences on the medieval and early modern English law of sanctuary' (1991) 2 Ecc LJ 222. For the modern history, see Teresa Sutton. 'Modern sanctuary' (1996) 4 Ecc LJ 487. (Teresa Field became Teresa Sutton when she married.)

[12] See 'Sanctuary family given right to stay', *The Times*, 4 July 1997, page 6, 'Family can stay in UK', *Church Times*, 11 July 1997, page 5.

[13] Section 25 (2). Section 25 (1) has been extended by the Asylum and Immigration Act 1996, but section 25 (2) is not altered by the 1996 Act.

[14] 24 (1) (b) refers to someone who stays longer than he has been allowed. Section 24 (1) (c) refers to seamen and aircrews who come to England temporarily while employed on a ship or aircraft, and then stay after their ship or aircraft leaves.

[15] Asylum and Immigration Act 1996, section 8.

Part III

Church Property

Chapter 19

SECURITY

1. INTRODUCTION

Some four hundred fires happen in church buildings in England each year. Some of the fires are small, but others cause damages costing many thousands of pounds. Smoke from a small fire can cause major damage to decorations and furnishings far from the scene of the fire, and water used to put out the fire can itself cause further damage. Each year, about one in four churches suffers from theft or vandalism. This chapter sets out some of the steps you can take to protect your church. This chapter also looks at the personal security of the parish priest, his family, and others involved with the church.

2. BASIC STEPS

The Ecclesiastical Insurance Group issues a questionnaire entitled *How secure is your church?* The questionnaire covers 16 steps which the Ecclesiastical Insurance Group recommend to churches. The recommended steps are as follows:

- Have a responsible person in the church whenever it is open.

This is by far the most important security step any church can take. Leaving a church open during the day makes it a target for vandals,

especially in urban areas. Someone responsible should always be there.
This can be done by a rota of people. Churches should always be locked
at night.

- Keep the vestry locked, and don't 'hide' the key in the church.

  The vestry is an obvious target for thieves.

- Have chimneys and flues swept and inspected each year.

  A fractured flue or dirty chimney is a real fire risk. Inspection of the
  chimney is not usually part of a maintenance contract with a heating
  engineer, so you should discuss this with the church architect, and then
  make sure that it is done.

- Take special care with portable heaters.

  These, too, are a major fire risk. Keep them at least 3 feet from
  anything which could catch fire. Paraffin and oil fired heaters should
  never be used, even as a temporary measure. Calorgas heaters are OK if
  they have a guard, and you keep an eye on them.

- Take extra care when workmen are in the buildings.

  Workmen can easily start a fire. They should be shown the position
  of fire extinguishers and how to use them. Smoking should not be
  allowed in the church. The church should be inspected at the end of
  every day. Ladders should be put away under lock and key so that they
  cannot be used by intruders.

- Keep the gates locked at night.

  This prevents cars being driven close to the church, and is a deterrent
  to theft.

- Have the lightning conductor professionally checked at least once
  every five years.

  A lightning conductor system which is not in perfect order is a
  positive danger, because lightning will be attracted to the terminals, and
  then will not be able to go down to the earth. They should be examined
  and tested by a competent specialist firm, in line with the Code of
  Practice for earthing BS 7430: 1991.

- Have fire extinguishers in the church, and make sure they are inspected regularly.

For general use, water type extinguishers are best. There should also be a carbon dioxide type near the organ and the mains electric distribution board. Check every month to see if they have been used or damaged, or have been moved from where they should be kept. They should be serviced every year.

Small churches should have at least two, medium size churches should have three, and large churches should have four or more extinguishers in the main area of the church.

In addition, a fire extinguisher should be in the boiler house, and the kitchen should have both a fire extinguisher and a fire blanket.

- Train people to use them.

The parish priest, the churchwardens, PCC members, all staff, and as many responsible members of the congregation as possible should know how to use them.

- Keep inflammable materials such as matches, candles, oil, incense, charcoal, white spirit and petrol locked up.

They are a temptation to arsonists.

- Stop visitors going where smoking can take place unseen.

- Have all electrical wiring professionally checked every 5 years.

Numerous church fires are caused by faulty electric wiring or apparatus. Only electrical contractors enrolled with the National Inspection Council for Electrical Installation Contracting (NICEIC) should be employed for work in churches.

You should also check that the fuse boxes are clean, dry, and dust free. Make sure that the right fuses are to hand when needed, and that you keep a good supply of spares.

- Switch off all electrical circuits when not in use.

- The electrics in the organ and blowers should be inspected regularly.

A professional organ builder should carry out the inspection, and the electric organ blower and humidifying apparatus should be examined by an electrical engineer. Organ lights should be installed so that there is no danger of them setting fire to timber or music sheets if they are accidentally left on. The recommended trade practice is to inspect organ blowers and humidifying apparatus every six months.

- Valuables should be kept in a secure place.

All items such as silver or brass candlesticks should be locked away, as should small carpets and valuable pieces of small furniture when not in use.

- Internal doors should be kept closed if possible.

This prevents a fire spreading.

---

3.   RISK ANALYSIS QUESTIONNAIRE

The following questionnaire is designed to help you work out the risks of damage, loss and injury.

It is meant to show you any areas where you need to take action or advice. It is not meant to take the place of expert risk evaluation or advice, which you can obtain from specialists in security or insurance, or from the police and fire brigade.

If the answer to any of these questions is No, you should take action to put things right.

	Yes	No	N/A

General

1. Have you taken advice from the police, fire brigade and/or the security industry? ☐ ☐ ☐

2. Have you taken advice from the Archdeacon or inspecting architect? ☐ ☐ ☐

3. Have you carried out a risk evaluation survey and taken the action it recommended? ☐ ☐ ☐

4. Are staff/helpers warned to report suspicious behaviour? ☐ ☐ ☐

Building Security

5. Are your buildings in good repair and do they appear secure? ☐ ☐ ☐

6. Is damage, graffiti etc. quickly made good to stop copycat acts? ☐ ☐ ☐

7. Is the boundary clearly marked and in good repair? ☐ ☐ ☐

8. Have you cut down any foliage that can give cover to trespassers? ☐ ☐ ☐

9. Have you lit up any areas that can give cover to trespassers? ☐ ☐ ☐

10. Do you lock all gates, doors, windows and skylights when the buildings are not in use? ☐ ☐ ☐

11. Have you taken steps to stop access to the roof from neighbouring buildings, walls, downpipes etc.? ☐ ☐ ☐

12. Are all tools and ladders locked away when not in use? ☐ ☐ ☐

13. Has a burglar alarm system been fitted by an installer approved by NACOSS?[1] ☐ ☐ ☐

14. Is the burglar alarm system linked to the police via a central monitoring service? ☐ ☐ ☐

		Yes	No	N/A
15.	Is the burglar alarm operated only by people you have chosen and trained?	☐	☐	☐
16.	Is the burglar alarm regularly inspected and serviced?	☐	☐	☐

Keys and Locking Up

17.	Do you strictly control the issue of keys, and keep a list of names of those who have them?	☐	☐	☐
18.	Is there an established procedure for locking up?	☐	☐	☐
19.	Do you check to ensure that no-one is concealed in the buildings or in the grounds before locking up?	☐	☐	☐
20.	Do you routinely check security fittings such as locks and bolts from time to time?	☐	☐	☐
21.	Are occasional users of the building properly briefed on locking-up procedures?	☐	☐	☐

Security During Open Hours

22.	Is a responsible person always present during open hours?	☐	☐	☐
23.	Do you make sure that there is only one way in to the building?	☐	☐	☐
24.	Is it possible to check the arrival and departure of visitors?	☐	☐	☐
25.	Are visitors prevented from entering private areas without permission?	☐	☐	☐

Security Outside Open Hours

26.	Are the buildings routinely locked outside open hours?	☐	☐	☐
27.	Is the outside of the building lit at night?	☐	☐	☐
28.	Is the building clearly visible to neighbours and passers by?	☐	☐	☐

	Yes	No	N/A
29. Is there a caretaker or someone else easy to contact?	☐	☐	☐
30. Can that person quickly obtain the services of police /fire brigade /security company?	☐	☐	☐

Theft

	Yes	No	N/A
31. Do you have somewhere secure and /or a locked safe for valuable items?	☐	☐	☐
32. Is your property marked, listed in an inventory, and photographed?	☐	☐	☐
33. Do you display 'property marking' signs to deter thieves?[2]	☐	☐	☐

Fire

	Yes	No	N/A
34. Does the congregation know where all the fire exits are?	☐	☐	☐
35. Are all the aisles and passageways leading to exits clear?	☐	☐	☐
36. Have you checked that all potential emergency exits are easily opened and that the locks work freely?	☐	☐	☐
37. Is the heating system regularly serviced?	☐	☐	☐
38. Are any portable heaters placed where they do not block access to exits?	☐	☐	☐
39. Are any portable heaters placed at least 1 metre from furnishings?	☐	☐	☐
40. Are electrical installations in good condition?	☐	☐	☐
41. Are all electrical sockets protected by residual current devices not exceeding 30 mA?	☐	☐	☐
42. Is your lightning conductor regularly inspected, and tested every 5 years?	☐	☐	☐
43. Are all inflammable materials e.g. petrol, paraffin, candles etc. securely stored?	☐	☐	☐

PART III.   CHURCH PROPERTY

		Yes	No	N/A
44.	Are cleaning rags impregnated with wax polish kept in a container with a metal lid and locked up?	☐	☐	☐
45.	If fire alarms are fitted, are they tested each week?	☐	☐	☐
46.	When the building is empty, do you carry out a fire security check?	☐	☐	☐
47.	Are the recommended number of fire extinguishers positioned where they are easily seen and immediately available?	☐	☐	☐
48.	Are fire extinguishers regularly maintained?	☐	☐	☐
49.	Is there a notice by the main entrance giving the names and addresses of key holders?	☐	☐	☐
50.	Is there a notice by the main entrance saying where the nearest telephone to call the emergency services is?	☐	☐	☐

---

4.   PERSONAL SECURITY

The most important advice on security is to have a responsible person always present when the church is open. A duty rota could be drawn up and kept in a suitable place (out of the public view). There are many older people who would be willing to give up an hour for such a reason. The personal security of those serving on the duty rota should be considered, especially in the case of older people. Older people should never be asked to guard the church alone. It may be right to issue personal alarms. A telephone should be available: a portable phone should be considered.

Security is also important when dealing with casual callers. It is not unusual in London to find at the vicarage, church, or parish office door, young people asking for or even demanding money. They are sometimes drunk or on drugs, sometimes mentally ill, often with no-one else to turn to. Others are homeless and asking for a bed.

300

There are both pastoral and practical things to think about when caring for the casual caller. These are fully considered in *Knocking at Heaven's Door*, a report by Christian Action and Response in Society made in 1996. A booklet with the same title is also available giving a summary of the full report. *Knocking at Heaven's Door* suggests that local churches should decide whether they should simply give information to casual callers, or whether to give further help such as food and money.

Each church should always have a printed list of resource centres to hand, so that it can be given to callers. This should list local shelters, social security offices, the psychiatric social worker, the emergency social worker, the Citizen's Advice Bureaux, Alcoholics Anonymous, CRUISE, and Relate. Keep the list by the inside of the main door to the church.

Knocking at Heaven's Door gives helpful advice concerning security:

- Consider installing at the vicarage, the church and the church office some of the following: spy-holes in the door, door-chains, panic buttons, personal alarm, visible security alarm, mobile phone, security mirrors, entry-phone, video-entry-phone, security lighting, window locks, double glazing, even a dog!
- If you have a porch, it needs good lighting. Provide a seat and interview people there. Keep the door to the house locked. If you think the seat may be stolen, fasten it to the floor.
- Be cautious about letting strangers in. If you consider there is any risk, keep them out of the family home, and interview them on the doorstep.
- If leaving the door to use the phone, lock the door with the caller outside.
- Be careful before interviewing on your own, whether in the church, parish office, or the vicarage. If possible ensure that someone else is in earshot and within reach of a telephone.
- If you become anxious when you are with a caller, listen carefully, avoid sudden movement or change in attitude, appear calm, give a sense of security and ensure that boundaries are clear. Avoid physical contact. It is lawful to use self-defence if it is reasonable, but the best

course of action is escape. Make an excuse to leave the room to get a drink for yourself or the caller.

- If you feel in danger, call 999 and ask for the police. Remember that help can take up to 20 minutes to arrive.
- All incidents where there are any problems should be recorded, however minor.
- Records should also be kept of all dealings with casual callers, noting the name of the person, the time and date, the request made, and the help offered.
- Agree this policy with the PCC.

Knocking at Heaven's Door recommends additional security measures which should be taken by what it describes as special caring projects, that is churches and organisations with a special ministry to the homeless and other people needing help.

5.   DO YOU NEED A FACULTY?

Faculties are considered fully in Chapter 20, 'Repairs and maintenance'. In general, before you carry out any major repairs or changes to a church building, either inside or outside, or its furniture, you need to obtain permission, known as a faculty, from the diocese. Before you install burglar alarms, security lights, or any other security devices in your church, contact the archdeacon, who will tell you what the form is for your diocese. Some dioceses are more strict than others about the need for a faculty for ordinary security devices.

6.   SECURITY PROCEDURES FOR CHURCH FUNDS

The subject of theft of church money by those inside the church, and how best to prevent this, is dealt with in Chapter 4, 'The Treasurer'.

7.   FURTHER INFORMATION

Geoff Crago and Graham Jeffery, *Safe and Sound? A guide to church security* (Church House Publishing, 1996).

Church Security (Diocese of Chichester, undated). This excellent 35-page book was sponsored by the Ecclesiastical Insurance Group. It contains advice from the Staffordshire and Sussex Police, and from the Sussex and Kent Fire Brigades.

Knocking at Heaven's Door, a report by Christian Action and Response in Society (CARIS) made in 1996. A booklet with the same title is also available giving a summary of the full report, though it does not list all the security recommendations made in the full report.

Clergy Security: a discussion paper (Advisory Board of Ministry, 1998, available from diocesan offices). This new report urges parishes to take the safety of their priests seriously.

Lighting your Church (Church House Publishing, 1997).

Wiring your Church (Church House Publishing, 1997).

ECCLESIASTICAL INSURANCE GROUP
Beaufort House,
Brunswick Road,
Gloucester GL1 1JZ.

Tel: 01452 528533.

The Ecclesiastical Insurance Group publishes a series of guidance notes for churches.

- *Guidance Notes for Churches. Section 1: Fire*
- *Guidance Notes for Churches. Section 2: Security*
- *Guidance Notes for Churches. Section 3: Health and Safety*
- *Guidance Notes for Churches. Section 4: General*

For a summary of their contents, see pages 352–3.

THE CRIME PREVENTION OFFICER OF YOUR LOCAL POLICE STATION.

THE FIRE PREVENTION OFFICER OF YOUR LOCAL FIRE STATION.

ENGLISH HERITAGE
23 Savile Row,
London W1X 1AB

Tel: 0171 973 3000.

Fax: 0171 973 3001

PART III.   CHURCH PROPERTY

THE COUNCIL FOR THE CARE OF CHURCHES
Fielden House,
Little College Street,
London SW1P 3SH

Tel: 0171 222 3793.

Fax: 0171 222 3794

THE FIRE PROTECTION ASSOCIATION
Melrose Avenue,
Borehamwood,
Herts WD6 2BJ

Tel: 0181 207 2345.

Fax: 01452 423557

LOCAL DIOCESAN ADVISORY COMMITTEES.

THE INSTITUTE OF BRITISH ORGAN BUILDING
49 Chelmsford Road,
Woodford,
London E18 2BW

Tel: 0181 559 7477

NATIONAL APPROVAL COUNCIL FOR SECURITY SYSTEMS (NACOSS)
Queensgate House,
14 Cookham Road,
Maidenhead,
Berkshire SL6 8AJ

Tel: 01628 37512

---

[1] The National Approval Council for Security Systems.
[2] Property marking means putting your postcode and the number of the building or part of the name onto an object. You can use an ultra-violet pen, engraving, a ceramic marker, punching dies, or chemical solutions.

Chapter 20

REPAIRS AND MAINTENANCE

1.   INTRODUCTION

C hurch repairs and maintenance is a big subject, involving both practical skills and legal requirements. The practical side needs no introduction, but the legal requirements may be new to you. They fall into two parts: the duty to inspect and report on the state of the building at regular intervals, and the need to obtain a formal permission known as a faculty for all but the most minor repairs.

2.   PRACTICAL POINTS ON REPAIRS

(a)   Essential repairs

Some problems require immediate attention. A broken step leading up to the church, or a leaking gas fire, are a danger to the public. Broken windows affect the security of a building. A broken water pipe needs to be repaired urgently. A slipped slate on the roof should be replaced to avoid water getting into the church. These and similar small repairs should be put in hand without delay. Each diocese issues guidance as to what items can be carried out without the need for a faculty, and such items as these usually fall within this category. If you have any doubt, a telephone call to the archdeacon or the diocesan surveyor will confirm whether or not you can go ahead immediately.

(b)   Routine maintenance

The following are typical items of routine maintenance.

- Gutters and downpipes should be cleaned out twice a year – more if trees are nearby.
- Central heating systems should be inspected every year.
- Lightning conductors should be inspected and tested every 5 years.
- Fire extinguishers should be inspected every year – check ones near cookers and fires more often.

- The electrics in the organ and the humidifying apparatus should be inspected every six months.

(c)   Churchyards

(i)   Wildlife and flowers

Some churchyards are full of wild flowers and other plants. *The Churchyard's Handbook* by Peter Burman and Henry Stapleton (Church House Publishing, 1988)[1] gives details for the management of churchyards with this in mind, and has the following suggestions:

- Do not cut the grass in May or June when most of the churchyard species will be in flower.
- At the end of the season (early October) grass can be cut quite short.
- All areas rich in flowers should be raked after cutting.
- Try to prevent the build-up of coarse tussocks of grass.

Even if the PCC does not want to encourage wildlife in all parts of the churchyard, it should be allowed to grow in at least some areas.

Churchyards are also of importance for lichen conservation. Many churchyards have well over 100 species on walls and tombstones. Some lichens are protected species under the Wildlife and Countryside Act 1981[2], but these protected species are very rare, and most unlikely to be found in churchyards.[3]

For advice on lichens and their conservation, contact

THE SECRETARY, THE BRITISH LICHEN SOCIETY
c/o Botany Department,
The National History Museum,
Cromwell Road,
London SW7 5BD

Tel: 0171 938 9123

(ii)   Buried treasure and other finds

Using a metal detector without the consent of the Secretary of State in a place which is of archaeological importance is a criminal offence. Churches which are in use do not count as monuments under the Ancient Monuments and Archaeological Areas Act 1979.[4] So it is not an offence for a person to use a metal detector in the churchyard of a parish church which is in regular use.

Under the Treasure Act 1996 *treasure* normally refers to coins or precious metal at least 300 years old.[5] If a person finds treasure, it should be reported to the coroner within 14 days. If the find is indeed treasure, it then belongs to the Crown. The Crown may make an award to the finder of the treasure, and may also make an award to the landowner – in the case of the parish church, the parish priest.[6] There is a code of practice covering the making of awards. This may be obtained from:

DEPARTMENT OF NATIONAL HERITAGE
2–4 Cockspur Street,
London SW1 5DH

Tel: 0171 211 6000

If the object found is not treasure, and the true owner cannot be found, it belongs to the church (technically, to the parish priest) if it is attached to or is in the land, and also if it is simply lying on the surface of the churchyard.[7]

(d)   Trees

Every PCC has the responsibility for the care of the trees in the churchyard, which are among its traditional features.[8] This responsibility extends to the planting of trees as well as to every aspect of their maintenance and, ultimately, their felling.

Many local authorities employ a tree officer,[9] who should be able to give advice as to the safety of a tree in a churchyard, and as to the type of maintenance work required. Where necessary the PCC may wish to take advice from a tree consultant or a tree surgeon. There is a directory of tree consultants and tree surgeons maintained by the Arboricultural Association, which is a registered charity concerned with tree care. The address is:

THE ARBORICULTURAL ASSOCIATION
Ampfield House,
Ampfield,
Near Romsey,
Hants SO51 9PA

Tel: 01794 368717

Each diocese is supposed to issue written guidance to PCCs on the care of trees in churchyards.

There are statutory restrictions against cutting down, topping, lopping, uprooting or damaging trees in churchyards which are in conservation areas. There are also restrictions where a tree is subject to a tree preservation orders. Registers of tree preservation orders and conservation areas are kept by the local planning authorities. Where this applies, the PCC should obtain the consent of the local authority before doing any work on a tree. The only exception is where a tree is dying, is already dead, or has become dangerous.[10]

Any PCC wishing to plant a tree should consult the archdeacon before purchasing the tree. A tree planted in an unsuitable place may prevent the building of an extension to the church at some time in the future, or the roots may interfere with the foundations or the fabric of the building.

Trees should be inspected every five years as part of the quinquennial inspection. This is in fact obligatory in the case of any tree which is subject to a tree preservation order.

(e)   *Electrical installations*

All contractors engaged to carry out electrical installations should be enrolled with the National Inspection Council for Electrical Installation Contracting (NECEIC).

NATIONAL INSPECTION COUNCIL FOR ELECTRICAL INSTALLATION
CONTRACTING (NICEIC)
Vintage House
37 Albert Embankment
London SE1 7UJ

Tel: 0171 582 7746

PART III.   CHURCH PROPERTY

All work should be up to the standards set by current electrical regulations. The Council for the Care of Churches publish two books on the subject: *Lighting your church*, and *Wiring your church*. These replace the now out-of-print publication *Lighting and Wiring of Churches*.

(f)   Gas safety and inspection

The Gas Safety (Installation and Use) Regulations 1994[11] apply to gas installations in buildings owned by the church. Under these regulations the PCC and the parish priest should make sure:

- that gas pipework is easy to recognise. New gas pipework is yellow.
- that nothing which runs on gas is used if it is in a dangerous condition.
- that the gas supply is shut off if gas escapes, and that the supplier is notified.
- that gas appliances and installation pipe-work are maintained in a safe condition.
- that they are inspected every year.
- that a record of the inspection is kept for two years.
- that any work to gas fittings should be carried out only by a competent person, that is, someone recognised as such by the Health and Safety Executive.

Horror stories abound in newspapers of gas accidents. All churches with gas installations are covered by the 1994 regulations. Every PCC should make sure that all gas appliances in the church are properly serviced every year by a CORGI[12] registered gas installer, and that a record of this is kept. Church halls and other church property should also be checked and serviced in the same way.

THE COUNCIL FOR REGISTERED GAS INSTALLERS (CORGI)
1 Elmwood, Crockford Lane,
Chineham Business Park,
Basingstoke, Hampshire RG8 8WG

Tel: 01256 372300

(g) *Cold weather*

Quite a lot of country churches do not have any water at all. But for churches that do, PCCs may not realise how easy it is to protect their buildings from having a burst pipe in the winter. In 1996 the Ecclesiastical Insurance Group published a very helpful leaflet called *The cold weather code for churches.* This covers:

- what to do before the cold weather arrives: what sort of lagging and insulation to use for pipes and tanks.
- what to do overnight during winter: leave some heating on, and leave loft trap doors open.
- what to do if pipes or tanks have frozen: turn off the water at the stopcock, and how to thaw out the pipes.
- what to do if a pipe has burst.
- how to dry out the system.

The full text is printed in Appendix 5.

3. INSPECTIONS AND REPORTS

(a) *Churchwardens' annual inspections*

Every year the churchwardens should discuss the state of the building with the parish priest, and should:

- inspect the building and articles belonging to it, or arrange for them to be inspected.
- make an annual fabric report to the PCC. The word *fabric* means the building itself – stones, bricks and mortar, but the report should also cover the contents of the building. So, for example, the purchase of a computer system and photocopier are items for the fabric report. The report should say:
  * what repairs were carried out in the previous year.
  * which of these repairs were recommended by the church architect in the quinquennial report.
  * what repairs the church intended to carry out in the previous year, but did not in fact carry out.
  * which of these outstanding repairs were recommended by the church architect in the quinquennial report.

- make sure that all repairs and other building works which have been carried out to the church over the previous year have been entered up in the church's log book.

The fabric report is presented to the PCC at the meeting before the annual parochial church meeting. The PCC can change the report, and it is then given to the annual parochial church meeting.

(b)   Five-yearly (quinquennial) inspection and report

Every five years the inspecting architect makes a report on the state of the church building. The report will usually list urgent works, works of a less urgent nature, and longer-term points for future planning and budgeting.

The quinquennial report should also cover the churchyard, the state of the boundary walls, and any movable article of outstanding architectural, artistic, historical, archaeological or monetary value. It will deal also with any tree which is subject to a tree preservation order.

The quinquennial report is every churchwarden's dread, but it can be a great help in deciding what repairs are urgent, and what can be left for a little while. For those churchwardens whose skills lie in other areas, the quinquennial inspection is a vital health check on the state of the building. In at least one diocese[13] the inspecting architect pays a visit to the PCC some weeks after the report is published to discuss how it will be handled. This extra visit is all covered in the quinquennial inspection fee paid by the diocese.

Even though the quinquennial report recommends an item of repair the PCC still needs to obtain a faculty before doing it (unless it is a minor repair which does not need a faculty).

(c)   Articles of enquiry, and archdeacon's visitations

Every year the diocesan office sends to the churchwardens of every parish a set of forms asking questions about many aspects of church life in the parish. These questions are known as the archdeacon's *Articles of Enquiry*, and they should be answered in time for the *archdeacon's visitation*, which is the formal occasion when new churchwardens take up their position as an officer of the bishop. For a description of what happens at a visitation, see Chapter 2, 'The Churchwardens'.[14]

Some of the questions in the articles of enquiry relate to repairs. So, for example, the articles of enquiry in use in the diocese of Blackburn in 1997 has the following item:

CHURCH BUILDINGS

In what year was the last quinquennial inspection?

Have the recommended repairs been

    (i)   completed?

    (ii) more than half completed?

    (iii) less than half completed?

    (iv) not started?

The articles of enquiry for the diocese of London in 1997 asks about the repairs mentioned in the quinquennial inspection report. It asks about gutters and drainpipes. It asks whether any alterations have been done and whether a faculty was obtained before doing them. It asks whether the inventory has been checked, and what records are kept of church key holders.

(d)   Archdeacon's inspections

Canon F 18 requires each archdeacon to inspect every church in his area at least once every three years, either in person or by the rural dean.

The quinquennial inspection is an occasion when the state of the building is professionally inspected. The archdeacon's inspection covers a lot more than just the state of the building. It is a time for the archdeacon to check that the church administration is being run properly. The archdeacon is likely to want to check all church records, to ask about finance, to check that valuables have not gone missing, as well as checking that the gutters and downpipes are working properly.

One handbook for archdeacons[15] describes the archdeacon's inspection as covering four headings.

(i)   Church records

This includes:[16]

- service records.

- baptism, marriage, and burial registers.
- the terrier and inventory.
- the electoral roll.
- the minute book of the PCC meetings and of the annual parochial church meetings.

(ii)   Church finance

- annual church accounts.
- insurance policies.

(iii)   Church contents

- church plate.
- other valuables such as stained glass and monuments.
- photographs of any items of value, for use in case of an insurance claim.
- altar linen.

(iv)   Church building and churchyard

- the quinquennial inspection report.
- the church log book.
- copies of all faculties obtained for work done in the church.
- any grave-space plan for the churchyard.
- gutters and down pipes.
- checking on security.

The archdeacon will want to inspect the church if any major works or repairs are proposed. So will members of the diocesan advisory committee when their advice is sought about a proposed faculty application.

4.   FACULTIES

(a)   Why bother?

A church is a place of worship, not a museum. Some Christians (and, sadly, even some clergy) consider that because this is so, they should be free to do what they like to their church buildings. They consider that the need to obtain a faculty is an unbearable interference with this freedom, and with the work of the Holy Spirit.

There are four reasons why such people are wrong in their thinking.

(i)   The alternative is control by the local planning authority

If the Church did not exercise control over church buildings, the local planning authority would do so. Surely Christians rather than non-Christians should be the judges of what should be done to church buildings.[17] Some changes to churches involve very difficult issues of churchmanship and theology, and such issues would not be properly appreciated by the secular planning authorities. The plain fact is that most architecturally important buildings have to obtain listed building consent before they are altered. The church is privileged, because it does not have to do this. Instead, churches have to obtain a faculty from the diocese. This is a delicate issue in the relationship between the Church and the State. If parish priests and PCCs do not obtain a faculty before carrying out alterations and major repairs to a church building, the Church of England will lose its privilege of being able to decide what should happen to its own property, and church buildings will become controlled by the State.

(ii)   Advice from the diocesan advisory committee

One of the first stages in the faculty process is to discuss your proposals with the diocesan advisory committee. (The diocesan advisory committee is often referred to as the DAC.) The job of the diocesan advisory committee is to *advise.* First of all its advice is usually sought informally by PCCs and anybody else who is applying for a faculty. Later, it gives advice to the chancellor on whether or not it considers the faculty should be granted.

The diocesan advisory committee is very well qualified to give advice. It has members with knowledge of the history, development and use of church buildings, Church of England liturgy and worship, architecture, archaeology, art and history. These members of the DAC give their services free, as their offering to the church. No one church is likely to have available such expertise within its own congregation. The DAC is there to help you, and to offer *helpful* advice on your proposals, free of charge.

(iii)   *The legitimate interests of the community*

The community as a whole has an interest in the care of churches, as part of our national heritage. The church building may remain for centuries, for many future generations to enjoy. It is right that bodies such as English Heritage should be consulted before, for example, unique examples of Jacobean woodwork are removed from a church. In some cases, even if English Heritage is against a proposal, a faculty may be granted.[18]

·(iv)   *The need for church laws*

Rules and laws are necessary for the church to do its work,[19] and are there to be followed. Church laws assist the church to follow Christ, and to carry out His mission in the world. The Holy Spirit can work through church laws; some would even say, despite them. As one Roman Catholic writer said, 'there should be no opposition between the *charismatic* [his italics] and the juridical[20] elements in the Church'.[21]

On a practical level, the faculty rules protect the church's property from the whim of a parish priest or the PCC. For example, someone may give a pair of candlesticks to a church in memory of a departed relative. If no faculty is obtained, the next parish priest might take a dislike to them, take them out, and put in some he liked better, and the originals would have no protection.

So, please, do not regard the need to get a faculty as red tape, or as something which prevents you running your church the way you want to run it. The Holy Spirit works through it all. And if your parish priest wants to go ahead with some building works without applying for a faculty, you should stop him, and contact the archdeacon without delay. Do not be afraid, or think you are telling tales.

Where work has been done *without* a faculty, the PCC should apply without delay for a *confirmatory faculty*. If the archdeacon and the DAC approve of what has been done, and there is no opposition to what has been done, the chancellor is likely to authorise the works which have already been carried out. But he does have power to order the church to be restored to its previous state: in one case, a church hall which had been built without a faculty had to be pulled down.[22]

316

So, do check with the archdeacon, and apply for a faculty whenever one is required.

(b)   *When is a faculty needed?*

You need a faculty for almost anything you do in a church building. You need a faculty for any repair to your church building, and any changes or additions to it. You need a faculty for any changes to its contents, for bringing in new items such as an electric piano or a new carpet, and for removing existing items. And you need a faculty for any alteration or new addition to your churchyard or to land adjoining your church building.

The faculty rules apply to all consecrated churches and churchyards. They do not apply to other properties which may be owned by the PCC, and which are not on consecrated land, or to the vicarage.

Very minor items of everyday maintenance and repair do not need a faculty. The chancellor of each diocese publishes written guidance as to what he considers falls within this rule. You should make sure you have a copy of it.

Any change to the building or its contents not mentioned in the chancellor's guidance *probably* requires a faculty. You should discuss it with the archdeacon before doing it. He can and often does authorise items to be carried out without the need for a formal faculty, if they are within the spirit of the chancellor's guidance. But if he has any doubts about what you are proposing, he will ask you to apply for a faculty.

During my time as churchwarden we were fortunate in not having to carry out any major repairs. But we did do some pretty major changes, and obtained faculties for the following variety of items:

- the moving of a large stone font from one position in the church to another.
- the erection of a notice board to advertise an *Alpha* course.
- the removal of the choir stalls.
- the removal of the Victorian pews and replacing them with chairs.
- the installation of an office, a kitchen and lavatories.
- a new gate for the car park.

PART III.   CHURCH PROPERTY

We also acquired various items of computer equipment and a photocopier for the church office. The computer equipment and the photocopier fell within the spirit if not the letter of the chancellor's guidance as to things which did not need a faculty.[23]

(c)   Trivial matters which do not need a faculty

As mentioned, in each diocese the chancellor consults with the DAC and then issues written guidance to PCCs, parish priests and churchwardens. This guidance sets out the matters which the chancellor considers to be of such a minor nature that they may be done without a faculty.

The guidance varies from diocese to diocese, but the ones I have seen have many items in common. Chancellors do change their guidance from time to time (after consultation with the DAC) to reflect the needs of their diocese. So make sure you have the latest version. The list is sometimes known as the *de minimis* list: this name comes from the legal phrase *de minimis non curat lex* meaning *the law does not concern itself with trifles.*

Examples of the sort of items which are likely to be covered in a *de minimis* list are the following.

- Cruets.[24]
- Vases.
- Kneelers, hassocks and cushions.
- Vestments and choir robes.
- Authorised service books.
- Hymn books, song books, bibles, and choir and organ music.
- Replacement of altar linen.
- Temporary decorative banners.
- Furniture in church halls.
- Furniture and furnishings in vestries.
- Fire extinguishers.
- Small display stands and book cases.
- Replacement of carpets or curtains..
- Routine repairs and maintenance up to a certain financial limit: in 1998 the limit is often £500 or £1000 plus VAT.

- Routine tuning and minor repairs to the organ.
- Routine repairs to the bell ropes, bell-frames, and pulleys.
- Routine maintenance of church clocks.
- Purchase and maintenance of lawnmowers and other churchyard equipment.
- Routine maintenance of paths.
- Repairs to notice boards.

Some lists are very brief, others go into quite a lot of detail. It is not always easy to decide whether what you want to do requires a faculty, or whether it is covered by the *de minimis* list. For example, a *de minimis* list might say that minor roof repairs do not need a faculty; but how many tiles make a *major* repair? If you have any doubt about the matter, contact the archdeacon, who will either say that you do not need a faculty, or will tell you to apply for one.

(d)   Churchyards

The faculty rules apply to churchyards as well as to church buildings. No faculty is needed for a person to be buried in a churchyard,[25] though a faculty is needed if a person wants to reserve a particular plot to be buried in. In practice, faculties relating to churchyards are normally for monuments and headstones to be relocated, and for kerbstones to be removed. Useful guidance can be found in *The Churchyard's Handbook*.

The chancellor issues guidance on the care of churchyards, and what type of monuments may be put up without the need for a faculty. It is the parish priest's responsibility to ensure that these guidelines are followed. If a proposed monument falls outside the guidelines the parish priest tells the relatives of the deceased that they will need to apply for a faculty.

Some families like to plant a tree in a graveyard in memory of the person who has died. No faculty is needed to plant a tree, but as it will be for the PCC to look after the tree, they should agree to it being planted.

(e)   *Temporary alterations*

There is a special informal system to deal with temporary changes. The archdeacon can give permission for up to 12 months for any changes inside a church as long as no structural work to the building is needed. So, for example, at the church where I was churchwarden, when we were considering removing the Victorian pews and replacing them with chairs, the archdeacon used this procedure. He suggested that we remove the front three rows as a temporary measure, to see whether we liked the result, before we applied for a full faculty. We did this, and a year later we applied for a faculty to remove the rest of the pews.

(f)   *How to obtain a faculty*

1. The first step is to make outline plans and proposals, and for the parish priest and churchwardens to discuss them within the standing committee and then the PCC. Ask the church architect for advice, and possibly for a sketch plan. It is a good idea to inform the archdeacon of your ideas at this early stage.

2. It is often helpful next to have an informal meeting with the DAC. Contact the DAC secretary who will arrange a time. It may be that the local planning authority, national amenity societies, English Heritage, the Council for the Care of Churches or English Nature will have an interest in the proposals.

3. You will then know whether the DAC is likely to object to what you propose, and what their views are at this stage. To go ahead and produce detailed plans[26] before discussing your proposal at least in outline with the DAC may be a huge waste of time and money.

4. The PCC should be asked to pass a resolution agreeing to what is proposed. The PCC should also consider how it is going to pay for the work, as it will have to mention this in the application for a faculty.

5. The DAC will then send you a faculty application form. Complete the form and send it back with all necessary specifications, plans, drawings, illustrations, photographs, written approval by the

320

Ecclesiastical Insurance Group for any proposed electrical works, and any other important documents.

6. The DAC merely gives advice, to you and to the chancellor. It does not actually grant you permission, nor can it refuse permission. That is for the chancellor to do. The DAC will send you a certificate which:

   - may recommend the proposal.
   - may be neutral, and say that the DAC does not object to the proposal.
   - may be against you, and not recommend the proposal.

   If it does not recommend your proposal it will tell you why.

7. Even if the DAC recommends your proposal you still have to apply for a faculty. The chancellor sees the views of the DAC, but he forms his own judgment, and he may grant you a faculty even if the DAC does not recommend the proposal.[27]

8. The diocesan registry will send you a 'Form of Petition'. This is the faculty application. Fill it in carefully, and return it to the registry, together with the same plans and diagrams that you sent to the DAC.

9. You should then put a notice called a *citation* on the church door for at least 14 days. This should include one Sunday when the church is used for worship. In some cases the diocese will ask you to put the notice up for 28 days. The citation tells people that you are applying for a faculty, and says that any person who wishes to object should write to the registrar within 21 days. The registrar then writes to any objectors sending them a form to fill in on which they set out the grounds of their objection.

10. If no objections are received, and if the DAC recommends the work, a faculty will usually be granted straight away.

11. If objections are received, the chancellor will decide how to proceed. A very small number of cases end up in what is known as a *consistory court*, with people giving evidence, and the chancellor giving his judgment at the end. In most cases, there is no need for people to give evidence in court. In those cases the chancellor can

321

decide whether to grant a faculty after reading written arguments from each side. This is usually much more convenient.

In straightforward cases the whole process will probably take three to four months from start to finish, and this should be taken into account when planning the work. If the proposals are objected to, and a court hearing is needed, the process is likely to take a lot longer and can be very expensive.

(g)   An example

Alpha is the name of a ten week-course which is used by many churches in England and abroad. In 1995 the church where I was churchwarden decided to run an *Alpha* course, and put up a big wooden board outside the church to advertise it. The PCC did not realise that a faculty would be needed for this. Various neighbours complained to the diocesan office, and the registrar said that we should apply for a faculty if we wanted to keep it there.

We prepared drawings and photographs, and sent these to the DAC, who had no objection to our proposal. We put up a citation on the notice board. Several people gave notice of objection. Many people said that we had enough notice boards already in the church grounds. One person said the message on the board was meaningless. Another person complained that we had put up the board already before applying for the faculty. Someone else said that the board would be up continually, even when an *Alpha* course was not running.

Then the chancellor wrote to us asking us whether we would agree to the sign being exhibited for not more than nine days at a time on three occasions during the year, to coincide with the timing of the *Alpha* courses. If we agreed, the chancellor would then write to the objectors asking if they would agree to this.

We agreed, the objectors agreed also, and the chancellor granted a faculty in accordance with her suggestion. She commented:

> As a satisfactory outcome has now been achieved I am granting a faculty in the terms already indicated. It is however essential that the time periods are not exceeded and I am placing the full responsibility for this on the Churchwardens as it is in matters of this kind that they should relieve the Incumbent of

responsibility. I am sure they will be meticulous so that there can be no cause for complaint. A record of the date should be kept in case of any query.

A satisfactory outcome following an inspired suggestion from the chancellor.

5.   PLANNING PERMISSION

Planning permission may be needed for works affecting the *outside* of the church building, or for change of use of part of the church, or for works in the churchyard. Planning permission is not required for any alterations *inside* a church (apart from a change of use).

6.   GRANTS AND LOANS

There are a number of grant-making bodies. The diocesan office or the archdeacon should be able to give you details of the main public bodies and of any local charities. Local authorities are allowed to give money for the repair of historic buildings, and there is also English Heritage and the Heritage Lottery Fund.

English Heritage and the Heritage Lottery Fund have a joint scheme for offering grants. Under the joint scheme

> churches must be of *significant heritage interest* to be considered for grant. Those which are not listed and are outside conservation areas are unlikely to be eligible.

A PCC can opt to apply only for English Heritage funding if it has objections to receiving Lottery Funds. English Heritage is more restricted in the grants it makes, and only covers funding for major and urgent repairs to the historic fabric of Grade I and Grade II listed buildings. The Lottery Fund covers both structural and non-structural repairs (e.g. churchyard monuments, gates and organs) and covers new facilities such as lavatories or catering spaces.

In other words, there is much more money available from the Lottery Fund, and it has a much wider use.

Full details of the Joint Grant Scheme: *Guidance Notes for Applicants* can be obtained from

PART III.   CHURCH PROPERTY

ENGLISH HERITAGE

Tel: 0171 973 3434

   or

THE HERITAGE LOTTERY FUND

Tel: 0171 947 2032 and 0171 947 2034

Two other possible sources of funding are the Historic Churches Preservation Trust and the Incorporated Church Building Society. They share the same address and telephone number. Application forms are available from the Secretary.

THE HISTORIC CHURCHES PRESERVATION TRUST
Fulham Palace,
London SW6 6EA

Tel: 0171 736 3054

THE INCORPORATED CHURCH BUILDING SOCIETY
Fulham Palace,
London SW6 6EA

Tel: 0171 736 3054

There are also over thirty county historic churches trusts and various other independent charities raising money and helping to repair churches and chapels. A list of addresses is given in Appendix 6.

7.   SAFETY

The Construction (Design and Management) Regulations 1994 apply to any major building project carried out by the church. Under these regulations the PCC has to appoint and pay for a planning supervisor, whose job is to look after the health and safety aspects of the project design and the initial planning. Full details are in Chapter 23, 'Safety'.

8.   FURTHER INFORMATION

The Council for the Care of Churches publishes a wide range of specialist and general booklets on conservation and the care of churches and churchyards. The most useful ones are the following:

Topic	Title
Adaptations	*Church Extensions and Adaptations* (1996)
Bats	*Bats in Churches* (1987)
Bells and bell-frames	*Code of Practice/Conservation of Bells and Bell-frames* (1993)
Churchwardens	*The Churchwarden's Year* (A calendar of maintenance) (1989)
Churchyards	*The Churchyard's Handbook* (1988)
Cleaning	*Handle with Prayer* (Church Cleaner's notebook) (1992)
Clocks	*Clocks, Turret: Guidelines for Repair/Auto Winders* (1996)
Fire precautions	*Fire Precautions Guide* (1992)
Floors	*Church Floors and Floor Coverings* (1992)
Glass	*Repair and Maintenance of Glass in Churches* (1991)
Heating	*Heating your Church* (1996)
Inspection and repair	*A Guide to Church Inspection and Repair* (1995)
Lighting	*Lighting your Church* (1997)
Lightning	*The Protection of Churches Against Lightning* (1988)
Log book	*The Church Log Book* (1996)
Looking after your church	*How to Look after your Church* (1991)
Looking after your church	*Looking after your church* (video) (1991)
Loose stones	*Architectural/Fragments in Churches* (1985)
Organs	*Repair/Replace? A guide for considering the future of organs* (1990)
Plate	*Care of Church Plate* (1991)
Redecorating	*Redecorating Your Church* (1986)
Roofing	*Church Roofing* (1988)
Security	*Safe and Sound: A guide to Church Security* (1996)
Sound	*Acoustic Treatment of Places of Worship* (1981)
Sound	*Sound Amplification in Churches* (1990)

PART III.   CHURCH PROPERTY

Topic	Title
Stonework	*Mortars, Plasters and Renders in Conservation* (1984)
Terrier and inventory	*Church Property Register* (1995)
Textiles	*Guidelines for the Care of Textiles* (1984)
Tourism	*Helping the Stones to Speak* (1989)
Wall paintings	*Conservation of Wall Paintings* (1986)
Wildlife	*Wildlife in Church and Churchyard* (1995)
Wiring	*Wiring your Church* (1997)

COUNCIL FOR THE CARE OF CHURCHES
Fielden House,
Little College Street,
London SW1P 3SH

Tel: 0171 222 3793.

Fax: 0171 222 3794

---

[1] A new edition is in the course of preparation, for publication in 1998.

[2] Wildlife and Countryside Act 1981 Section 13 and Schedule 8.

[3] I am grateful to Mr Donald Smith, the British Lichen Society representative for Yorkshire and Lancashire, for this information.

[4] Ancient Monuments and Archaeological Areas Act 1979, section 61 (8).

[5] The definition of treasure in section 1 of the Treasure Act 1996 is quite complicated. This is a simplification.

[6] See Mark Hill, *Ecclesiastical Law* (Butterworths 1995), page 101.

[7] This assumes that the PCC had been exercising control over the churchyard by looking after it properly: see *Waverley Borough Council v Fletcher* [1996] QB 334.

[8] Care of Churches and Ecclesiastical Jurisdiction Measure 1991 section 6.

[9] Known as an arboricultural officer.

[10] See generally the Town and Country Planning Act 1990 sections 198 and 211.

[11] As amended by the Gas Safety (Installation and Use) (Amendment) Regulations 1996 and the Gas Safety (Installation and Use) (Amendment) (No 2) Regulations 1996. For further details, see *Legal Opinions concerning the Church of England* (Church House Publishing, 1994 plus 1997 supplement) page 136a (1st supplement).

[12] The Council for Registered Gas Installers.

[13] In the East Riding of Yorkshire.

[14] Page 20.

[15] Hugh Buckingham, *Oculus Episcopi: a handbook for new archdeacons* (1997, privately published, available from the House of Bishops Training Committee), page 32. Hugh Buckingham is the archdeacon of the East Riding.

[16] See Chapter 24, 'Church Records', for a more complete list.

[17] See 1 Cor. 6: 1–6.

[18] For example, *Re St Helen's, Bishopsgate* (1993) 3 Ecc LJ 256.

[19] Both the Catholic Church and the Church of England are in agreement on this issue. For the Catholic position see James Coriden, *An Introduction to Canon Law* (Paulist Press, 1991), pages 5–6; for the Church of England position, see the *Report of the Archbishops' Commission on Canon Law* (SPCK, 1947), page 5.

[20] 'Juridical' means 'legal'.

[21] *The Christian and Canon Law*, by George Lobo, quoted in Jordan Hite and Daniel Ward, *Readings, Cases, Materials in Canon Law. A textbook for ministerial students* (Liturgical Press, 1990), page 30.

[22] My source for this information is Mr Roy Martin, the synodical secretary for the diocese of London. The parish concerned was in the diocese of Chichester.

[23] Item 2 under the heading Furniture and Fixtures in the guidance for London: Introduction of furniture and furnishings and minor fixtures (excluding wall safes) in vestries.

[24] Cruets are the glass or precious metal bottles in which the wine and water used for Holy Communion are brought to the altar.

[25] Strictly, provided the person was a parishioner, or on the electoral roll, or a person who died in the parish.

[26] If you are planning a major scheme of alteration, your plans will have to be properly prepared by an architect, and you will need to allow for the cost of this in the overall cost of the scheme. See *Re St George the Martyr, Holborn* (1997) 5 Ecc LJ 67. The case concerned a listed church, but the principle is surely not limited to such churches.

[27] See George H. Newsom and George L. Newsom, *Faculty Jurisdiction of the Church of England*, 2nd edn. (Sweet & Maxwell, 1993). page 45. Or the chancellor can overrule the DAC's objections as to particular items, as in *Re St Helen's, Bishopsgate* (1993) 3 Ecc LJ 256. In that case the DAC's objections to alterations to the south transept were overruled by the chancellor (see pages 67–69 of the judgment). The chancellor was also in favour of a new window, even though the DAC were divided on the subject (see page 74 of the judgment).

Chapter 21

INSURANCE

1.   INTRODUCTION

There were 88 serious church fires in England in the 10-year period from January 1985 to December 1994. The estimated loss was over £33,000,000.[1]

Vandalism, theft, burglary and arson at churches are very serious problems. Up to 70 per cent of fires in churches are started deliberately. The other main causes of church fires are electrical faults and contractors. Currently one in four churches can expect an incident of vandalism, theft, burglary or arson each year. Fires of course vary in their size and damage. In the worst cases, all that is left of a church may be the four walls and the tower or spire.

PART III.   CHURCH PROPERTY

2.   ECCLESIASTICAL INSURANCE GROUP

Ecclesiastical Insurance Group insure about 95 per cent of the 16,000 Anglican churches in the United Kingdom. Their profits from church business are shared between many churches, including the Church of England. They are the only insurance company to advise their clients how much to insure for.

Many dioceses have arranged a group insurance scheme with the Ecclesiastical Insurance Group. Any PCC in the diocese may then subscribe to the scheme and pay a lower premium than if it negotiated directly with Ecclesiastical Insurance Group.

The Ecclesiastical Insurance Group's current standard policy for churches is known as its Parishguard Policy. Some churches are still insured under an older form of contract. The Parishguard Policy has been in use since 1996.

3.   HOW MUCH SHOULD YOU INSURE FOR?

PCCs should seek the advice of Ecclesiastical Insurance Group as to the right level of insurance for their church. The ideal, and most expensive option, is to insure the church for the costs of restoring it, in the event of its destruction, to its existing condition. This includes the cost of professional fees and other ancillary expenses, and the cost of hiring a substitute building for use during the rebuilding work.

In practice the Ecclesiastical Insurance Group knows that many PCCs prefer to pay lower premiums in return for a lower level of insurance. This can be done by insuring the church for the cost of a good modern replacement, rather than the cost of building an exact replica of the original church.

If a church is under-insured without agreeing this in advance with the Ecclesiastical Insurance Group, then in the event of a claim, you would receive only a proportion of your loss.[2] If the value of the church has been agreed in advance, then Ecclesiastical Insurance Group will pay out the full loss up to the limit you have agreed to.

Diocesan offices can usually give you information about what cover can be obtained for different levels of premium.

Most policies offer a reduced premium for a £100 excess on all claims. Higher voluntary excesses are available.

Some churches have valuable church treasures, such as silver, gold, and pictures, which are extremely expensive to insure for their full value. Also, the Ecclesiastical Insurance Group is likely to require extra security precautions in the case of such items. The PCC may decide that the cost of insuring these treasures for their full value could be better spent elsewhere. If so, they should insure these items for the value of a suitable modern replacement only, and they should explain to the Ecclesiastical Insurance Group that they are doing this.[3]

Another option is for valuable items to be locked up in the bank, and brought out on certain named days by arrangement. This should reduce the cost of insuring them.

4.   THIRD PARTY LIABILITY INSURANCE

Every PCC should take out insurance against liability for claims for injury by persons using the church, churchyard and church hall, and for injury suffered by any employees through their employment. The Ecclesiastical Insurance Group offers suitable cover for this as part of its Parishguard Policy.[4] The limit of indemnity should be not less than £2,000,000, as damages for personal injuries in a serious accident can reach this level.

The Ecclesiastical Insurance Group Parishguard Policy covers you for injury suffered by employees and also by voluntary workers. It covers you for injury suffered by anybody else (including children) in connection with your church business or activities anywhere in the British Isles.

The Parishguard Policy does not cover you for liability arising from any counselling or advice given by someone associated with your church to another individual.

PART III.   CHURCH PROPERTY

5.   CHECK LISTS

The check lists below cover questions which should be asked when considering insurance. They cover the main areas of insurance which churches need.

(a)   Property

- Are all risks covered?
- Is the sum insured sufficient? Is there index linking?
- Is the policy subject to *average*? This means, does it say that if the property is under-insured, you will recover only a proportion of your loss?
- Is there a regular review of values? Who undertakes this?
- Has the value of alterations and additions to a building been added to the last sum insured?
- If the PCC is the tenant of a property, what does the lease say about insurance?
- What limits does the policy have about contents? For example, the Parishguard Policy only gives cover for £2,000 for office equipment, unless you have agreed a higher figure.

(b)   Fire

- Are the contents properly valued?
- Is cover on an *indemnity* or a *replacement* basis? That means, if the building is destroyed will the insurance company pay you the market value of the building, or what it costs to rebuild it (which may be much more than its market value)? The Parishguard Policy is on a replacement basis – they pay the cost of repairs up to the limit of the sum insured. The same applies to contents.
- Is there a reinstatement clause in the policy? That means, do you *have* to rebuild the property with the insurance money following a claim? In the Parishguard Policy, the answer is No.
- Is the cost of rebuilding properly calculated? Are site clearance costs and professional fees covered?
- Does the policy cater for additional risks such as storm, flood, burst pipes and impact damage? In the Parishguard Policy these are covered.

332

- Is there cover for consequential loss? This means loss of income while a property is being repaired. An example would be church hall bookings. The Parishguard Policy provides cover for this.
- If the PCC is the tenant of the property, what does the lease say about insurance?

(c) Theft and financial loss

- Does the policy cover cash? The Parishguard Policy gives sufficient cover for most churches.
- Does the policy cover 'walk in' theft? The Parishguard Policy does.
- Is property on loan to the church covered? Under the Parishguard Policy, there is a small amount of cover for property which is on loan for an exhibition, a festival or an event. Otherwise, No.
- Can premiums be reduced by taking extra security precautions?
- Is there cover for property while it is off the premises? Under the Parishguard Policy there is cover for musical instruments and portable items up to £500 per item and £5,000 any one claim. Items removed for repair or while being taken to and from the bank are covered up to £1,000.
- What exclusions are there? For example, under the Parishguard Policy, theft from a car is excluded unless the items are hidden from view and the car properly locked.
- Is there cover for fraud and dishonesty? Under the Parishguard Policy, there is cover for up to £10,000 provided the loss is discovered quickly.

(d) Employer's liability

- Is the certificate of insurance displayed?
- Who is the legal employer? (Usually, the PCC).

(e) Public liability

- Is cover sufficient?
- Are disclaimer notices displayed (for example, a notice saying that all property is left at the owner's risk, and the PCC accepts no responsibility for cars or their contents left in the car park)?
- Does the policy cover risks to unpaid volunteers? Yes, under the Parishguard Policy.

- Does the policy cover negligent acts by a volunteer? Yes, under the Parishguard Policy, but not for counselling or advice.
- Is there a need for professional indemnity insurance? Probably not for most PCCs.
- Is there a need for personal accident policies? The Parishguard Policy provides a very small amount of cover for the clergy, church employees and volunteer workers. It also provides £5,000 life cover for these people.

(f)   Motor insurance

- Does the insurer know the uses to which the vehicles will be put?
- Is the cover adequate: comprehensive or third party only?
- Who is covered to drive the vehicles?

6.   PREVENTION IS BETTER THAN CURE

Chapter 19, 'Security', sets out steps which each church can take to minimise the risk of theft and fire.

Computer security is discussed in Chapter 12, 'Computers'.

7.   WHAT IF THE MONEY IS NOT THERE?

The PCC is under a duty to insure the church and other buildings in the parish, and the goods and ornaments of the church, against all usual risks. Strictly, this is not an absolute duty: the PCC should consider the other proper claims on its income as well as insurance, and if the money is not available from church funds, the members of the PCC are not obliged to pay the insurance premiums out of their own pockets.[5]

In practice, PCCs should regard insurance as of the highest priority. Insurance is likely to represent the second highest item in the church's expenditure, after payment of the diocesan quota. Any PCC unable to afford to insure the church building should discuss this with the archdeacon immediately.

Churches by law should have public liability insurance. They should also have employers' liability insurance if they have any employees.

8.   FURTHER INFORMATION

ECCLESIASTICAL INSURANCE GROUP
Beaufort House,
Brunswick Road,
Gloucester GL1 1JZ.

Tel: 01452 528533

Safe and Sound: A guide to church security, published by the Council for the Care of Churches.

Church Security, published by the diocese of Winchester.

Parishguard Policy, and advice leaflets concerning church security, available from the Ecclesiastical Insurance Group.

Parishguard Summary of Cover (Ecclesiastical Insurance Group, 1997)

The Ecclesiastical Insurance Group publish a series of guidance notes for churches.

- *Guidance Notes for Churches. Section 1: Fire*
- *Guidance Notes for Churches. Section 2: Security*
- *Guidance Notes for Churches. Section 3: Health and Safety*
- *Guidance Notes for Churches. Section 4: General*

For a summary of their contents, see pages 352–3.

---

[1] See Bryan Hunt's 'Fire precautions in places of public worship', a paper dated 7 November 1995 prepared for a conference in the St Albans diocese The statistics were compiled by the Ecclesiastical Insurance Group.

[2] In insurance law terms, this is known as the *rule of average.*

[3] If they do not agree this with the Ecclesiastical Insurance Group, they would be under-insured, and the Ecclesiastical Insurance Group would only pay out a proportion of any loss.

[4] Section 5 of the Ecclesiastical Insurance Group Parishguard Policy.

[5] The power to insure is in the Parochial Church Councils (Powers) Measure 1956 section 4 (1) (ii) b). The extent of the duty to insure is considered in *Legal Opinions concerning the Church of England* (Church House Publishing, 1994 plus 1997 supplement), page 152.

Chapter 22

CHARITABLE TRUSTS

Now it is required that those who have been given a trust must prove faithful.[1]

PART III.   CHURCH PROPERTY

1.   INTRODUCTION

Many parish priests, churchwardens and PCCs find themselves involved with a charitable trust related to their church. Money is sometimes left by a will to the PCC for charitable use in the parish. Some land may also be held on a charitable trust. The trustees need some knowledge of the rules about charities, so that these trusts are run properly.

2.   WHAT IS SPECIAL ABOUT A CHARITY?

A charity is a form of trust. The big advantage charities have over other forms of trust is that charities are exempt from income tax, capital gains tax, and inheritance tax. Charities are also exempt from paying rates. When a tax payer makes a gift to a charity using a four-year covenant or the Gift Aid scheme, the charity can add to the value of the gift by reclaiming tax at the basic rate from the Inland Revenue.

The other side of the coin is that charities are subject to certain rules to stop fraud. Most charities should be registered with the Charity Commissioners, and registered charities are subject to rules about the way they prepare their accounts.

3.   BECOMING A CHARITY TRUSTEE

(a)   Who can be a trustee of a charity?

Anyone over 18 years of age can be a trustee unless they:

- have been convicted of an offence involving deception or dishonesty.
- are an undischarged bankrupt.
- are disqualified from being a company director.
- or have been removed from being a trustee by the court or the Charity Commissioners.

If you are disqualified on one of these grounds, you should not act as a trustee unless the Charity Commissioners agree. If you act as a trustee without their agreement, you can be prosecuted.[2]

(b) *How do trustees get appointed, or retire?*

A charitable trust is usually set up by a trust deed, a will, or a scheme under the Charities Act 1993. Usually the trust deed, the will or the scheme says who can appoint a new trustee. Many church trusts say that the parish priest or the parish priest and the churchwardens are to be the trustees. (For this reason, they are often known as *vicar and warden trusts*.) When this is the case, there is no need for any legal document to be signed each time the churchwardens or the parish priest changes. The new churchwardens and the parish priest take over as trustees straight away.

The normal way for a trustee to retire is by having someone else appointed to replace him. If there is any difficulty, the Charity Commissioners can both appoint and remove trustees from a charity.[3]

(c) *Suitability of trustees*

A trustee should be suitable for the type of trust he is to run. He should support the work the trust does. He should be efficient, with new ideas and drive, and know that he is doing an important job. In the case of a religious trust which is only for the benefit of members of a particular church, only members of the church should be appointed trustees.

In the case of a charity which is for the benefit of something linked to a particular parish church, the parish priest and churchwardens are natural choices, but there may be other people who would do the job well. When the Charity Commissioners set up a scheme for the benefit of one parish, they usually state that one or more members of the PCC should be on the board of trustees.

Charity trustees should be active in carrying out their duties. They should be involved in the running of the charity. They cannot be charity trustees in name only, and leave the running of the charity to others. They can employ staff or obtain professional help paid for by the charity, but it is the charity trustees who should make sure that the charity is run properly.

PART III.   CHURCH PROPERTY

4.   RESPONSIBILITIES OF CHARITY TRUSTEES

(a)   What are the first steps a new charity trustee should do?

They should obtain a copy of the trust deed or will or the document setting up the trust. Some trusts have been changed by the Charity Commissioners into a scheme, and the Charity Commissioners will be able to provide a copy of the scheme. Trust deeds are usually written in technical legal language. A trustee should look to see what the aim of the trust is, in other words, what the money can be spent on. A typical church trust may say as follows:

> The Trustees shall apply the income of the Charity in furthering the religious and other charitable work of the Church of England in the Ecclesiastical Parish of [name and address of church].

Charity trustees should use the money and investments of the charity for the purposes set out in the trust deed, and not for other purposes.

The trustees should find out what property is subject to the trust: money in the bank, investments, land, or whatever.

They should meet the other trustees, and find out as much as they can about the trust.

They should look at the latest accounts, and satisfy themselves that they know what is going on.

(b)   How should they look after the charity's assets?

Trustees should use as much care as a sensible businessman would use in dealing with his own private affairs. They should protect the charity's property. They need to repair it when necessary, and they need to keep it insured. They should invest money which they do not need straight away. They may need to take advice on how they should invest the trust money. They should check that all income due to the charity is received, and that all tax and rate reliefs are claimed. So, for example, if they invest charity funds in companies which deduct income tax before paying dividends, they should submit a claim to the Inland Revenue to recover the tax.[4]

For details on how to claim tax back on gifts made to charities, see Chapter 25, 'Covenants and Gift Aid'.

(c)   How often should trustees meet?

This depends on the size and nature of the trust. They should meet at least once a year. Some trustees meet every month. They should keep minutes of their meetings.

(d)   Disagreements between the trustees

Charity trustees do not have all to agree on their decisions. In general, decisions are made by a majority vote. However, if a trustee considers that what the other trustees propose to do is not only wrong, but improper, he should contact the Charity Commissioners, who will give advice, and take action if necessary.

(e)   Can trustees be paid?

Usually, No. Trustees can be paid their expenses, but they are not entitled to be paid for their time or work unless the trust document says that they can.

(f)   Personal dealings between the trustees and the charity

Sometimes a trustee would like to make some private arrangement between himself and the charity. There is a strict rule that they cannot do this, because of the risk of fraud. Trustees should not borrow money from the trust, or enter into contracts with it. They should not purchase property from the trust, or live in any property belonging to the trust. They should not use their position as trustees for their own benefit.

In a special case the Charity Commissioners may agree to a trustee making a private arrangement with the charitable trust, but they will need to be sure that it is in the best interests of the charity. And you should ask the Charity Commissioners first.

Sometimes the trustees may need to decide something which might affect one of themselves. When this happens, the trustee who might be affected by the decision should leave the room while the others discuss and vote on the matter.

(g)   Can trustees delegate?

There is nothing to stop trustees appointing professional help to deal with matters such as investment. Large charities have employees to deal with the day-to-day running of the charity. But the trustees should maintain overall control.

(h)   How should trustees invest their funds?

There are rules in the Trustee Investment Act 1961 on how trustees should invest the charity funds. For example, the rules say that a charity may invest up to 50 per cent of its funds in *wide-range investments*, such as debentures, stocks and shares in public companies. The rest should under the Act be invested in *narrow-range investments* such as bank deposits and government securities.

Under section 24 of the Charities Act 1993 trustees may now also invest in what are known as *common investment funds*. There are two well known investment funds which may be used:

- The Central Board of Finance of the Church of England Investment Fund.
- Equities Investment Fund for Charities (Charifund).

The trust documents may gives the trustees special powers of investment, so that they can invest in other things. But unless it does, they should follow these rules.

If the sums involved are large, charity trustees should obtain professional advice on the best means of investing their money.

Ordinary trading companies have to deduct income tax at the basic rate before paying dividends to their shareholders. If charity trustees choose to invest in such companies, they should make sure that they send a claim form to the Inland Revenue to recover the tax. Dividends from common investment funds are paid gross, so there is no tax for the trustees to have to reclaim.

The Charities Aid Foundation offer an investment service for charity trustees in their own common investment funds. These are managed for the Charities Aid Foundation by Cazenove Fund Management Ltd. The minimum initial investment is £5,000, and there is no upper limit. For further details contact

THE CHARITIES AID FOUNDATION
Kings Hill,
West Malling,
Kent ME19 4TA

Tel: 01732 520 000

(i)   Should charities be registered?

In general, any charity with an annual income of over £1,000, or which uses or occupies any land, or which has permanent endowment (that is, some or all of its assets are required to be held as capital which cannot be spent as though it were income), needs to register with the Charity Commission.[5]

But many religious charities do not have to register. Under the Charities (Exception from Registration) Regulations 1996, a religious charity connected with the Church of England does not have to register as a charity if:

- its trustee is a corporation connected with the Church of England, or
- the trust was set up wholly or mainly to make provision for public worship.

Diocesan boards of finance and PCCs are all corporations. So if the PCC or a diocesan board of finance is a trustee of a Christian charity, that charity does not need to be registered.[6]

Some people give money to charity on condition that a particular grave, tomb or personal monument is maintained. A Christian trust which requires a grave, tomb or monument to be maintained does not have to be registered as a charity if the income of the trust is no more than £1,000 a year.[7]

The 1996 regulations do not apply to all vicar and warden trusts. A vicar and warden trust should be registered unless its purpose is wholly or mainly to make provision for public religious worship. Look once again at the typical charitable trust mentioned above:

> The Trustees shall apply the income of the Charity in furthering the religious and other charitable work of the Church of England in the Ecclesiastical Parish of [name and address of church].

This trust allows the money to be spent on much more than just public religious worship. The trust should therefore be registered. Trustees should take advice from the Charity Commissioners if they are in any doubt whether or not they should register their charity.

The Charity Commissioners produce a registration pack, free of charge, which explains how to register a charity, and what happens afterwards.

Any registered charity with an annual income of over £5,000 should state that it is a registered charity in all its letters, on any notices and advertisements, and on all its cheques, invoices, receipts and bills.[8]

(j)   Land held by a PCC

Land held by a PCC should be held in the name of the Diocesan Board of Finance as custodian trustee.[9]

(k)   Charity accounts

Registered charities have to send a set of accounts and an annual report to the Charity Commissioners every year. There are detailed rules which describe the form of these accounts, and which require the accounts to be independently examined or audited.[10]

- If the income or the money spent by the charity in a year is over £10,000, the accounts should be examined by what the Charities Act 1993 calls an *independent examiner*.
- If the income or the money spent is over £100,000, the accounts should be prepared using what is known as the *accruals basis* for accounts.
- If the income or the money spent by the charity in the current year or in either of the two previous years is over £250,000, the accounts should be audited.

Chapter 26, 'Church accounts', explains in detail how PCCs have to prepare the church accounts. This should provide guidance for trustees dealing with other registered charities.[11]

(l) Appeals for money

A permit should be obtained from the local authority before making any public charitable collection.[12] This does not apply to an ordinary collection in church.[13]

(m) Can a trustee be sued personally?

It is most unlikely that a charity trustee who acts honestly and reasonably will be sued. But a charity trustee can be made personally liable if:

- he causes loss to the charity by acting unlawfully, unwisely, or outside the terms of the trust deed or governing document.
- he commits the charity to debts which amount to more than its assets.

5. THE CHARITY COMMISSIONERS

The Charity Commissioners have four main functions.

- They maintain a public register of charities.
- They investigate misconduct and the abuse of charitable assets, and can take action to protect the assets of charities.
- They give free advice to charity trustees on any matter to do with charity.
- They make schemes which alter the way the charity money can be spent, and which give additional powers to the trustees so that the charity can be run better.

They publish a wide range of leaflets and publications which provide information and advice about the role of the Charity Commission, the duties of trustees, and charity law. These are all available free of charge from any of the Commission's offices, and they are also published on the Internet at http://www.charity-commission.gov.uk.

The following leaflets are likely to be the most useful for church trusts.

Charity Commission Publications (1997)	CC1
Charities and the Charity Commission(1995)	CC2
Responsibilities of Charity Trustees (1996)	CC3
Charities for the Relief of Sickness (1994)	CC6
Internal Financial Controls for Charities (1996)	CC8

PART III.   CHURCH PROPERTY

The Charity Commissioners are always most willing to give help and advice – that is one of their functions. They have three offices:

CHARITY COMMISSIONERS
St Alban's House,
57–60 Haymarket,
London SW1Y 4QX

Tel: 0171 210 4477

CHARITY COMMISSIONERS
2nd Floor,
20 Kings Parade,

Queens Dock,
Liverpool L3 4DQ

Tel: 0151 703 1500

CHARITY COMMISSIONERS
Woodfield House,
Tangier,
Taunton,
Somerset TA1 4BL

Tel: 01823 345000

---

[1] 1 Corinthians 4:2.

[2] Charities Act 1993, section 72.

[3] Charities Act 1993, section 16.

[4] The government in its July 1997 Budget announced that over the next seven years, charities will lose their tax credits from dividends.

[5] Charities Act 1993, section 3. No charity is required to be registered in respect of a registered place of religious worship.

[6] Charities (Exception from Registration) Regulations 1996 paragraph 4. This regulation applies until 1 March 2001.

[7] Charities (Exception from Registration) Regulations 1996 paragraph 5.

[8] Charities Act 1993, section 5.

[9] Parochial Church Councils (Powers) Measure 1956 section 6.

[10] Charities Act 1993, sections 41–48, the Charities (Accounts and Reports) Regulations 1995.

[11] The rules for PCCs are based on the rules which govern other charities.

[12] Charities Act 1992, sections 66 and 67.

[13] Charities Act 1992, sections 65 (2) (b).

Chapter 23

SAFETY

1.   INTRODUCTION

Health and safety laws cover many aspects of church life. These include safety at work, food safety, the safety of buildings, the personal safety of clergy and church workers, and the safety of children. Here is a brief reminder of each of these items:

(a)   *Safety at work*

This is covered in Chapter 6, 'Employees and office holders'. PCCs employing a verger, an organist, a secretary, an administrator, lay workers, or any other staff, need to make sure they follow the requirements set out in chapter 6.

(b)   *Food safety*

Food safety is covered in Chapter 20, 'Food and drink'. The topics covered include registering the church kitchen with the local authority, preventing food contamination, and training food handlers. Any church with a kitchen, or which prepares food for church activities, should make sure that it follows the steps set out in Chapter 20.

(c)   The safety of buildings

This is mainly covered in Chapter 20, 'Repairs and maintenance'. The subjects covered include gas and electricity installations, and the safety of trees in the churchyard. The safety of buildings is also covered in Chapter 19, 'Security', which describes what you can do to prevent fire and theft.

(d)   The personal safety of clergy and church workers

The protection of clergy and church workers against casual callers who may be drunk, on drugs, and violent, is described in Chapter 19 'Security'.

(e)   The safety of children

The safety of children is covered in Chapter 8, 'Children'. The chapter covers far more than just protecting them against child abuse. It includes also the safety of church premises for children's work, first aid and medication, travel in cars and minibuses, and insurance.

PCCs should know about one more area of health and safety law: health and safety during major building projects.

2.   THE CDM REGULATIONS

Serious injury and death happen regularly as a result of construction work. The Construction (Design and Management) Regulations 1994 were made into law to help prevent accidents and ill-health in the construction industry. They are known as the CDM regulations.

(a)   When do the CDM regulations apply to the church?

The CDM regulations apply to construction work which:
- lasts for more than 30 days, or
- which involves five or more people on site at any one time, or

- which will involve more than 500 'person days' of work. (If 30 people are involved for 20 days, that is 600 'person days' of work.)

It applies to any design work no matter how long the work lasts or how many workers are involved on site.

If the work includes demolition, the CDM regulations also apply, regardless of the length of time or the number of workers.

In summary, the CDM regulations apply to any major building project for the church.

(b)   What does the church have to do under the regulations?

The main requirement is that the PCC should appoint (and pay for) a planning supervisor, whose job is to look after the health and safety aspects of the project design and the initial planning. This is an extra cost which now has to be paid for when the PCC wants to carry out any large building project on the church.

But that is not all. The PCC should keep in mind health and safety both at the planning stage of the project and during the building work. This means:

- choosing and appointing a competent planning supervisor and the main contractor.
- being satisfied that the planning supervisor and the principal contractor are properly skilled, and that they will set apart enough resources for health and safety. Resources means money, people, equipment, and making sure sufficient time is allowed for all stages of the project.
- being satisfied that the designers and contractors are also properly skilled, and that they too will set apart enough resources for health and safety when making arrangements for the building work.
- giving to the planning supervisor all the information he needs which is relevant to health and safety on the project.
- making sure that the building work does not start until the principal contractor has prepared a satisfactory health and safety plan.

(c)   The health and safety plan

The health and safety plan is drawn up by the planning supervisor during the pre-tender stage. The plan will include:

- a general description of the work.
- details of timings within the project.
- details of risks to workers.
- other information for preparing a health and safety plan for the construction phase of the work.

After the tender has been accepted, the principal contractor has to develop the health and safety plan and carry it out while the building work is taking place.

(d)   The health and safety file

The new building work may need maintenance and repair at some future date. During the course of the building project the planning supervisor prepares what is called a *health and safety file*. This is a record of anything to do with health and safety risks for the new building which the PCC needs to know about for the future. The PCC should keep this file for when it is needed.

3.   FURTHER INFORMATION

CDM Regulations: How the Regulations affect you! published by the Health and Safety Executive.

HSE BOOKS
PO Box 199
Sudbury
Suffolk CO10 6FS

Tel: 01787 881165

The Ecclesiastical Insurance Group publish a series of guidance notes for churches. These guidance notes cover many aspects of church safety.

- *Guidance Notes for Churches. Section 1: Fire.* This covers electrical wiring in churches, fire-fighting equipment in churches, installation and use of basket fryers, heating in churches, church repairs and restoration, and the installation of fire alarms.

- *Guidance Notes for Churches. Section 2: Security.* This covers church security, protection and use of parish computer equipment, installation of closed circuit television systems, purchase and installation of safes, and the installation of intruder alarms.
- *Guidance Notes for Churches. Section 3: Health and Safety.* This covers tower tours, general precautions, churchyard safety, conditions of use applying to change-ringing bells, the Construction (Design and Management) Regulations 1994, building works, use of inflatable bouncy castles, preparation and sale of food on church premises, and a questionnaire to determine how safe is your church and church hall.
- *Guidance Notes for Churches. Section 4: General.* This covers a variety of subjects, including making an insurance claim, protection of stained-glass windows, organisation of bonfire and firework displays, organisation of charity walks, hiring agreements and signing indemnities, and parishes involved in youth work.

Chapter 24

CHURCH RECORDS

1.   INTRODUCTION

Every parish has a number of official registers and records. Most of these records have been discussed in previous chapters, so they are not described in detail here. It is useful to have a list of the registers and records which a church should have when preparing for an archdeacon's inspection. You also need to check the records and registers each year before the annual parochial church meeting.

2.   BAPTISM AND OTHER REGISTERS

Ballpoint pens should not be used for official registers. The registers should be written up in a quality ink suitable for permanent records. The official registers are the following:

- Service register.
- Baptism register.
- Confirmation register.
- Banns of marriage register.

- Marriage register.
- Burial register (where the churchyard is still used for burials).

3.   CLOSING REGISTERS

A register should be closed as soon as its oldest entry is 150 years old. That means that no further entries should be made in it. The only exception is marriage registers begun after June 1837, which are allowed to stay in use.

To close a register, draw a line in ink across the page beneath the last entry in the register, and write the following:

> This register is now closed so that it can be deposited in the [name of diocese] Diocesan Record Office under the Parochial Registers and Records Measure 1978.

followed by the date and the parish priest's signature.

4.   DEPOSITING OLD REGISTERS IN THE DIOCESAN RECORDS OFFICE

All registers which have been closed should be deposited in the diocesan record office.

Any register whose last entry is over 100 years old should also be deposited in the diocesan record office.

You do not need a faculty in order to deposit registers in the diocesan records office.

If the PCC wants to retain these old registers it should write to the bishop asking for permission to keep the records in the parish. The PCC will have to agree to very strict standards for their preservation.[1] These include:

- keeping the registers in a wood-lined, rust-proofed, vented steel cabinet, fitted with a multi-lever lock.
- The cupboard should be loosely packed, and opened *every week* to allow free air circulation. Nothing except books or documents may be kept in the cupboard.
- The temperature and humidity should be checked *every week* and kept within strict limits. Records of all temperature and humidity

readings should be kept for at least a year, and made available to the archdeacon for inspection.

- The temperature in the cabinet should not be allowed to rise above 18°C, and should not be allowed to vary by more than 10°C in any week.
- The relative humidity inside the cupboard should be maintained between 50 per cent and 65 per cent.
- If the temperature and humidity cannot be consistently maintained within these limits, dehumidifying equipment and/or heating systems will need to be installed.

It is far simpler to agree to deposit the registers in the diocesan records office!

So, just to be clear:

- Close a register where the oldest entry (the first entry in the book) is 150 years old (unless it is a marriage register begun after June 1837). Then deposit the register in the diocesan office.
- Also deposit a register in the diocesan record office where the newest entry (the last entry in the book) is 100 years old.

5.   INVENTORIES AND PROPERTY LOG BOOKS

There should be the following records of the church property:

- A terrier of all lands belonging to the church.[2]
- An inventory of all articles belonging to the church.[3]
- Photographs of valuables.[4]
- The church log book to record building work and alterations.[5]
- Copies of all faculties obtained for work done in the church.[6]
- Copies of any planning permissions obtained for work done to the outside of the church.[7]
- Any local authority consents needed for work to trees in the churchyard.[8]
- Insurance certificates.[9]
- The quinquennial inspection report.[10]
- Any grave-space plan for the churchyard.[11]

PART III.   CHURCH PROPERTY

6.   RECORDS OF CHURCH BUSINESS

These are the main records you should have:

- The electoral roll.[12]
- The minute book of the PCC meetings.[13]
- The minute book of the annual parochial church meetings.[14]
- Correspondence file for the PCC.
- Contracts entered into by the PCC.
- Local authority licences, permits or registrations.[15]

7.   FINANCIAL RECORDS

The following records are kept, normally by the treasurer:

- Church accounts.[16]
- Covenant and Gift Aid records.[17]
- Cash book and other normal financial records.[18]

8.   SAFETY RECORDS

You should have the following:

- An *insurance certificate* for third party liability.[19]
- An *accident book*, if you have employees, to record any accidents at work.[20]
- If you have five or more employees, you should have a record of your *health and safety risk assessment.*[21]
- If you have five or more employees, you should also have a *written health and safety statement.*[22]
- If you have a children's church or any youth activities, you should have an *accident book* and a *log book* to record any unusual events such as fights or odd behaviour involving a child.[23]
- If you carry out any major building project, you will need to have a *health and safety file.* This is a record of anything to do with health and safety risks for the new building which the PCC needs to know about for the future.[24]
- A gas safety inspection certificate.[25]

9. PERSONNEL RECORDS

This will include:

- References taken for employees.[26]
- Job specifications and contracts of employment.[27]
- Declarations by employees to comply with child protection procedures.[28]
- Any written disciplinary warnings to employees, and a note of any other disciplinary procedures.[29]
- A record of any notice of dismissal and written reasons for dismissal.[30]

These records are likely to be particularly sensitive, and you should make sure that they are kept secure. You should consider carefully who should have access to them.

10. COMPUTER RECORDS

Not all churches have computers. But if you do, you should know what records you have on your computer, and what steps you are taking to keep these records secure.[31]

11. FURTHER INFORMATION

The Guide to the Parochial Registers and Records Measure 1978, (Church House Publishing), contains information, practical suggestions, and advice for all who have care of parish records.

---

[1] They are set out in Schedule 2 to the Church of England (Miscellaneous Provisions) Measure 1992.

[2] See Chapter 2, 'The churchwardens', Chapter 3, 'The PCC'.

[3] See Chapter 2, 'The churchwardens', Chapter 3, 'The PCC'.

[4] See Chapter 19, 'Security'.

[5] See Chapter 2, 'The churchwardens', Chapter 3, 'The PCC'.

[6] See Chapter 20, 'Repairs and maintenance'.

[7] See Chapter 20, 'Repairs and maintenance'.

[8] See Chapter 20, 'Repairs and maintenance'.

[9] See Chapter 21, 'Insurance'.

---

[10] See Chapter 20, 'Repairs and maintenance'.

[11] See Chapter 20, 'Repairs and maintenance'.

[12] See Chapter 10, 'The annual parochial church meeting'.

[13] See Chapter 3, 'The PCC', and Chapter 5, 'The PCC Secretary'.

[14] See Chapter 10, 'The annual parochial church meeting'.

[15] See Chapter 8, 'Children', Chapter 11, 'Food and drink', Chapter 22, 'Charitable trusts', and Chapter 18, 'Lotteries and other matters'.

[16] See Chapter 26, 'Church Accounts'.

[17] See Chapter 25, 'Covenants and Gift Aid'.

[18] See Chapter 4, 'The Treasurer'.

[19] See Chapter 21, 'Insurance'.

[20] See Chapter 6, 'Employees and office holders'.

[21] See Chapter 6, 'Employees and office holders'.

[22] See Chapter 6, 'Employees and office holders'.

[23] See Chapter 8, 'Children'.

[24] See Chapter 23, 'Safety'.

[25] See Chapter 20, 'Repairs and maintenance'.

[26] See Chapter 6, 'Employees and office holders'.

[27] See Chapter 6, 'Employees and office holders'.

[28] See Chapter 6, 'Employees and office holders', and Chapter 8, 'Children'.

[29] See Chapter 6, 'Employees and office holders'.

[30] See Chapter 6, 'Employees and office holders'.

[31] See Chapter 12, 'Computers'.

Part IV

Church Finance

Chapter 25

COVENANTS AND GIFT AID

1. DEEDS OF COVENANT

(a) What is a deed of covenant?

A deed of covenant is a way of giving money to the church (or any registered charity). It enables the church to receive more than you actually give! The difference is paid to the church by the Inland Revenue. It is a very popular way of giving money.

You can only make a gift using a covenant if you pay income tax. You agree to make regular payments to the church for a period of four years. The payments can be made in weekly, monthly, quarterly or annual instalments. You fill in a simple printed form saying how much you wish to give, and when the donations will begin, and then sign it in front of a witness. The form is then given to the church. At the end of the first year you also have to sign a certificate of deduction of tax, confirming that you have made the agreed payments, and that you pay UK income tax.

The church can then claim from the Inland Revenue a refund of tax amounting to almost 30 per cent of the amount you have given. In effect therefore, a covenanted gift is worth almost 30 per cent more to the church.

(b) How does a covenant work?

You pay tax at the basic rate of 23 per cent.[1] You sign a covenant to pay, say, £100 out of your taxed income to your church each year.

(i)   *From the tax payer's point of view*

You earn	£129.87
Less tax @ 23 per cent	– £29.87
Net amount you donate	£100.00

Provided you pay to the church £100 each year, the church can then recover from the Inland Revenue the £29.87 tax which you have paid, at no extra cost to yourself.

(ii)   *From the church's point of view*

The church receives from you each year	£100.00
It reclaims the tax you have paid from the Inland Revenue	+ £29.87
Total amount received by the church	£129.87

The £100 it has cost you to make your gift is worth £129.87 to the church, at no extra cost to you.

The £100 is called the *net* donation, and the £129.87 is called the *gross* donation.

How did I calculate the figure £129.87? This is known as *grossing up* the gift. The arithmetic is as follows:

The covenantor[2] pays £100 to church	£100.00

To calculate gross payment @ 23 per cent basic rate

$$£100 \times \frac{100}{(100 \text{ minus basic rate})} = £100 \times \frac{100}{77} \qquad £129.87$$

Amount which can be claimed from the Inland Revenue	£29.87

The Inland Revenue will supply tax calculation tables on request. Or you can use the table on page 388.

(c)   **Husbands and wives**

Since 6 April 1990 married couples have been treated as individual tax payers. Therefore a spouse should only make a covenant if he or she personally pays income tax at the standard rate or higher.

(d)   Cancelling a covenant

A covenant should be capable of lasting for at least four years. The only 'escape clause' which the Inland Revenue allows is a provision that it comes to an end on death. A provision such as 'for as long as I remain on the electoral roll of St Mark's' makes the deed invalid.

Yet there are genuine reasons why the donor[3] may not be able to keep up his covenant, and proper reasons why he may not want to. He may have suffered some misfortune such as unemployment or sickness, and so to keep up his payments would cause hardship; or he may have moved to a new church and would prefer to give his money to that church rather than to the old one.

Church covenants are a promise to pay money for the Lord's work, and they should therefore be honoured. But we do not have to be like Jephthah in Judges 11:35, and consider them immutable. The Roman Catholic Church allows people to be released from their vows in suitable circumstances,[4] and so does the Church of England. If a person is in genuine difficulty in keeping up payments, he should raise the matter with his parish priest or with the church treasurer. The covenant may then be cancelled, or the church may agree to accept a lower payment. The church can then claim tax back on the lower payments actually made.[5]

If a person moves to another church and wants to transfer his covenant to that church, the easiest way is for the old church to cancel the old covenant, and for the person then to enter into a new covenant with his new church. Although no one has a right to demand that a church release them from a covenant, in practice churches do agree to do so when a person wishes to give his financial support to another church.[6]

A covenant can be released by a letter from the church. Strictly, a deed (a formal legal document) is required,[7] but in practice a letter should suffice. An example of a suitable letter is on page 385.

Proper record keeping is essential in order to recover the tax from the Inland Revenue. How to do this is explained under *Covenant administration and reclaiming tax*.[8] Proper records will show whenever a covenantor is getting into arrears. The covenant secretary or the treasurer can then discuss any financial problems with him or her at an early stage.

(e)   Replacement covenants

If a person wants to increase his covenant before its four years are up, he can do this in one of two ways. He can make an additional covenant to run jointly with the old covenant: the new covenant should be for four years, and so will continue after the first covenant has ended. Or the church can release the old covenant and accept a new one for a larger sum. If the old covenant is to be released, the Inland Revenue insist that the new covenant should be for a higher amount.

Not many people know when their covenants are due to expire. It is up to the church to remind them, and to ask them to sign a new covenant form so that there is no gap. Each church should therefore keep a list of expiry dates of covenants.

(f)   Higher rate tax payers

From 6 April 1998 the current rates of income tax are:

- Lower rate band: 20% on the first £4,300 taxable income.
- Basic rate band: 23% on the next £22,800 of taxable income.
- Higher rate band: 40% on all other taxable income.

The church can only claim tax at the basic rate on deeds of covenant. But a higher rate tax payer receives the benefit of tax relief at his or her highest rate. This means that the net cost of a gift made under a deed of covenant is less to a higher rate tax payer than it is to a basic rate tax payer. Put another way, a higher rate tax payer should be encouraged to increase the amount he covenants to a church. This obviously benefits the church, and the net cost to him is the same as a smaller gift made by a person who only pays tax at the basic rate.

Let me explain using figures. Suppose a higher rate tax payer wishes to make a gift under a deed of covenant which costs him £200 net. He should do the following calculation

$$\text{Net amount of gift} \ \times \ \frac{(100 - \text{basic rate of tax})}{(100 - \text{highest rate of tax})}$$

The basic rate is 23 per cent, and the highest rate is 40 per cent. So this calculation becomes £200 x $\frac{(100-23)}{(100-40)}$, which is £200 x $\frac{77}{60}$. This equals £256.67 per annum, and this is the net amount to enter on the deed.

(i)   *From the church's point of view*

The church receives from the person making the gift each year	£256.67
It reclaims basic rate tax on this figure	+ £76.66
Total amount received by the church	£333.33

(ii)   *From the higher rate tax payer's point of view*

The taxpayer enters an amount of £256.67 on his tax return. This, grossed up at the standard rate, produces £333.33 (the value of his gift to the church). But he is entitled to higher rate tax relief equal to

£333.33 x (40% – 23%) = £333.33 x 17% = £56.67.

So the result is as follows:

The tax payer earns	£427.78
Tax is deducted @ 40 per cent	– £171.11
Net amount he receives	£256.67
This is the same amount as he pays to the church	£256.67
He then claims higher rate tax relief	– £56.67
So the net cost to him of the gift is	£200.00

Using this method, a higher rate tax payer can increase the value of his gift from £200 to £333, that is, by 67 per cent.

(g)   *Lower rate tax payers*

People who pay income tax at the lower rate only should realise that the church is reclaiming tax at the basic rate on their covenanted payment. This means that the Revenue may be paying to the church more than the tax paid by the person making the gift. Strictly the

Revenue can claim from them the difference if this happens, but in practice the Revenue does not do so.[9]

(h)　Filling in the deed of covenant

Have a look at the *Deed of covenant and banker's order* on page 383.

Check that:

- The name and address of the donor (the person giving the money) are clearly legible.
- The deed is witnessed. A wife can witness her husband's signature, and a husband can witness his wife's signature.
- The church name is inserted. Many parishes print their own covenant forms so that this does not have to be filled in by the donor.
- The frequency of the payments is shown, and the unwanted options are crossed out.
- The total amount per year is arithmetically correct.
- The date the first payment is due is on or after the date the deed is signed. It is not possible to backdate a deed.
- If any amendments are made, they are initialled by the covenantor.
- It is not strictly necessary for the deed to ask for details of the covenantor's tax district and National Insurance Number, but this information will be needed when the Inland Revenue claim forms are filled in by the church, so it is useful to obtain it at the start. It also helps to confirm that the donor does pay income tax.
- If payments are being made by banker's order, check that all details are completed fully, and that the payment instructions matches the covenant.
- Make sure it is clear whether the new deed replaces any existing covenant, or whether it is intended as an additional covenant.

(i)　How are payments made?

Payments can be made by cheque, banker's order, or cash through the envelope scheme. They can be made weekly, monthly, quarterly or annually, whichever is most convenient to the donor.

Money paid under a covenant should not just be placed loose in the collection plate. It is essential that accurate records are maintained to prove that the money was indeed given by the person making the covenant. This cannot be done if loose money is put in the collection plate. It is therefore essential to use one of the other methods. See *Covenant administration*[10] for more details.

(j)   *Deposited covenants*

A covenant has to run over four years. A person may not wish to commit himself to making the same payments over four years. He may prefer to make a single gift without committing himself to making further gifts in future years. Before Gift Aid was introduced, the deposited covenant was a scheme to dress up a one-off gift into the form of a four-year covenant.

It worked as follows. Suppose a person wanted to make a gift of £1,000 to a church. He signed a covenant to pay to the church £250 each year for four years. He then wrote a letter to the church enclosing a cheque for £1,000. The letter said that he was making an interest free loan of £1,000 to the church, and that £250 of this £1,000 was to be used each year as his payment under the deed of covenant. Of course he never intended the loan to be repaid, and it was not repaid. But this arrangement enabled the church to recover tax from the Inland Revenue as though he had made a covenant for £250 for four years.

The whole arrangement was a fiction. The government realised this, and in 1990 brought out the much simpler Gift Aid scheme, which can now be used for all gifts of £250 or more. Whenever a person wants to make a single gift of £250 or more, he should now use Gift Aid. Deposited covenants should only be used for gifts of under £250.

Two forms are needed to set up a deposited covenant: a deed of covenant, and a letter of loan. A draft letter of loan is set out at the end of this chapter. It is most important that the deed of covenant and the letter of loan are dated the same date as the cheque. A lump sum gift cannot be converted into a deposited covenant after it has been made.

2.   GIFT AID

The Gift Aid scheme is available for individual payments of £250 or more. It is not available where you make a series of smaller payments which, over a period, total £250. If two people – say, a husband and wife – join forces to make a single gift of £250, the gift should be treated as made by only one of them in order to qualify. You can make more than one Gift Aid gift to the same charity in a year, but each gift should be over £250 to qualify for the tax benefit.

You can make the gift in cash, by cheque, or by bank transfer. It is not possible to make a gift of some other kind of asset and obtain the benefit of Gift Aid. It is not possible to forgive a loan and claim the benefit of Gift Aid – instead, the loan should be repaid by the church, and the donor should then give the money by a separate cheque back to the church.

You should be an income tax payer, and the amount of income tax you pay should be at least the same as the church is going to recover on your gift (just under 30 per cent of your gift, as with a covenant).

The gift should be an outright gift, with no significant benefit to the donor in return. (Strictly, there is allowed a trivial benefit worth up to 2½ per cent of the gift, up to a maximum value of £250.)

No forms have to be filled in before the gift is made. All that is required is that at some stage you fill in a Gift Aid Certificate, so that the church can recover the tax.

You can use the Gift Aid scheme to 'top up' a covenant if you decide you want to give additional money, but you cannot use the Gift Aid scheme for money which you have already promised under a covenant.

Gift Aid has the same advantages for higher rate tax payers as covenants.

You can recover the tax on a Gift Aid payment immediately. It is not spread over four years like a covenant. Church members can use this method for their regular giving, so that they can decide each year how much they want to give. The disadvantage is that unless they are conscientious in their giving, they may need to be reminded each year.

If a person wants to give £100 a month to the church, and asks you how he should do it, you have two options. You can ask him to make a four-year covenant to pay £100 each month. Or you can ask him to pay £300 to the church four times a year, and ask him to fill in four Gift Aid forms. The total cost to him is of course £1,200 a year in both cases. The difference is that under a covenant he is committed to giving this money for four years, whereas using Gift Aid he can change the amount he gives you each year.

The advantages of Gift Aid are:

- the church receives 30 per cent more than your gift.
- it gives flexibility to make payments when you wish.
- it is useful for those who have irregular income, and for those for whom annual bonuses constitute a large part of their earnings.
- it can be used to meet one-off appeals and needs.

Companies as well as individuals can give money to charities under the Gift Aid Scheme. Companies should be resident in the UK, and not be charities themselves for the gift to qualify. A company has to fill in the Inland Revenue form R240 (SD), whereas an individual has to fill in the Inland Revenue form R190 (SD).

3.   COVENANT ADMINISTRATION AND RECLAIMING TAX

(a)   *The covenant secretary*

The PCC should appoint a covenant secretary. In some churches the treasurer acts as covenant secretary; in others they are two different people.

(b)   *Acknowledgement of covenants and Gift Aid*

The covenant secretary should acknowledge all covenants and Gift Aid firstly for the sake of courtesy, but also to provide the donor with a record of the date of the covenant and the amount agreed to be paid, to help the donor with his or her income tax return. Some donors ask for photocopies of deeds of covenant and Gift Aid donations.

(c)   *What records are needed?*

For the Inland Revenue, the basic requirement is that you are able to show that your claims are correct. Your records should be sufficient to identify each covenantor's donation from the moment it is received right through until it is banked or spent.

(i)   Deeds of covenant

The first important document is the deed of covenant. This will demonstrate that payments received by the church were made under a legal obligation. Therefore, you should keep the deeds of covenant as part of your records. It is best not to mark deeds in any way, or punch holes in them, as this can lead to problems with the Inland Revenue.[11]

You should also keep any correspondence between the covenantor and the church concerning the deed.

For convenience when preparing claims you should keep the covenants in alphabetical order according to the name of the covenantor.

The Inland Revenue does not normally ask to see original deeds made by individuals. The Inland Revenue does ask to see deeds made by companies, and if they carry out an inspection of a church's records, they will ask to see all its deeds of covenant. If you do need to send original deeds to the Revenue, make a photocopy of all the deeds you send, in case the originals are lost.

If a deed of covenant is lost, the Inland Revenue will accept a photocopy, provided it is accompanied by a certificate signed by the covenant secretary saying

> A properly executed deed, in the form of the copy attached, was received by me on .... (date).
> The original has been lost, and all attempts to trace it have failed.

(ii)   A covenant register

This register will list all the covenantors, and show details of all payments made by them. You should have one record sheet for each covenantor. The register needs to show the following information.

- Name and address of each covenantor.
- Payment method.

  Payment may be by cash, cheque, or standing order. If payment is by standing order you should record the name, address, and account number of the covenantor's bank. If payment is by envelope, insert the unique number of the covenantor's envelope. For other cash payments, record the Cash book page number.

- Date of deed of covenant.

    This is the date the deed was signed.

- Date of last payment.

    This is the date on which the last payment under the deed falls
    due. This information helps you to make sure, for example, that you
    do not make a claim for a fifth year under a four-year deed.

- The net amount payable in the year.

    This is the 'net' amount due under the deed.

- Weeks 1–53.

    This allows you to record weekly payments. If payments are
    made monthly or at other intervals, record them in the month in
    which you receive them. For example, if a covenantor pays nothing
    in week 15 but pays double the normal amount in week 16, your
    records should show this.

- Total paid in the year.
- The consecutive number of the payment. If, for example, this is the
  2nd payment under a 4-year deed, the records should show
  number '2'.
- A record number. You will need this record number when you fill in
  the claim form to reclaim tax.

(iii)   Cash book

You may wish to keep a cash book which will show details of cash
and cheques received, and of cash spent or banked.

(iv)   Bank statements, paying in books

You should keep copies of bank statements and paying in books,
particularly where covenantors pay directly into the bank account by
standing order.

(v)   Envelope schemes

Where covenants are in favour of a church, many people want to
make their payments in cash at the church services.

A practical way to provide satisfactory records of this is to introduce
an envelope scheme. Each covenantor is given a set of envelopes with a

unique number. Every week the amount in each envelope is counted, and the amount paid is entered in the line for that week on each covenantor's record. In this way, a clear record is kept that individual covenantors have paid the proper amounts. If the covenant register is not written up there and then, the amount contained in each envelope should be written in ink on the envelopes.

You can use the donor's record number as his or her envelope number. Or you may prefer to have a separate series of numbers just for those people who give using the envelope scheme. If you do the latter, don't confuse the two sets of numbers.

(vi)   Deposited covenants

Money received under a deposited covenant has to be recorded differently. Here the donor pays the whole amount of the gift at the start. This is treated as a loan to the church for four years, and each year one quarter of the loan is used to pay the amount due under the covenant. Therefore, each year the church can claim back the tax on one quarter of the gift.

(vii)   General points

Do enter the actual amount received, not simply a tick, on the record card for the donor.

Covenanted payments should not be made in loose cash placed in the collection bag at services. This is because there is no way to distinguish one person's gift from somebody else's, and so it cannot be proved that any particular covenantor made the payments due under his covenant.

Some dioceses have their own forms which are suitable to use as records in the covenant register. One which I have designed is shown at the end of the chapter.

(d)   How long should records be kept?

Keep each deed of covenant for 6 years from the date of the final claim on the deed.

Keep other records in support of a claim for 6 years from the date you submit the claim.

You should keep a representative sample of the envelopes used in the envelope scheme for 6 years. The Inland Revenue recommend that you should keep all the envelopes used over a one-month period each year.

(e)   *How to make a covenant claim*

You will need a supply of the following forms:

Covenants

R185	Income Tax deduction certificate for individual
R185 (AP)	Income Tax deduction certificate for limited companies
R68A	A form to list all the covenants on which you are claiming repayment
R68A (Summary)	Summary of listing forms
R68	Tax repayment claim form. This form is also used for Gift Aid claims

Gift Aid

R190 (SD)	Single payment by an individual to a charity
R240 (SD)	Single payment by a limited company to a charity
R68 (Gift Aid Insert)	Summary of single donations

You can obtain them from your local tax office, or from the Inland Revenue address on page 381.

You start by filling in Form R68A. Some of the column headings are obvious. Some need explanation. The columns are as follows.

- *The name of the covenantor.*
- *The date of the deed.*
- *The consecutive number of payment.* If it is the first year of the deed, you enter 1, if the second, you enter 2, etc.
- *The net amount received.* This of course is the actual payments you have received.

- *The tax deducted.* This is the amount received x $\frac{23}{77}$, this fraction being $\frac{\text{basic rate of tax}}{(100 - \text{basic rate of tax})}$. The Inland Revenue supply tables, so you can look up the tax rather than having to calculate it.
- *The date of receipt.* This is the date the last payment was made in the tax period which you are claiming for. So if you are claiming for the period up to April 5, it is the last payment received before that date.
- *Cash book folio or page number.* Enter here the record number on the covenantor's record card.
- *Tick if first claim under this deed.*
- *Tick if company covenant.*

You can list up to 42 covenants on one form R68A. Fill in as many forms R68A as you need, and then summarise them all on form R68A (Summary). Finally, fill in form R68 which is the actual tax reclaim form.

There is no need to submit deeds of covenant made by individuals. You should however keep them for inspection if an Inland Revenue auditor visits you. You do need to enclose the deeds for first claims under company covenants.

You should also include completed form R185 (Covenant) for all first-year payments by individuals, and a completed form R185(AP) each year for all payments under company covenants. Form R185 (Covenant) is a certificate given by the covenantor declaring that he or she has made one or more covenanted payments, and deducted basic rate tax. You should obtain and enclose one of these forms signed by the covenantor with your first claim relating to that covenant. You do not need to ask the covenantor to complete Form R185 for any later claims under the deed.

Many charities try to help the covenantor by filling in as much of the form R185 (Covenant) as possible. The form requires the donor to give details of his tax office, income tax reference number, and national insurance number. The model deed of covenant included at the end of this chapter asks the donor to give this information when he fills in the covenant form. The covenant administrator can then fill in these details on the form R185 (Covenant) before sending it to the covenantor for signature.

(f)   A check list

When you submit your claim, please check that you have:

- listed all the covenants for which you are claiming on form R68A.
- completed and signed the form R68A (Summary).
- enclosed completed forms R185(Covenant) for all *first-year* payments by individuals.
- enclosed completed forms R185(AP) for all payments under company covenants.
- enclosed the deeds for all first claims under company covenants.

You can also claim the tax back on Gift Aid Schemes at the same time. For this you fill in a special insert to the claim form R68. The details to be shown are similar to those for covenanted payments.

There are separate sections on the form for gifts by individuals, close companies, and non-close companies. (A close company is a company which is under the control of five or fewer persons, or under the control of their directors. Small family companies are typical close companies.) Each gift should be shown separately and accompanied by the form R190 (SD) for individuals or R240(SD) for companies.

(g)   When should a claim be made?

You can claim repayment of tax on any payment made under a deed once the payment has become due, and has been paid. So, for example, if a deed says that John will pay £300 to St Mark's every quarter for four years, a claim can be made every quarter once the church has received the £300 which is due.

In practice, most churches find it convenient to make one claim a year for ordinary covenants. Claims made under the Gift Aid scheme (especially if they are for large amounts) should be made more frequently.

(h)   Inland Revenue audits

From time to time the Inland Revenue undertakes an inspection of a charity's records to check the accuracy of claims for repayment of income tax on covenants and Gift Aid payments. Charities are only entitled to repayment of tax if the money received has been used for charitable purposes. The inspection therefore includes evidence of payments as well as evidence of receipts.

When they inspected the church where I was churchwarden in December 1994 the inspection took most of a day. They gave us about six weeks' notice. They asked to see:

- statements, paying in books and cheque book stubs for all bank accounts in the name of the church from 6 April 1990 to the time of the inspection (i.e. for the last four tax years).
- cash books from 6 April 1990 to the time of the inspection.
- any index or register of covenantors and Gift Aid payments.
- all deeds of covenant, both current and expired, in favour of the church.
- copies of claims submitted to the claims branch.
- a specimen copy of current deeds.
- any correspondence connected with Gift Aid or deeds of covenant.

I am happy to report that we emerged almost unscathed. (They always find one or two little things to justify their visit!)

(i)   Computer software

Several computer programs have been written to assist churches with their covenant administration. *Covenant* handles the reclaiming of tax for both covenants and Gift Aid. It covers multiple claims per covenant per year, standing orders, and bank reconciliation. *Donate* handles envelope schemes, pledge and stewardship campaigns, regular giving and general fund-raising within the Church. The two programs have links to each other. They cost £69 each, including VAT, and are available from Data Developments Ltd, the creators of the program, from Sunrise Software, and from many Christian book shops.

Part IV. Church Finance

Data Developments Ltd
Wolverhampton Science Park,
Stafford Road,
Wolverhampton,
West Midlands WV10 9RU

Tel: 01902 824044

Fax: 01902 824046

Sunrise Software
Scorrier Park,
Scorrier,
Cornwall TR16 5AU.

Tel: 01209 821821

Fax: 01209 822125

One well-established system for administering covenants is the *Kubernesis Deeds of Covenant System* (KDC). (*Kubernesis* is the New Testament Greek word for *administration*.) The program generates R185 and R68A forms, with all tax listings in a form approved by the Inland Revenue. It can be used on its own, or with other systems, forming a suite of programs for administration of membership, giving, and covenants. KDC on its own is priced at £175. An optional Windows support pack is available, but it can also be used directly from DOS on non-Windows machines. KDC is produced by

The Kubernesis Partnership
36 Acomb Wood Drive,
York YO2 2XN,

Tel: 01904 788885

(j)   The Charities Aid Foundation

The Charities Aid Foundation offers a service for churches (and other charities) in which it handles all the administration and tax claims connected with covenants. There is an annual charge for each covenant the Charities Aid Foundation handles for the church. For further details contact

THE CHARITIES AID FOUNDATION
Kings Hill,
West Malling,
Kent ME19 4TA

Tel: 01732 520 000

4.   FURTHER INFORMATION

The following stationery items are available from the Inland Revenue.

- Charity Tax Pack.
- Booklet: *Deeds of Covenant – Guidance for Charities.*
- Booklet: *Gift Aid – Guidance for Charities.*
- Grossing up tables to show tax calculations on net covenants.
- All the Inland Revenue Forms which are needed.

INLAND REVENUE
Financial Intermediaries and Claims Office
(Repayments)
St John's House,
Merton Road,
Bootle,
Merseyside L69 9BB

Tel: 0151 472 6037 (covenants)

Tel: 0151 472 6038 (Gift Aid)

5.   MODEL FORMS

(a)   *Gift Aid form*

GIFT AID

in favour of [*NAME OF CHURCH*]

(This form applies if you are a **tax-payer** and wish to make a lump-sum gift of £250 or more to [*name of church*]. Please complete this form and send it with your cheque (made out to [*name of church*] to the Covenant Secretary, [*name and address of church*], who will then send you the appropriate Gift Aid Certificate for tax purposes.)

I, (Dr/Mr/Mrs/Miss) ....
of ....
        address in capitals
....*post code*..............................
enclose a donation of £............... for [*name of church*], the gift to be administered under the Gift Aid scheme.
Please send me a Gift Aid Certificate (R 190 SD) for tax purposes.

Thank you for your generosity and support

(b)   ***Deed of covenant and banker's order***

DEED OF COVENANT FOR [*NAME OF CHURCH*]

I, (Dr/Mr/Mrs/Miss) ....

of ....
       address in capitals

....*post code*..............................

promise to pay the Parochial Church Council of [*name of church and address*] for four years or during my lifetime (whichever is shorter), such, a sum as, after deduction of income tax at the basic rate, amounts to:

£.............................
Enter the amount you will give in each instalment, i.e. if £20 per month, enter £20; if £200 per month, enter £200.

Each month/quarter/year
Delete whichever period is inappropriate, i.e. if giving monthly, cross out quarter and year.

From the .... day of ....19.........
Enter the date the payments will start. This date should not be earlier than the date of signing the deed of covenant.

This deed supersedes any previous deed.
Cross out this line if this is your first deed of covenant to [name of church].

Signed and delivered by ....Date.....................

Witnessed by ....

Full name of witness ....

Address of witness ....

....

Occupation of witness ....

Note

We will need the following details in order to recover the tax on your payments. It will help us if you can give us these details now, but if you do not have them to hand, please let us have them as soon as possible.

The name of my Tax Office is ....

My Income Tax reference number is ....

My National Insurance Number is...

PART IV.   CHURCH FINANCE

BANKER'S ORDER

To the Manager of .... Bank plc
Address of branch ....
....

Please pay to the Parochial Church Council of [Name of Church and address], account number .... (sort code ....) at the [Name and address of the Church's bank]

the sum of £......... (in figures) ....(in words)

on the .... day of .... 19......... and on the same date in each succeeding month/quarter/year until further notice.

Please debit my account number .... with each payment made.

Please cancel my previous standing order for £......... per month/quarter/year (*delete as necessary*)
Signed .... Date ....
Address ....
....

(c)   *Letter to accompany a deposited covenant*[12]

Dear Sir,

I am enclosing a cheque for £.................. as an interest free loan to [*name of church*] for four years.

I am also enclosing a deed of covenant under which I promise to pay to [*name of church*] the sum of £............ each year for four years.

Each year would you please take one quarter of the money I have loaned to you, and treat that as my payment to you under the covenant.

If I should die within the four years, please treat the balance of the loan as an absolute gift to [*name of church*].

Yours faithfully,

Signed ....Date ....

Address ....

....

Note: You also need to execute a deed of covenant for one quarter of the total gift each year.

(d)   *Letter releasing a person from a covenant*

Dear John,

I am pleased to hear that you have now joined St Barnabas. I quite understand that you wish to cancel your covenant with St Luke's so that you can support St Barnabas financially.

On behalf of the PCC I agree to your deed of covenant with St Luke's being cancelled. May I thank you once again very much for all the financial support you have given us in the past.

With best wishes

(signature of the parish priest or the treasurer of the PCC or the covenant secretary)

(e)   Covenant record card

Front of card, or page 1

Name				Record No			
Address							
Date of deed			Payment method		Cash Cheque Standing Order Dep. Covt.		
Last payment due			Envelope Number				
Name, address and account number of the covenantor's bank							
Year number of the deed (1 to 4)			Net amount payable per year				

Week	Net Amt	Date of Receipt	Ref	Week	Net Amt	Date of Receipt	Ref
1				14			
2				15			
3				16			
4				17			
5				18			
6				19			
7				20			
8				21			
9				22			
10				23			
11				24			
12				25			
13				26			
Total (A)				Total (B)			

In the column headed *Ref* you insert a reference number to some other record showing the receipt of the money paid by the covenantor. So, depending on the circumstances, you show here a page number of the cash book, or a page number of a bank statement, or whatever record is appropriate.

Rear of card, or page 2

Name					Record No		
Week	Net Amt	Date of Receipt	Ref	Week	Net Amt	Date of Receipt	Ref
27				40			
28				41			
29				42			
30				43			
31				44			
32				45			
33				46			
34				47			
35				48			
36				49			
37				50			
38				51			
39				52			
				53			
Total (C)				Total (D)			
Total Net Amount (A+B+C+D)				Tax deducted (to be claimed)			
Total Gross Amount							
Date R185 sent				Date R185 received			
Date tax claimed				Date tax received			

The card shown is for weekly payments, and therefore has 53 payment boxes. For monthly, quarterly or annual payments, a card with 12 payment boxes is more convenient.

6.   Tax tables

The table on this and the next page shows the gross value of net deeds at various rates of tax. For example, a net gift of £80 equals a gross gift of £103.90 when the basic rate of tax is 23 per cent.

Net amount	23%	24%	25%	26%	27%	28%
£	£	£	£	£	£	£
1.00	1.30	1.32	1.33	1.35	1.37	1.39
2.00	2.60	2.63	2.67	2.70	2.74	2.78
3.00	3.90	3.95	4.00	4.05	4.11	4.17
4.00	5.19	5.26	5.33	5.41	5.48	5.56
5.00	6.49	6.58	6.67	6.76	6.85	6.94
6.00	7.79	7.89	8.00	8.11	8.22	8.33
7.00	9.09	9.21	9.33	9.46	9.59	9.72
8.00	10.39	10.53	10.67	10.81	10.96	11.11
9.00	11.69	11.84	12.00	12.16	12.33	12.50
10.00	12.99	13.16	13.33	13.51	13.70	13.89
11.00	14.29	14.47	14.67	14.86	15.07	15.28
12.00	15.58	15.79	16.00	16.22	16.44	16.67
15.00	19.48	19.74	20.00	20.27	20.55	20.83
20.00	25.97	26.32	26.67	27.03	27.40	27.78
25.00	32.47	32.89	33.33	33.78	34.25	34.72
26.00	33.77	34.21	34.67	35.14	35.62	36.11
30.00	38.96	39.47	40.00	40.54	41.10	41.67
35.00	45.45	46.05	46.67	47.30	47.95	48.61
40.00	51.95	52.63	53.33	54.05	54.79	55.56
45.00	58.44	59.21	60.00	60.81	61.64	62.50
50.00	64.94	65.79	66.67	67.57	68.49	69.44
52.00	67.53	68.42	69.33	70.27	71.23	72.22
60.00	77.92	78.95	80.00	81.08	82.19	83.33
70.00	90.91	92.11	93.33	94.59	95.89	97.22
80.00	103.90	105.26	106.67	108.11	109.59	111.11
90.00	116.88	118.42	120.00	121.62	123.29	125.00
100.00	129.87	131.58	133.33	135.14	136.99	138.89

Net amount	23%	24%	25%	26%	27%	28%
£	£	£	£	£	£	£
100.00	129.87	131.58	133.33	135.14	136.99	138.89
200.00	259.74	263.16	266.67	270.27	273.97	277.78
300.00	389.61	394.74	400.00	405.41	410.96	416.67
400.00	519.48	526.32	533.33	540.54	547.95	555.56
500.00	649.35	657.89	666.67	675.68	684.93	694.44
600.00	779.22	789.47	800.00	810.81	821.92	833.33
700.00	909.09	921.05	933.33	945.95	958.90	972.22
800.00	1,038.96	1,052.63	1,066.67	1,081.08	1,095.89	1,111.11
900.00	1,168.83	1,184.21	1,200.00	1,216.22	1,232.88	1,250.00
1,000.00	1,298.70	1,315.79	1,333.33	1,351.35	1,369.86	1,388.89

---

[1] The basic rate from 6 April 1998. Higher rate tax payers are discussed on page 367.

[2] The *covenantor* means the person who signs the deed of covenant, the person giving the money.

[3] The *donor* means the person giving the money.

[4] Canon 1196 of the *Code of Canon Law*. An excellent guide to the Roman Catholic *Code of Canon Law* is the *Code of Canon Law Annotated*, edited by Ernest Caparros, Michel Thériault and Jean Thorn (Wilson and Lafleur Limitée, Montreal, 1993).

[5] In legal terms it is the PCC who should release the covenant, because the covenant is to pay money to the PCC. But this can be done privately on behalf of the PCC by the parish priest, the church treasurer or the covenant secretary.

[6] The donor could if necessary appeal to the bishop, and the parish priest and the PCC would have to obey the bishop's direction.

[7] See *Chitty on Contracts* 27th edn. (Sweet & Maxwell, 1994) paragraph 22–003.

[8] See page 372.

[9] This is an unwritten concession, and it cannot be relied on as certain.

[10] Page 372.

[11] See the Diocese of Truro Covenant handbook (written in 1991), page 12. Even though the Inland Revenue no longer ask to see every deed, I think the advice is still good.

[12] When people used to make significant gifts of thousands of pounds using deposited covenants, it was a matter of concern that if they died, their executors might seek to recover the balance of the loan (and if the beneficiaries insisted, the executors would be bound to do so). In order to avoid this difficulty, properly drafted letters of loan included a clause similar to ones seen on wills, showing that two witnesses had witnessed the signing of the letter.

Now that deposited covenants are normally only used for gifts under £250, it is not worth the bother of requiring them to be witnessed with this formality. If the donor dies and repayment is sought by his executors, this is unlikely to cause a church serious financial difficulty.

I know of no good reason to use a deposited covenant instead of Gift Aid for a gift over £250.

Chapter 26

CHURCH ACCOUNTS

We want to avoid any criticism of the way we administer this liberal gift. For we are taking pains to do what is right, not only in the eyes of the Lord but also in the eyes of men.[1]

PART IV.   CHURCH FINANCE

1.   INTRODUCTION

The Charities Act 1993 introduced new accounting rules for almost all charities, including money given to the Church.[2] To help PCCs prepare accounts which comply with the new law, General Synod has introduced its own set of rules for churches, the *Church Accounting Regulations* 1997. The Church of England Central Board of Finance (the CBF) has prepared a set of guidance notes, and these are published together with the regulations under the title *The Charities Act 1993 and the PCC* (Church House Publishing, 1997).[3]

PCCs should follow these new rules and the CBF guidance when they prepare the accounts for the 1998 annual parochial church meeting and thereafter. This chapter is an introduction to the new rules.

2.   AN ANNUAL REPORT

The best way to understand the new rules is to look at an example of what is now required. The first new requirement is for what is called an *annual report*. This has to contain more information than has usually been included in the PCC report for the annual parochial church meeting. The annual report should contain:

- a section on the matters that have been discussed at PCC meetings.
- a section on the financial activities of the parish.
- a lot of information which church members might take for granted, like how the PCC operates, and the names of its members.
- a review of progress and achievements, giving a flavour of the main areas of church life.

St Mark's Church, Bishopstown

**Annual Report
and
Financial Statements
of the
Parochial Church Council**

for the year ended 31 December 1997

Incumbent:
Name and address of the parish priest

Bank:
Name and address of the bank

Independent examination:
Name and address of the independent examiner

St Mark's Church, Bishopstown – Annual Report for 1997

Background

St Mark's Church, Bishopstown has the responsibility of co-operating with the incumbent, *Name*, in promoting in the ecclesiastical parish the whole mission of the Church, pastoral, evangelistic, social and ecumenical.

Membership

The PCC is a charity excepted from registration with the Charity Commission. Members of the PCC are either ex officio or elected by the annual parochial church meeting in accordance with the Church Representation Rules.

During the year the following served as members of the PCC:

The Incumbent: *Name*, the chairman.
The churchwardens: *Names*. *Name* was vice-chairman.
The representatives on the Deanery Synod were *Names*.
The elected members up to the APCM 1997 were *Names*.
The elected members from the APCM 1997 were *Names*.
The treasurer was *Name*.

PART IV.   CHURCH FINANCE

The secretary was *Name.*

Committees

Standing Committee

This is the only committee required by law. It has power to transact the business of the PCC between its meetings, subject to any directions given by the Council.

List any other committees and explain their function.

Church attendance

There are ...... parishioners on the Church Electoral Roll, ... of whom are not resident within the parish. ...... names were added during the year and ...... were removed either through death or because they moved away from the parish. The usual Sunday attendance, counted during May, was ......, [*but the number increased at festivals. Over 400 people came to the church during the Christmas period.*]

Review of the year

The full PCC met ...... times during the year with an average level of attendance of ...... per cent. The standing committee [*and any other committee*] met between meetings, and minutes of their meetings were received by the full PCC and discussed where necessary.

[*Continue with a report on the main proceedings of the PCC and the activities in the parish.*

Summarise also the major financial highlights of the year. This is discussed below.]

On behalf of the PCC

The Revd *Name* (Chairman)

Date

As this example shows, the annual report has to contain certain information:[4]

- the full name of the church and the town: St Mark's Church, Bishopstown, or whatever.

- the location of the church (or address if it has one), and the correspondence address – (the address of the church office, the parish priest or a churchwarden).
- a statement that the PCC is required, as stated in the Parochial Church Councils (Powers) Measure 1956, to co-operate with the parish priest in promoting in the parish the whole mission of the Church, pastoral, evangelistic, social and ecumenical.
- the names of the members of the PCC who have served since the commencement of the financial year until the approval of the accounts. The financial year begins in January. PCC members are elected at the annual parochial church meeting, which has to be held not later than 30 April. So the report should include the names of the people on the PCC *over two years*. The names of the churchwardens, treasurer and secretary to the PCC should be stated.
- a brief description of the way the PCC organises itself in order to carry out its business.
- the number on the electoral roll, and the number of usual Sunday worshippers.

The name and address or the independent examiner or auditor should be given,[5] also the address of the bankers, and legal and other advisers to the PCC.[6]

The review of the year should include any significant developments and achievements, and any significant changes over the year. Any important events which have affected what the PCC has done, and any likely future developments should also be included.

Consider mentioning:

- how the church's work has developed towards fulfilling its aims.
- what progress has been made in specific projects.
- how the church has responded to important events.
- the *value* of the church, and not just what it costs.

The review of the year should summarise the financial activities of the church. Examples of the sort of items to mention are given in *The Charities Act 1993 and the PCC*.[7] They include:

- major transactions:

> The repairs to the church roof cost £6,000, but we received a grant of £2,000 from a local trust fund towards this.

- a comment on the planned giving.
- legacies received.
- fund-raising efforts.
- donations to other charities.
- payments made to members of the PCC if not shown in the accounts, such as payments to the organist or the verger.

3.   A SET OF ACCOUNTS FOR A MEDIUM SIZE CHURCH

Here is a set of accounts for a church whose gross income is under £100,000.[8] The CBF estimates that 12,000 of the 13,000 PCCs in England have an income under £100,000, so the example shown below should cover by far the majority of churches.

If the gross income of a church for the current year is under £100,000, the accounts may be prepared using what is known as the *receipts and payments basis*. This is the way most churches have done their accounts in the past, and so should not be difficult to understand. Churches whose gross income exceed £100,000 have to prepare their accounts using what is known as the *accruals basis*, which is less familiar to most people.[9]

A set of accounts prepared using the *receipts and payments* basis has two parts: one or more receipts and payments accounts, and a statement of assets and liabilities.

(a)   A receipts and payments account

A receipts and payments account is a summary of the money received and paid out during the financial year.

The CBF strongly recommends[10] that churches should adopt certain specific headings in their receipts and payments accounts.[11] These headings may be new to you. Under receipts, the headings are:

- Incoming resources from donors.
  This means covenants, income tax recovered, Sunday collections, gifts made at gift days.
- Other voluntary incoming resources.

Such as grants from local authorities, special donations, legacies, fetes and bazaars.

- Income from investments.
  Dividends, bank and building society interest, rent from land and buildings.
- Income from charitable and ancillary trading.
  Such as income from the bookstall, church hall lettings, magazines, fees for weddings.
- Income from non-charitable trading.
  Where the PCC funds were not put at risk.
- Other ordinary incoming resources.
  Insurance claims, and sale proceeds when assets are sold.

The headings for expenses are:

- Grants.
- Activities directly relating to the work of the church.
- Church management and administration.
- Fund-raising and publicity.

These headings for expenses are explained in Chapter 4, 'The Treasurer'. [12]

The accounts should show the comparable figures for the previous year for each entry. In the example shown below, to make the accounts easier to understand I have shown where the figures should appear for the previous year, but have filled in ✱✱✱✱ instead of actual figures.

In Chapter 4, 'The Treasurer', I explained the three different type of fund: unrestricted funds, restricted funds, and endowments.

- *Unrestricted funds* can be spent by the PCC on anything related to the church.
- *Restricted funds* can only be used for the purposes for which they were given.
- *Endowment funds* are where (in general) only the income from the funds can be spent.

I mentioned also that churches may have one or more *designated funds*, which are a type of unrestricted fund. The money in a designated fund could if necessary be spent on any general church purpose, but the

PCC has *designated*, in other words *set aside*, the money in the fund for a particular purpose.

If the church has both restricted and unrestricted funds, the church should show a separate receipts and payments account for each type of fund.

Let us start with the *general fund receipts and payments account*. It shows what has been received into and paid out of the *general fund*. The general fund is an unrestricted fund. The general fund receipts and payments account is likely to be by far the most complicated of the receipts and payments accounts which need to be prepared.

(i)   A general fund account

St Mark's Church, Bishopstown

Financial Statement for the Year ended 31 December 1997

General Fund Receipts and Payments Account

	1997		1996	
	£	£	£	£
Receipts				
Incoming resources from donors				
Planned giving	34,500		****	
Collections and other giving	4,500		****	
Income tax recovered	9,600		****	
		48,600		****
Other voluntary incoming resources				
Legacy	4,500		****	
Donations	1,800		****	
Summer fete	800		****	
		7,100		****
Income from investments				
Bank interest		250		****
Income from charitable and ancillary trading				
Church bookshop	2,500		****	
Rent from church hall	6,200		****	
Fees	600		****	
Magazine sales	300		****	
		9,600		****
Total Receipts		**65,550**		****

Payments

Grants
Overseas mission and relief agencies		5,300	****

Activities directly relating to the work of the church
Diocesan quota	35,000		****
Church running expenses	7,800		****
Clergy expenses	3,600		****
Cost of services	2,500		****
Printing magazine	900		****
Buildings maintenance	5,200		****
Designated to the choir fund	1000		****
Materials for *Alpha* course	500		****
		56,500	****

Church management and administration
Printing and stationery	500		****
Salary to administrator	2,000		****
		2,500	****
Total Payments		**64,300**	****

Excess of Receipts over Payments		**1,250**	****
Bank current and deposit accounts at 1 Jan. 1997		3,400	****
Bank current and deposit accounts at 31 Dec. 1997		4,650	****

For those not familiar with accounts, at the most basic level this account shows that the receipts of the church amounted to £65,550 over the year, and the payments amounted to £64,300, so the church ended up with a surplus for the year of £1,250 (the figures shown in bold in the table). The figures for the bank account at the start and the end of the year show a difference of £1,250, which corresponds with the surplus for the year.

At a more detailed level, this account shows the different categories of receipts and payments, which make up these two totals. Each group of figures in the first column of numbers is added together, and the total shown in the second column. Thus, the three figures shown under the first heading *Incoming resources from donors* £34,500, £4,500 and

£9,600 produce the total £48,600 shown in the second column of numbers. There is only one item shown under the heading *Income from investments*, so it goes straight into the second column. The £65,550 shown for *Total Receipts* is the total of the four items above it in the second column. The rest of the account should now be clear to you.

What you do not see mentioned specifically in these accounts are the usual items such as heating and lighting, and insurance. They are there, but they are included in the item *church running expenses*. *The Charities Act 1993 and the PCC*, pages 16–17 sets out a whole range of typical church expenses, and what items these should now come under in the accounts. (Items such as heating, lighting and insurance *can* be shown separately if it would help people understand the accounts better.[13])

The General Fund account shows a payment of £1,000 designated to the choir fund. So there should be a receipts and payments account for the choir fund. Here it is.

(ii)   A designated fund account

Choir Fund Receipts and Payments Account – Designated Fund

	1997 £	£	1996 £	£
Receipts				
Interest from CBF Deposit Fund		300		****
Payments				
Choir music	250		****	
Payments to professional singers	1200		****	
Total Payments		1,450		****
Deficiency of Receipts over Payments		(1,150)		****
Transfers				
Designated income from general fund		1,000		****
Bank current and deposit accounts at 1 Jan. 1997		2,300		****
Bank current and deposit accounts at 31 Dec. 1997		2,150		****

This shows that the choir fund paid out more than it received. Its receipts were £300 and its payments £1,450, so it made a deficit of £1,150. Negative figures are usually shown in accounts with round brackets rather than a minus sign. The choir fund received a contribution of £1,000 from the general fund, so if you take the starting figure in the bank of £2,300, add the £1,000 transferred to the account, and subtract the £1,150 loss, you end up with the closing figure in the account, £2,150.

The fund of £2,300 at the start of the year had been built up from previous years as a designated fund. The only money received by the choir fund was interest on a deposit account, and the money transferred to it from the general fund.

Note that there were no donations to the choir fund. All the money in the choir fund is simply money which the PCC has directed towards the choir, but which could be used for other purposes if need be. If money had been given by people to the choir fund specifically for the music in the church, that money would have had to be kept in a separate *restricted* fund choir account, and could not be used by the PCC for any other purpose. There would then be two funds: the existing designated fund and the new restricted fund.

The church also has a restricted fund, the Church Fabric Fund, consisting of gifts given to the church specifically for the church building and contents. There were no transfers to the Church Fabric Fund from the general fund (or else they would have been shown in the receipts and payments account for the general fund). On the next page is the receipts and payments account for the Church Fabric Fund.

(iii)   A restricted fund account

Church Fabric Fund Receipts and Payments Account – Restricted Fund

	1997 £	£	1996 £	£
Receipts				
Interest from CBF Deposit Fund	540		****	
Restricted donations	19,600		****	
		20,140		****
Payments				
New sound system	3,400		****	
New kitchen	12,500		****	
Photocopier	3,000		****	
Total Payments		18,900		****
Excess of Receipts over Payments		**1,240**		****
Bank current and deposit accounts at 1 Jan. 1997		3,500		****
Bank current and deposit accounts at 31 Dec. 1997		4,740		****

Here the receipts include large donations specifically for the fabric of the building. This includes the fittings, so the purchase of the photocopier and the new sound system was a proper use of the money (as of course was the new church kitchen). The account shows a profit of £1,240, and this is reflected in the increase in the Fabric Fund's bank account.

One more account is needed for this church, a *Statement of Assets and Liabilities* at the end of the financial year.

(b)   A statement of assets and liabilities

A statement of assets and liabilities is not a balance sheet, but simply a list of the PCC's significant possessions and obligations at the year end. Assets will include:

- all funds owned by the PCC.
- debts owed to the PCC (adequately explained).

- investments (shown at their original cost with, if desired, a note of their year-end market value).
- land, buildings and equipment.

The statements of assets and liabilities should show the different types of funds separately. Here is the statement of assets and liabilities for our imaginary church St Mark's.

Statement of Assets and Liabilities at 31 December 1997

	General Fund £	Fabric Fund £	Choir Fund £	Total 1997 £	Total 1996 £
Monetary assets					
Bank current and deposit account	4,650	4,740	2,150	11,540	****
CBF Deposit fund	4,500	15,000	4,000	23,500	****
Total cash	9,150	19,740	6,150	35,040	****
Debtors					
End of year income tax claim (received Jan 98)	3,200			3,200	****
Other assets					
Church hall					
Photocopier					
Liabilities					
Hire of coach for Christmas outing	250				

There is no need to value assets for a statement of assets and liabilities. In this example, assets such as the church hall and the photocopier should be mentioned, but it is not necessary to give a value for them.

The bank current and deposit accounts figures in this statement should agree with the figures shown in each of the receipts and payments accounts. For example, the balance at 31 December 1997 in the general fund account was £4,650, and this appears in both the receipts and payments account and in the statement of assets and liabilities.

From this account you can see the overall picture of the church's material wealth. It has cash assets of £35,040, plus some tax to be repaid. It owns its church hall, and its photocopier. It has no large outstanding debts from the previous year, just one debt which became due over the Christmas period.

In outline, this is the format for a set of church accounts for an average size church. In practice, life is not often quite as simple as this, and you will need to read *The Charities Act 1993 and the PCC* to see how the new rules apply to your situation. In particular, there are special rules which apply in the following situations:

- team and group ministries.
- district church councils.
- Vicar and warden trusts administered by the PCC.
- 'Friends' and other organisations connected to the church.

For example, team and group ministries which consist of a number of separate parishes now need to produce separate accounts for each parish. Where there is a single parish but more than one place of worship, accounts need to be produced for the parish as a whole. Even if district church councils have been accustomed to producing their own separate accounts, accounts should now be produced for the parish as a whole, unless the bishop's council has given permission for them to produce their own separate accounts.[14] If the total income or expenditure is over £100,000, these accounts should be prepared on the accruals basis rather than the receipts and payments basis. Chapter 1 of *The Charities Act 1993 and the PCC* covers team ministries and these other topics.

4.   ACCOUNTS FOR A LARGER CHURCH

Where the gross income of the church in the current year is more than £100,000 then the accounts should be prepared using the *accruals basis*. Instead of a receipts and payments account there should now be a *statement of financial activities*, and instead of a statement of assets and liabilities there should now be a *balance sheet*. There should also be *notes to the accounts*, which explain the accounting policies adopted and provide other useful information.

In a set of accounts prepared on the receipts and payments basis, debts owing by the church are shown in the accounts only when they are actually paid, and income is shown only when it is actually received. In a set of accounts prepared on the accruals basis, debts are shown when they have accrued due, rather than when they are paid; likewise income is shown when it has accrued due to the church, not when it is actually received. That is the fundamental difference between the two ways of preparing accounts. Most traders and all companies prepare their accounts on the accruals basis rather than the receipts and payments basis.

(a)   A statement of financial activities

The *statement of financial activities* shows all resources made available to the PCC and all expenditure incurred by the PCC. Income is referred to as *incoming resources*, and has to be set out under the following headings:

- incoming resources from donors.
- other voluntary incoming resources.
- income from investments.
- income from charitable and ancillary trading.
- income from non-charitable trading.
- other ordinary incoming resources.

In the section 'A receipts and payments account',[15] I said that these headings are strongly recommended. In a *statement of financial activities* these headings have to be used.

Expenditure is referred to as *resources used*, and has to be set out under the following headings:

- grants.
- activities directly relating to the work of the church.
- fund-raising and publicity.
- church management and administration.

The same rule applies here. In a receipts and payments accounts, these headings are strongly recommended. In a statement of financial activities they have to be used.

The complete statement of financial activities has to be set out so as to show the following information:[16]

- total incoming resources (a).
- total expenditure (b).
- transfers between funds (c).

- net incoming resources (d). This is (a) – (b) – (c).
- gains and losses on investments (e).
- net movement in funds (f). This is (d) + (e).
- balances brought forward at 1 January (g).
- balances carried forward at 31 December. This is (f) + (g).

This sounds very technical, but it is not as fearsome as it seems. The best way to understand what is required is to look at the example statement of financial activities in *The Charities Act 1993 and the PCC*, page 53, and the notes at pages 55–56.

(b)   A balance sheet

The *balance sheet* shows the assets, liabilities and funds of the PCC. The form is similar to that used for company accounts. It has to be set out so as to show the following information:[17]

- fixed assets (a).
- current assets (b).
- current liabilities (creditors due within one year) (c).
- net current assets (d). This is (b) – (c).
- total assets after deduction of current liabilities (e). This is (a) + (d).
- creditors due after one year (f).
- provision for liabilities or charges (g).
- net assets. This is (e) – (f) – (g).
- the funds of the PCC divided into unrestricted funds, restricted funds and endowment funds.

A look at the example balance sheet in *The Charities Act 1993 and the PCC*, page 54, and the notes at page 57 will explain what is required.

5.   INDEPENDENT EXAMINER OR AUDITOR

Any church whose income or expenditure is over £250,000 should have its accounts professionally audited. So should any church whose income or expenditure was over £250,000 in either of the last two years, even if the current year is less than this figure. Every other church should have its accounts independently examined rather than audited.

(a)   What is an independent examination?

An independent examination is a review of the accounting records kept by the PCC and of the accounts themselves. It is a formal exercise, involving a number of set tasks. It is not as stringent as an audit, but it needs to be properly planned, controlled and recorded. *The Charities Act 1993 and the PCC* contains a work programme[18] setting out the tasks which the independent examiner should carry out to check that the accounts and financial records are in order. *The Charities Act 1993 and the PCC*, pages 58 and 59 sets out examples of the report which the independent examiner has to give once he has examined the accounts and records of the church.

(b)   Selection of an independent examiner

The annual parochial church meeting appoints an independent examiner. Before recommending a person to the annual parochial church meeting for appointment, the PCC should consider carefully his suitability, as the annual parochial church meeting will not be able to do this.

The Charities Act 1993 section 43 describes an independent examiner as:

> an independent person who is reasonably believed by the trustees to have the requisite ability and practical experience to carry out a competent examination of the accounts.

The PCC should therefore check that the person they recommend:

- is independent, and
- has both the ability and the practical experience to carry out the task.

(i)   Independence

Being *independent* means he or she should not be connected with the PCC. So he or she should not be:

- a member of the PCC.
- a member of a PCC committee.
- employed by the PCC.

Nor should a close relative, a business partner, or an employee of any of these persons be appointed.

An independent examiner can however be a member of the church with their name on the electoral roll.

(ii)   The necessary ability and practical experience

This depends very much on the size and complexity of the PCC's accounts.

For small PCCs with an income of less than about £5,000, and accounts prepared on the receipts and payments basis, anyone with basic book-keeping skills should be able to carry out the necessary work.

For larger PCCs with an income of up to £100,000, and with accounts prepared on the receipts and payments basis, the person needs to be more familiar with business and financial matters, but does not need not to be a qualified accountant. For a PCC with an income close to £100,000 a finance manager of a large commercial organisation would be suitable; for lower incomes, a bank or building society manager, or a local authority treasurer would be suitable; for a small PCC a businessman or school teacher may have the necessary skill.

If the PCC has an income over £100,000, it should consider appointing a qualified accountant to carry out the independent examination. If it has an income over £250,000 a fully qualified auditor should be appointed.

(c)   Payment to the independent examiner

Some people may be willing to carry out an independent examination free of charge. Others will expect to be paid a reasonable fee. Before appointing someone who may be willing to do the work for nothing, the PCC should be sure that he can do the job properly.

[1] 2 Cor. 8: 20–21.
[2] The detailed statutory regulations are contained in the Charities (Accounts and Reports) Regulations 1995 and a Statement of Recommended Practice *Accounting by Charities* issued by the Charity Commission in 1995.
[3] ISBN 0 7151 8095 9.
[4] Church Accounting Regulations 1997, regulation 27.
[5] Church Accounting Regulations 1997, regulations 19 and 25.
[6] *The Charities Act 1993 and the PCC* at page 31.

---

[7] *The Charities Act 1993 and the PCC* guidance at page 31, and the example annual report at page 49.

[8] See Chapter 2 of *The Charities Act 1993 and the PCC* for a definition of gross income.

[9] Churches whose income or expenditure is under £100,000 can if they wish prepare their accounts on the accruals basis. Most churches with an income under £100,000 have prepared their accounts in the past on the receipts and payments basis, and will continue to do so.

[10] *The Charities Act 1993 and the PCC*, page 16.

[11] These headings are compulsory where accounts are prepared on the accruals basis and the gross income for the year is greater than £100,000.

[12] See also *The Charities Act 1993 and the PCC*, chapter 6.

[13] In a set of accrual accounts, the figures for heating, lighting and insurance could be set out in the notes which accompany the accounts. A set of receipt and payments accounts does not normally have any notes accompanying the accounts.

[14] As from March 1998 a PCC can apply to the bishop's council of the diocese for the DCC to be treated as a parish for the purpose of producing financial statements. If the bishop's council agrees, the DCC then produces financial statements in respect of the district instead of consolidating its own financial statements in the statements of the whole parish: see Rule 18 of the Church Representation Rules as amended by the Church Representation Rules (Amendment) Resolution 1998, SI 1998 No. 319.

[15] See page 396.

[16] Church Accounting Regulations 1997, regulation 10 and appendix I.

[17] Church Accounting Regulations 1997, regulation 12 and appendix II.

[18] *The Charities Act 1993 and the PCC*, pages 40 and 41. These pages may be photocopied and given to the independent examiner.

Chapter 27

VAT

1.   INTRODUCTION

V alue Added Tax does not affect the normal activities of churches such as weddings, funerals, and Sunday services. It applies only when goods or services are sold for money as part of a business. So the church has to pay VAT on many of the things it buys or pays for.

Some goods and services likely to affect churches are exempt from VAT or subject to VAT at a reduced rate. Other goods and services are liable to VAT at the standard rate. Churches should know what goods and services are subject to VAT, what goods are exempt, and when a reduced rate of VAT is payable, so that they do not pay more VAT than they need.

Most churches do not need to register for VAT as they do not supply goods or services which are subject to VAT worth more than £49,000 in a year.

2.   AN OUTLINE OF THE VAT SYSTEM

(a)   General

VAT is a tax which, with a few exceptions, applies to everything sold or supplied in the course of a business. The standard rate of VAT is 17.5 per cent. Whenever a business sells goods or services, it has to charge VAT at 17.5 per cent to the person or business it supplies them to.

If the person buying the goods or services is himself in business, that person pays VAT whenever his business buys things, and he charges VAT whenever his business sells things. He has to keep an account of both the VAT which he pays when his business buys things, and the VAT which he charges when his business sells them. The VAT he pays when he buys things for his business is known as *input tax*, and the VAT he charges when his business sells things is known as *output tax*. At regular intervals he should fill in a tax form known as a VAT return, and send it to HM Customs and Excise. (VAT is run by HM Customs and Excise, not by the Inland Revenue.) If the return shows that his input tax is greater than his output tax, then HM Customs and Excise will repay to

412

him the difference. If his business is going well, it is more likely that his output tax will be greater than his input tax. If this is so, he has to pay to HM Customs and Excise the difference.

People who do not purchase goods as part of a business cannot recover the VAT they have paid. So people who buy goods for home use, and churches (unless they are registered for VAT), cannot recover the VAT they have paid when they buy goods and services.

(b)   Administration

When a person sells or supplies something in the course of his business, he has to give the purchaser a VAT invoice. This shows the name and address and the VAT registration number of the supplier, the name and address of the purchaser, the date and a description of the goods or services supplied. It also has to show the price and the VAT separately.

(c)   Registration

From 1 December 1997 a trader has to register for VAT if he has supplied more than £49,000 worth of goods or services in the last 12 months, or if he is likely to supply more than £49,000 worth of goods or services in the following 30 days.

Any church thinking of registering for VAT should take advice both from the local VAT office and from the diocesan office.

(d)   Zero-rated goods, and exempt goods

Some goods are *zero-rated* for VAT; others are *exempt* from VAT. In both cases, a person who buys the goods pays no VAT. The difference is that a person who trades in *zero-rated* goods can still claim back VAT from HM Customs and Excise, but a person who deals in *exempt* goods can not claim back any VAT which relates to those goods. In practice, this rule only applies if the VAT input tax relating to exempt goods is more than £7,500 a year, or unless it exceeds the VAT input tax for ordinary goods. For most churches registered for VAT, it should make no difference whether goods are zero-rated or exempt. If you are in any doubt about the matter, you should contact your local VAT office for advice.

Examples of zero-rated goods are:

- food for human consumption.
- books.
- advertisements for a charity.
- construction and sale by a builder of new buildings for a charity.
- alterations, but not repairs, to certain listed buildings including churches.

Food supplied by caterers is taxable at the standard rate (17.5 per cent), as are sweets and drinks.

Examples of supplies which are exempt from VAT are:

- leases, licenses and other rights over land. Business landlords can choose to charge tax, and frequently do so for business leases.
- insurance.
- post.
- betting, gaming and lotteries.
- dealing in stocks and shares and dealing in money.
- education.
- health and welfare.
- funeral arrangements.
- fund-raising events by charities.

3.   VAT ON SERVICES SUPPLIED TO THE CHURCH

(a)   Construction work

Most construction work is subject to VAT at the standard rate. This includes

- all repairs and maintenance of church buildings.
- all alterations and extensions to church buildings, unless they are listed buildings.

The following types of construction work are exempt from VAT. This means that the church does not have to pay VAT on them. You should ask the church architect to issue the builder with a certificate so that the builder does not have to charge VAT to the church.

(i)   Construction of a new church building

The construction of a new church building is exempt from VAT. To claim the exemption, the new church should either be a completely new building, or it should be built on the site of an old church which has been knocked down to ground level.

If you build the new church on the site of an old church, you may wish to use the foundations of the old church building. The new church is still exempt from VAT if you do so. In some cases, the local authority giving planning permission may require you to retain a single facade of the old church building, or a double facade on a corner site. If they do so, building the rest of the new church is exempt from VAT.

(ii)   Construction of a new church hall

The construction of a new church hall is exempt from VAT if the hall is to be used by the local community for social purposes or recreation.

(iii)   Construction of a new church annex

The construction of a church annex is exempt from VAT if certain conditions are satisfied.

- The annex should be connected to the church by a door or corridor.
- It should have its own separate entrance.
- It should be intended to be used as a church hall or for some charitable use.

(iv)   Alterations and extensions to listed buildings

If the church is a listed building, alterations and extensions which have been approved by the local planning authority are exempt from VAT.

(v)   Construction of a new vicarage

All new housing is exempt from VAT, so no VAT is payable where a new vicarage is built.

(vi)   Demolition work

Demolition work is normally subject to VAT. But if the demolition is part of building a new church, or one of the other types of building which is exempt from VAT, then there is no VAT to pay on the demolition work.

(b)   Bells and organ

The VAT position depends on whether the bells or the organ are to be installed in a new church or in an existing church. It also depends on whether or not an existing church is a listed building.

(i)   New church buildings

There is no VAT on the cost of installing bells or a fixed organ in a new church.

(ii)   Existing churches which are not listed buildings

The cost or installing or repairing bells or a fixed organ in an existing church which is not a listed building is subject to VAT.

(iii)   Existing churches which are listed buildings

If the church is a listed building, repairs are subject to VAT, but approved alterations are exempt from VAT. So, if the work on the organ and the bells is part of a scheme of approved alterations to a listed building, it will be exempt from VAT. Otherwise it will be subject to VAT at the standard rate.

(c)   Aids for handicapped persons

Most work to provide aids for handicapped persons on church premises is exempt from VAT. This covers such items as the construction of wheelchair ramps, widening doorways for wheelchair users, installing chair lifts for wheelchairs, installing and repairing an induction loop system for the deaf, and installing lavatories for the disabled.

(d)   Water, fuel and power

There is no VAT to pay on water supplied to churches. A reduced rate of VAT (5 per cent) is payable on fuel and power supplied to churches.[1]

(e)   *Professional fees*

Charges by solicitors, surveyors and accountants for professional services are subject to VAT at the standard rate.

(f)   *Pre-printed stationery used for fund-raising*

Pre-printed stationery, such as letters, envelopes, and collecting boxes, used for special church appeals are zero-rated. This does not include stationery used for regular giving such as the envelopes used in planned giving schemes. These are subject to VAT at the standard rate.

4.   SALES BY A CHURCH

If a church is registered for VAT it should charge VAT when it sells goods or services, unless they are zero-rated or exempt. If it is not registered for VAT then it does not charge VAT.

If the church is registered for VAT, it will need to charge VAT on:

- sales of goods bought for resale, for example at bazaars. But goods which have been *given* to the church are exempt from VAT when they are later sold by the church.
- catering – but see *Fund-raising events* and *Donations* below.
- admission charges.
- sale of slides, photographs, and postcards.
- printed orders of service.
- diaries and address books

Lettings of the church hall are exempt from VAT.

5.   SPECIAL CASES

(a)   *The quota or parish share*

There is no VAT on the quota or parish share paid to the diocese.

(b)   *Statutory fees*

There is no VAT on the statutory fees for marriages and funerals.

(c)   Fund-raising events

One-off fund-raising events such as a fete are exempt if the proceeds are for the church or some other charity. They should not form part of a series of regularly run or similar events.

So, catering at a fete, a coffee morning, or a church lunch to raise funds would be exempt from VAT. Catering for an *Alpha* course would be subject to VAT, because that is run on a series of evenings.[2]

(d)   Donations

Voluntary donations such as church collections and income from covenants are outside the scope of VAT.

If a church asks for a donation towards a meal, rather than charging a fixed price for it, the money received is outside the scope of VAT. It should be made clear that people can have the meal without paying, and that donations are entirely voluntary.[3]

6.   FURTHER INFORMATION

The following VAT Notices are likely to be useful. They are available from your local VAT office.

- *VAT: The VAT Guide* (VAT Notice 700, HM Customs and Excise, 1996). This is a general guide to VAT.
- *VAT: Charities* (VAT Notice 701/1, HM Customs and Excise, 1995) gives advice on VAT and charities.
- *VAT: Buildings and construction* (VAT Notice 708, HM Customs and Excise, 1997). This includes advice on the VAT exemption for the construction of churches and church halls.
- *VAT: VAT refunds for 'do-it-yourself' builders and converters* (VAT Notice 719, HM Customs and Excise, 1996) gives advice on the DIY Builders Scheme, which may be relevant to church buildings.
- *VAT: Burial, cremation and the commemoration of the dead* (VAT Notice 701/32, HM Customs and Excise, 1997) gives advice on VAT for goods supplied in connection with burial and cremation.

Further advice is available from your local VAT office. The national VAT office for enquires about property construction matters is

HM CUSTOMS AND EXCISE
Land and Property Division,
Thomas Paine House,
Angel Square,
Torrens Street,
London EC1V 1TA

Tel: 0171 865 3014

In 1997 the Churches' Main Committee published a useful booklet *Value Added Tax and the Churches*. This can be obtained from

THE CHURCHES' MAIN COMMITTEE
Fielden House,
Little College Street,
Westminster,
London SW1P 3JZ

Tel: 0171 222 4984

Fax: 0171 233 1104

---

[1] If the 'business' use of the church (for example, from admission charges or the letting of church buildings) amounts to more than 40 per cent of the total use of the building, then a proportion of the fuel is subject to VAT at the standard rate.
[2] For more on *Alpha* course catering, see Chapter 11, 'Food and drink'.
[3] Some charities have a sign saying that the meal costs (say) 50p, but they would like you to pay (say) £2.50 for the meal. In this case HM Customs and Excise would charge the charity VAT on the 50p, and treat the extra £2 as a donation. It should be clear to everyone buying a meal that anything above the 50p is entirely voluntary.

Appendices

APPENDICES

APPENDIX 1

DIOCESAN OFFICES ADDRESS LIST

The names of the diocesan secretaries are correct at the time of writing. The diocesan secretaries will change from time to time, but the addresses of the diocesan offices are likely to remain fairly constant.

BATH AND WELLS
Mr Nicholas Denison
The Diocesan Office,
The Old Deanery,
Wells,
Somerset BA5 2UG

Tel: 01749 670777

BIRMINGHAM
Mr Jim Drennan
175 Harborne Park Road,
Harborne,
Birmingham B17 0BH

Tel: 0121 427 5141

BLACKBURN
The Rev Michael Wedgeworth
Diocesan Offices,
Cathedral Close,
Blackburn,
Lancs BB1 5AA

Tel: 01254 54421

BRADFORD
Mr Malcolm Halliday
Cathedral Hall,
Stott Hill,
Bradford,
West Yorks BD1 4ET

TEL: 01274 725958

APPENDIX 1

BRISTOL
Mrs Lesley Farrall
Diocesan Church House,
23 Great George Street,
Bristol,
Avon BS1 5QZ

Tel: 0117 921 4411

CANTERBURY
Mr David Kemp
Diocesan House,
Lady Wootton's Green,
Canterbury CT1 1NQ

Tel: 01227 459401

CARLISLE
Canon Colin Hill
Church House,
West Walls,
Carlisle,
Cumbria CA3 8UE

Tel: 01228 22573

CHELMSFORD
Mr David Phillips
Guy Harlings,
53 New Street,
Chelmsford,
Essex CM1 1AT

Tel: 01245 266731

CHESTER
Mr Peter Mills
Diocesan House,
Raymond Street,
Chester CH1 4PN

Tel: 01244 379222

CHICHESTER
Mr Jonathan Prichard
Diocesan Church House,
211 New Church Road,
Hove,
East Sussex BN3 4ED

Tel: 01273 421021

COVENTRY
Mrs Isobel Chapman
Church House,
Palmerston Road,
Coventry CV5 6FJ

Tel: 01203 674328

DERBY
Mr Bob Carey
Derby Church House,
Full Street,
Derby DE1 3DR

Tel: 01332 382233

DURHAM
Mr W. Hurworth *(until June 1998)*
Diocesan Office,
Auckland Castle,
Market Place,
Bishop Auckland,
County Durham DL14 7QJ

Tel: 01388 604515

ELY
Dr M. E. Lavis
Bishop Woodford House,
Barton Road,
Ely,
Cambs CB7 4DX

Tel: 01353 663579

THE DIOCESE IN EUROPE
The Ven. Gordon Reid
14 Tufton Street,
Westminster,
London SW1P 3QZ

Tel: 0171 976 8001

EXETER
Mr Mark Beedell
Diocesan House,
Palace Gate,
Exeter,
Devon EX1 1HX

Tel: 01392 272686

GLOUCESTER
Mr Michael Williams
Church House,
College Green,
Gloucester GL1 2LY

Tel: 01452 410022

GUILDFORD
Mrs Kristina Ingate
Diocesan House,
Quarry Street,
Guildford,
Surrey GU1 3XG

Tel: 01483 571826

HEREFORD
Miss Sylvia Green
The Palace,
Hereford HR4 9BL

Tel: 01432 353863

LEICESTER
Mr Jonathan Cryer
Church House,
3/5 St Martin's East,
Leicester LE1 5FX

Tel: 0116 262 7445

LICHFIELD
Mr David Taylor
St Mary's House,
The Close,
Lichfield,
Staffs WS13 7LD

Tel: 01543 414551

LINCOLN
Mr Phil Hamlyn Williams
The Old Palace,
Lincoln LN2 1PU

Tel: 01522 529241

LIVERPOOL
Mr Keith Cawdron
Church House,
1 Hanover Street,
Liverpool L1 3DW

Tel: 0151 709 9722

425

LONDON
Mr Christopher Smith
London Diocesan House,
36 Causton Street,
London SW1P 4AU

Tel: 0171 932 1100

MANCHESTER
Mrs Jackie Park
Diocesan Church House,
90 Deansgate,
Manchester M3 2GH

Tel: 0161 833 9521

NEWCASTLE
Mr Michael Craster *(until June 1998)*
Church House,
Grainger Park Road,
Newcastle upon Tyne NE4 8SX

Tel: 0191 226 0622

NORWICH
Mr David Aveney
Diocesan House,
109 Dereham Road,
Easton,
Norwich,
Norfolk NR9 5ES

Tel: 01603 880853

OXFORD
Mr Terry Landsbert *(until July 1998)*
Diocesan Church House,
North Hinksey,
Oxford OX2 0NB

Tel: 01865 244566

PETERBOROUGH
Mr K. H. Hope-Jones
Diocesan Office,
The Palace,
Peterborough,
Cambs PE1 1YB

Tel: 01733 64448

PORTSMOUTH
Mr Michael Jordan
Cathedral House,
St Thomas's Street,
Portsmouth,
Hants PO1 2HA

Tel: 01705 825731

RIPON
Mr P. M. Erundel
Diocesan Office,
St Mary's Street,
Leeds LS9 7DP

Tel: 0113 248 7487

ROCHESTER
Mr Peter Law
St Nicholas Church,
Boley Hill,
Rochester,
Kent ME1 1SL

Tel: 01634 830333

ST ALBANS
Mr Lawrence Nicholls
Holywell Lodge,
41 Holywell Hill,
St Albans,
Herts AL1 1HE

Tel: 01727 854532

ST EDMUNDSBURY AND
IPSWICH
Mr Nicholas Edgell
Diocesan House,
13/15 Tower Street,
Ipswich,
Suffolk IP1 3BG

Tel: 01473 211028

SALISBURY
The Rev Karen Curnoch
Church House,
Crane Street,
Salisbury,
Wilts SP1 2QB

Tel: 01722 411922

SHEFFIELD
Mr Tony Beck
Diocesan Church House,
95–99 Effingham Street,
Rotherham S65 1BL

Tel: 01709 511116

SODOR AND MAN
The Hon Christopher Murphy
Cooil Voorath,
The Cronk,
Ballaugh,
Isle of Man IM7 5AX

Tel: 01624 897800

SOUTHWARK
*(The position of diocesan
secretary is currently vacant.)*
Trinity House,
4 Chapel Court,
Borough High Street,
London SE1 1HW

Tel: 0171 403 8686

SOUTHWELL
Mr Brian Noake
Dunham House,
Westgate,
Southwell,
Notts NG25 0JL

Tel: 01636 814331

TRURO
Mr Colin Gorton *(until July
1998)*
Diocesan House,
Kenwyn,
Truro,
Cornwall TR1 3DU

Tel: 01872 274351

WAKEFIELD
Mr William Smith
Church House,
1 South Parade,
Wakefield WF1 1LP

Tel: 01924 371802

APPENDIX 1

WINCHESTER
Mr Ray Anderton
Church House,
9 The Close,
Winchester,
Hants SO23 9LS

Tel: 01962 844644

WORCESTER
Mr John Stanbury
The Old Palace,
Deansway,
Worcester WR1 2JE

Tel: 01905 20537

YORK
Mr Colin Sheppard
Church House,
Ogleforth,
York YP1 2JE

Tel: 01904 611696

APPENDIX 2

THE HOUSE OF BISHOPS' POLICY DOCUMENT ON CHILD PROTECTION

The House of Bishops' Policy Document on Child Protection (Church House Publishing, 1995) is in the process of being revised. The new House of Bishops' Policy Document is expected to be issued in April or May 1998, after this book has gone to press. The material in this Appendix is taken from a draft for the revised document prepared in January 1998. The official version may be slightly different.

The policy document consists of a policy statement, a detailed set of recommendations as to how the policy statement should be implemented, and various annexes. This is the text of the policy statement.

1. Christians are called to recognise the unique status of children. There is a special need to respect them as individuals and protect them in their vulnerability. Jesus warned that those who exploited or abused children deserved profound condemnation. Within the Kingdom of God children matter in their own right and are to be taken seriously.

2. The church is required by God to foster relationships of the utmost integrity, truthfulness and trustworthiness. Clergy and laity who work with children within the Church in any paid or voluntary capacity need to operate within a carefully thought-out framework of good policy and practice which will ensure that children are safeguarded and nurtured physically and emotionally as well as spiritually. Clergy and laity need to exercise the greatest care in their use of power and authority. They must avoid taking advantage of trust.

3. The highest professional standards should therefore be maintained in all pastoral, counselling, educational, worship and recreational situations. The exploitation of any relationship for self-gratification will not be tolerated.

4. The Church of England accepts the principle enshrined in the Children Act 1989 that the welfare of the child is paramount.[1]

5. Allegations of abuse will be taken seriously and appropriate steps will be taken.

6. The Church of England will collaborate fully with the statutory and voluntary agencies concerned with child abuse. It will not conduct investigations on its own.

7. All those working or seeking to work with children will be properly recruited and trained, and subject to whatever supervision is appropriate.

8. All candidates for ordained ministry and accredited lay ministry will be asked to declare whether they have any criminal convictions or whether certain types of orders of the civil courts have been made against them, and whether they have caused significant harm to children or put them at risk of significant harm.

9. The following will be asked to complete and submit the confidential declaration form[2] set out in Annex 1A to this Policy Statement[3]:

   (a) all clergy, whether stipendiary or not, who hold or are seeking to hold an office, a licence or a permission to officiate or exercise their ministry[4];

   (b) all members of the accredited lay ministry (including lay workers within the meaning of Canon Law and readers) who hold or are seeking a licence or permission to exercise their ministry; and

   (c) all paid staff and volunteers working or seeking to work in a capacity which involves work with children or which is likely to involve opportunities for unsupervised contact with them.

10. A search in the Department of Health's Consultancy Service Index will be made against all candidates for ordained ministry or accredited lay ministry, all those in categories (a) and (b) in paragraph 9 and those working or seeking to work as paid staff as set out in category (c).

11. In the case of those seeking to do paid or unpaid work under category (c) in paragraph 9, references will be obtained which satisfy the recommendations in the Home Office's Guidelines 'Safe from Harm'.

12. The procedure under paragraphs 9–11 above will be repeated on the person concerned seeking to move to a new appointment or position or new work.

....

The recommendations as to how the policy statement should be implemented cover the following topics:

- The Bishop's representative
- Recruitment of people to work with children
- Diocesan and parish procedures
- Definitions of abuse
- Receiving reports of abuse
- Legal procedures following allegations of abuse
- Church concerns following allegations
- Risk of untrue allegations
- Notifications to the Department of Health

Annex 1A is the confidential declaration form to be filled in and signed by the person applying for the position.

Annex 1B is the procedure to be followed when appointing clergy or accredited lay ministers.

Annex 1C is the procedure to be followed on appointing a full or part time paid worker with children/young people.

Annex 1D are guidelines on the recruitment and support of paid staff and volunteers. These are based on the guidelines contained in *Safe from Harm*.

Annex 1E is a list of offences listed or treated as listed in Schedule 1 to the Children and Young Persons Act 1933, and a list of offences specified in the Schedule to the Disqualification for Caring with Children Regulations 1991. The confidential declaration forms require 'spent convictions' under the Rehabilitation of Offenders Act 1974 to be disclosed if they are amongst these offences.

Annex 1F describes the Department of Health's Consultancy Service. The Department of Health operates a consultancy service, which applies to England and Wales, whereby local authorities, private and voluntary organisations can check the suitability of those they propose to employ in a child-care post.

Annex 2 is a statement from the Ecclesiastical Insurance Group.

Finally there is a resource list, giving the names of various publications and organisations concerned with child abuse.

---

[1] The Children Act 1989 defines a child as a person under 18 for most purposes.

[2] The form includes questions as to whether the person concerned has any criminal convictions, whether certain types of orders of the civil courts have been made against them and whether they have or have been alleged to have caused significant harm to a child or put a child at risk of significant harm.

[3] In the case of new appointments, the procedures in Annexes 1B, C and D should be followed.

[4] This category includes those in episcopal orders; and retired clergy holding permission to officiate. It also includes clergy of other Anglican Churches, and clergy of other Churches acting on the basis of or seeking permission from one of the Archbishops to exercise their ministry in the Church of England. Clergy holding or seeking an office or employment with a body outside the Church and not involved in any other ministry are not required to submit the declaration, and the procedure under paragraph 10 will not be necessary, if they are subject to a corresponding process in relation to the office or employment in question. (This would cover chaplains in a variety of fields of ministry.)

APPENDIX 3

THE MAIN RECOMMENDATIONS IN *SAFE FROM HARM*

In order to safeguard the welfare of the children and young people in their charge, voluntary organisations should consider the issues raised by each of the following statements of principle and then, if they wish to do so, take any action which they deem to be appropriate in the light of their circumstances and structures, and the nature of their activities.

1. Adopt a policy statement on safeguarding the welfare of children.

2. Plan the work of the organisation so as to minimise situations where the abuse of children may occur.

3. Introduce a system whereby children may talk with an independent person.

4. Apply agreed procedures for protecting children to all paid staff and volunteers.

5. Give all paid staff and volunteers clear roles.

6. Use supervision as a means of protecting children.

7. Treat all would-be paid staff and volunteers as job applicants for any position involving contact with children.

8. Gain at least one reference from a person who has experience of the applicant's paid work or volunteering with children.

9. Explore all applicants' experience of working or contact with children in an interview before appointment.

10. Find out whether an applicant has any conviction for criminal offences against children.

11. Make paid and voluntary appointments conditional on the successful completion of a probationary period.

12. Issue guidelines on how to deal with the disclosure or discovery of abuse.

13. Train paid staff and volunteers, their line managers or supervisors, and policy makers in the prevention of child abuse.

APPENDIX 4

COMMUNION BEFORE CONFIRMATION

The guidelines agreed by the House of Bishops

a. Since 'communion before confirmation' is a departure from our inherited norm, it requires special permission. After consultation, every diocesan bishop will have the discretion to make a general policy whether or not to entertain new applications for 'communion before confirmation' to take place in his diocese. If he decides to do so, individual parishes must seek his agreement before introducing it. The bishop should satisfy himself that both the incumbent and the Parochial Church Council support any application, and that where appropriate ecumenical partners have been consulted. If the parties cannot agree, the bishop's direction shall be followed.

b. The incumbent must ensure that the policy adopted for his/her parish is clearly and widely understood. The policy should be considered within the general context both of the ministry that is carried out in the parish through initiation, and also of the continuing nurture of people in the Christian faith. The bishop should be satisfied that the programme of continuing Christian nurture is in place, leading to confirmation in due course.

c. Before admitting a person to communion, the priest must seek evidence of baptism. Baptism always precedes admission to holy communion.

d. There is a question regarding the age at which children may be admitted to holy communion. In general the time of the first receiving should be determined not so much by the child's chronological age as by his or her appreciation of the significance of the sacrament. Subject to the bishop's discretion, it is appropriate for the decision to be made by the parish priest after consultation with the parents or those who are responsible for the child's formation, with the parents' good will. An appropriate and serious pattern of preparation should be followed. The priest and parents share in continuing to educate the child in the significance of holy communion so that (s)he gains in understanding with increasing maturity.

e. The church needs to encourage awareness of many different levels of understanding, and support the inclusion of those with learning difficulties in the Christian community. Particular care needs to be taken with the preparation of any who have learning difficulties, including children. The incumbent should consult with those concerned in their care, education and support regarding questions of their discernment of the sacrament, their admission to holy communion, and their preparation for confirmation.

f. Before a person is first brought to holy communion, the significance of the occasion should be explained to him/her and to his/her parents, and marked in some suitable way before the whole congregation. Wherever possible, the person's family should be involved in the service.

g. A register should be kept of every person admitted to holy communion before confirmation, and each should be given a certificate (or, better, the baptismal certificate should be endorsed).

h. Whether or not a parish practises 'communion before confirmation', the incumbent should take care regarding the quality of teaching material, especially that used with the children and young people. The material should be reviewed regularly, and the advice of diocesan officers and other professional advisers taken into account.

i. The priest must decide exactly how much of the liturgy communicant children will attend. Even if there is a separate 'Ministry of the Word' for children, anyone who is to receive holy communion should be present in the main assembly at least for the eucharistic prayer.

j. No baptised person, child or adult, who has once been admitted to holy communion and remains in good standing with the Church, should be anywhere deprived of it. When, for example, a family moves to another area, the incumbent of the parish they are leaving should contact their new incumbent to ensure that there is no confusion regarding the communicant status of children. It is the responsibility of the new incumbent to discuss with the children and parents concerned when the children should be presented for confirmation. Such children should normally be presented at least by the age of 18.

k. Since baptism is at the heart of initiation, it is important for the bishop regularly to be the minister of holy baptism, and particularly at services where candidates will be both baptised and confirmed. It is generally inappropriate for candidates who are preparing for initiation into the Christian life in baptism and confirmation to receive baptism at a service other than the one in which they are to be confirmed.

l. In using rites of public re-affirmation of faith other than baptism and confirmation, care should be taken to avoid the impression that they are identical with confirmation. In the case of people who have not been confirmed, it will be more appropriate for the incumbent to propose that they be confirmed.

APPENDIX 5

THE COLD WEATHER CODE FOR CHURCHES

This guidance on how to avoid burst pipes is produced by the Ecclesiastical Insurance Group, and is for churches and halls with water pipes or water storage above ground.

BEFORE COLD WEATHER ARRIVES

- **Find your main stopcock** and make sure you can turn it on and off.
- **Repair any dripping taps.**
- **Fully lag all pipes and tanks which may be liable to freezing.**
  Use pre-formed insulation on all pipe runs – check with your Church Inspector to see how thick this should be.
  Wrap ends or hard-to-get-at pipes with securely fixed strips of insulation material.
- **Insulate the top and sides of the tank** with either ...
  ... a pre-formed plastic tank jacket filled with glass fibre matting;
  ... rigid polystyrene sheeting at least 25 mm (1 in.) thick;
  ... insulation matting, 150 mm (6 in.) thick.
  However, do not insulate under a tank – if you place insulation material below any water tank, warm air cannot rise from rooms below to help prevent freezing. Only header tanks (generally those for heating, raised above the level of joists in the roof space) are the exception to this – completely enclose them in an insulating jacket.
- **Check your loft insulation is thick enough and still intact, not damaged or disturbed since you last looked.**
  Ensure it covers pipes running between joists, enclosing them in the building's 'insulation envelope'. (If loft insulation is *under* the pipes, warm air cannot reach them from below, and they are more likely to freeze.)

OVERNIGHT DURING WINTER

- **In severe weather, or if it is forecast ...**
  ... try to leave heating on day and night at your usual temperature setting – this will help prevent pipes freezing.
- **Open any loft trap doors.**
  This allows warmth from other parts of the building to circulate in the loft, again helping to prevent frozen pipes. Background heating in roof spaces containing water pipes or storage tanks can be installed to raise ambient temperatures to above 0 degrees centigrade.
- **Have somebody visit the building daily.**
  If you suffer a burst pipe it will be spotted soon and damage minimised.

IF PIPES OR TANKS HAVE FROZEN

- **Turn off the water at the main stopcock.**
  If there is a stopcock on the system or header tank, it is to stop water leaving the tank, so turn this off too. Do this even if you only suspect pipes are frozen, since they could also have burst – turning off the water will minimise any consequent flood damage.
- **Before you start to thaw the system ...**
  ... protect or remove anything which might be damaged by thawing water running from the burst.
- **Thaw the pipe.**
  Use a hairdryer or hot-water bottle – *NOT A BLOW LAMP OR A HEAT GUN.*
  Open the tap closest to the frozen part of the pipe.
  Begin thawing the pipe from the tap side of the frozen area by heating it gently: work back towards the header tank.
- **If a pipe has burst ...**
  ... turn off the water at the main stopcock. At the same time, switch off the central heating and any other water-heating installation to avoid further damage or even an explosion.
  Open all taps to drain the system.

If water is coming through the ceiling, collect it in buckets. If the ceiling starts to bulge, pierce the plaster with a broom handle to let water through.

If your wiring or any electrical appliances have been affected DO NOT TOUCH THEM until they have been checked by a professional electrician. If in doubt, turn off your mains electricity.

Call in a professional plumber to make repairs.

Contact your insurers for information on how to make a claim.

DRYING OUT

- **Leave windows, doors and built-in cupboards open during the day** if your security is not compromised (for example, while premises are occupied).
- **Keep affected rooms heated**, but do not overheat them, since this could create more damage.
- **Store damaged items** in a dry place – your insurer may want to inspect them.

APPENDIX 6

CHARITABLE TRUSTS FOR THE REPAIR OF CHURCHES

(a) *COUNTY TRUST SECRETARIES*

(Arranged in County order)

The County historic churches trusts are all independent charities raising money and helping repair churches and chapels within their own boundaries. The list is up to date at the time of writing. The Historic Churches Preservation Trust keeps an up-to-date list, and can supply any changes of address.

BEDFORDSHIRE AND HERTFORDSHIRE HISTORIC CHURCHES TRUST
Mr R. Tomlins
80 Beaumont Avenue, St Albans, Hertfordshire AL1 4TP

ROYAL COUNTY OF BERKSHIRE CHURCHES TRUST
Mr W. Stebbings
6 Whitelands Drive, Mill Road, Ascot, Berks SL5 8LR

BUCKINGHAMSHIRE HISTORIC CHURCHES TRUST
Mrs P.J. Keens
The Pound House, Wicken, Milton Keynes, Buckinghamshire
MK19 6BN

CAMBRIDGESHIRE HISTORIC CHURCHES TRUST
Mr R. Walker
14 Clay Street, Histon, Cambs CB4 4EY

HISTORIC CHESHIRE CHURCHES PRESERVATION TRUST
Mr Nick Cummings
Birch Cullimore and Co, 20 White Friars, Chester, Cheshire CH1 1XS

CORNWALL HISTORIC CHURCHES TRUST
Mr R.G. Purser FCIS FHSM
17 Higher Trehaverne, Truro, Cornwall TR1 3PW

DERBYSHIRE HISTORIC CHURCHES AND CHAPELS TRUST
Mr M.A.B. Mallender
35 St Mary's Gate, Derby, Derbyshire DE1 3JU

DEVON HISTORIC CHURCHES TRUST
Mr P. Plumbley
Jarrah, Broadpath, Stoke Gabriel, Devon TQ9 6SQ

DORSET HISTORIC CHURCHES TRUST
Mr N.C. McClintock CBE
Lower Westport, Wareham, Dorset BH20 4PR

FRIENDS OF ESSEX CHURCHES
Mrs Mary Blaxall
Box F E C, Guy Harlings, 53 New Street, Chelmsford, Essex CM1 1AT

GLOUCESTERSHIRE HISTORIC CHURCHES PRESERVATION
TRUST
Mr C. Page
7 Dollar Street, Cirencester, Glos GL7 2AS

HAMPSHIRE AND THE ISLANDS HISTORIC CHURCHES TRUST
Mr B. Woods
19 St Peter's Street, Winchester, Hants SO23 8BU

HEREFORDSHIRE HISTORIC CHURCHES TRUST
Mrs C.J.A. Gallimore
Orchard House, Credenhill, Hereford HR4 7DA

FRIENDS OF KENT CHURCHES
Mr N.B. Whithead
Beemans, High Street, Cranbrook, Kent TN17 3DT

THE ROMNEY MARSH HISTORIC CHURCHES TRUST
Mrs E.A. Marshall
Lansdell House, Rolvenden, Nr Cranbrook, Kent, TN17 4LW

LEICESTERSHIRE HISTORIC CHURCHES TRUST
Lay Canon T.Y. Cocks
24 Beresford Drive, Leicester LE2 3LA

LINCOLNSHIRE OLD CHURCHES TRUST
Lt Cdr C.H.R.N. Rodwell
Lincolnshire Old Churches Trust, P O Box 195, Lincoln, Lincs
LN5 9XU

NORFOLK CHURCHES TRUST LTD
Mr M. Fisher
7 The Old Church, St Matthew's Road, Norwich, Norfolk NR1 1SP

NORTHAMPTONSHIRE HISTORIC CHURCHES TRUST
Mr J.A. White MA
7 Spencer Parade, Northampton, Northants NN1 5AB

NORTHUMBRIA HISTORIC CHURCHES TRUST
Rev. Canon J.E. Ruscoe
The Vicarage, South Hylton, Sunderland SR4 0QB

NOTTINGHAMSHIRE HISTORIC CHURCHES TRUST
Mr M. Stewart RIBA
c/o Mark Stewart Associates, 34A Musters Road, West Bridgford,
Nottingham NG2 7PL

OXFORDSHIRE HISTORIC CHURCHES TRUST
Mr R.H. Lethbridge
Fawler Manor, Charlbury, Oxford OX7 3AH

RUTLAND HISTORIC CHURCHES TRUST
Mrs L.I. Worrall
6 Redland Close, Barrowden, Oakham, Rutland LE15 8ES

SHROPSHIRE HISTORIC CHURCHES TRUST
The Ven. G. Frost MA
The Archdeacon of Salop, Tong Vicarage, Shifnal, Shropshire
TF11 8PW

FRIENDS OF SOMERSET CHURCHES AND CHAPELS
Lt Cdr C. Kerr, RN
Leeson's Cottage, Middle Twinhoe, Nr Midford, Bath, BA2 8QX

STAFFORDSHIRE HISTORIC CHURCHES TRUST
Dr J. Benton
1 Yew Tree Cottage, Slindon, Stafford ST21 6LX

SUFFOLK HISTORIC CHURCHES TRUST
Mr C.K. St J. Bird
Brinkleys, Hall Street, Long Melford, Suffolk CO10 9JR

SURREY CHURCHES PRESERVATION TRUST
Mr S.J. Osmond
Sylvans, Tilford Road, Farnham, Surrey GU9 8JB.

SUSSEX HISTORIC CHURCHES TRUST
Countess de la Warr
Buckhurst Park, Withyham, Near Hartfield, East Sussex TN7 4BL

WARWICKSHIRE AND COVENTRY HISTORIC CHURCHES
TRUST
Dr Charles Brown
42 High Street, Warwick CV34 4AS

WILTSHIRE HISTORIC CHURCHES TRUST
Mr J. Caunt
The Cottage, Barford St Martin, Salisbury, Wilts SP3 4AS

WORCESTER AND DUDLEY HISTORIC CHURCHES TRUST
Mr M. Shaw
The Pound, Chaddesley Corbett, Kidderminster, Worcestershire
DY10 4QL

YORKSHIRE HISTORIC CHURCHES TRUST
Dr C. Cubitt
Centre for Medieval Studies, University of York, The King's Manor,
York YO1 2EP

(b)   OTHER ORGANISATIONS

CADW (WELSH HISTORIC MONUMENTS)
9th Floor, Brunel House, Fitzalan Road, Cardiff CF2 1VU
Tel: 01222 465511

THE CHARITIES AID FOUNDATION
Kings Hill, West Malling, Kent ME19 4TA
Tel: 01732 520 000

The Charities Aid Foundation publishes every other year *The Directory of Grant Making Trusts*, two volumes containing the details of 2,500 grant making trusts in the UK. It is also published as a CD-ROM under the name *Grantseeker*.

THE COUNCIL FOR THE CARE OF CHURCHES
Fielden House, Little College Street, London SW1P 3SH

Tel: 0171 222 3793

The Council for the Care of Churches produce a helpful publication *Fund-raising for church repairs*. This lists many sources of grant aid, and summarises the grants which can be obtained and the conditions required.

ENGLISH HERITAGE
429 Oxford Street, London W1R 2HD

Tel: 0171 973 3000.

Fax: 0171 973 3001

THE ESMEE FAIRBAIRN CHARITABLE TRUST
1 Birdcage Walk, London SW1H 9JJ

Tel: 0171 222 7041

THE GLAZIERS TRUST
The Worshipful Company of Glaziers and Painters of Glass, The Glaziers Hall, 9 Montague Close, London Bridge, London SE1 9DD

Tel: 0171 403 3300

Grants are made for the conservation of stained glass of historic importance.

HERITAGE LOTTERY FUND
National Heritage Memorial Fund, 10 St James's Street, London SW1A 1EF

Tel: 0171 747 2032

HERITAGE MEMORIAL FUND
National Heritage Memorial Fund, 10 St James's Street, London SW1A 1EF

Tel: 0171 930 0963

HISTORIC CHURCHES PRESERVATION TRUST
Fulham Palace, London SW6 6EA

Tel: 0171 736 3054

THE LECHE TRUST
84 Cicada Road, London SW18 2NZ

Tel: 0181 870 6233

Grants are awarded by the Trust for the repair of church furniture, including monuments and bells, but not for structural repairs to the building.

MANIFOLD TRUST
21 Dean's Yard, Westminster, London SW1P 3PA

Tel: 0171 222 6581

THE MILLENNIUM FUND
The Millennium Commission, 2 Little Smith Street, London SW1P 3DH

Tel: 0171 340 2001

THE PILGRIM TRUST
Fielden House, Little College Street, London SW1P 3SH

Tel: 0171 222 4723

SAINSBURY FAMILY CHARITABLE TRUSTS
9 Red Lion Court, London EC4A 3EB

Tel: 0171 410 0330

SCOTTISH CHURCHES ARCHITECTURAL HERITAGE TRUST
15 North Bank Street, Edinburgh EH1 2LP

Tel: 0131 225 8644.

APPENDIX 7

SOURCES AND AUTHORITIES

CASES

STATUTES AND MEASURES

CANONS

REGULATIONS

BIBLIOGRAPHY

5 Steps to Risk Assessment (HSE Books, 1997) 105
A Guide to Church Inspection and Repair (Council for the Care of Churches,
    1995) 325
A meeting will be held (how to prepare agendas) (Administry) 89
Accident Book, form B1 510, (HMSO) 161
Accounting for the Smaller Charity (Charity Commission leaflet
    CC54, 1995) 346
Accruals accounts for the smaller charity (Charity Commission leaflet CC55,
    1995) 346
Acoustic Treatment of Places of Worship (Council for the Care of Churches,
    1981) 325
Advice for Victims of Sexual Assault (The Metropolitan Police) 158

APPENDIX 7

ORGANISATIONS

INDEX

For the many organisations referred to in this book, see also the table of organisations on page 462.